Thoma

SUPER COOKERY

Pasta &
Italian

p

This is a Parragon Publishing Book
This edition published in 2004

Parragon Publishing
Queen Street House
4 Queen Street
Bath BA1 1HE, UK

Copyright © Parragon 2000

ISBN: 0-75257-560-0

A copy of the CIP data for this book is available from the British
Library, upon request

Printed in China

Note
Cup measurements used in this book are for American cups.
Tablespoons are assumed to be 15 ml. Unless otherwise stated,
milk is assumed to be full fat, eggs are medium and pepper is
freshly ground black pepper.

Contents

Introduction

Pasta has existed since the days of the Roman Empire and remains one of the most versatile cooking ingredients: no storecupboard should be without it. It can be combined with meat, fish, vegetables, fruit, or even a simple herb sauce to create a mouthwatering and nutritious meal within minutes.

Most pasta is made from durum wheat flour and contains protein and carbohydrates. It is a good source of slow-release energy and has the additional advantage of being value for money.

There are many different types of pasta, some of which are listed on the opposite page. Many are available both dried and fresh. Unless you have access to a good, Italian delicatessen, it is probably not worth buying fresh unfilled pasta, but even supermarkets sell high-quality tortellini, capelletti, ravioli, and agnolotti.

Best of all is to make fresh pasta at home. It takes a little time, but is quite easy and well worth the effort. You can mix the dough by hand or prepare it in a food processor. Pasta may be colored and flavored with extra ingredients that are usually added with the beaten egg:

Black: add 1 tsp squid or cuttlefish ink.

Green: add 4 ounces, of well-drained, cooked spinach when kneading.

Purple: thoroughly process 1 large, cooked beet in a food processor, and add with an extra ½ cup flour.

Red: add 2 tbsp tomato paste.

To cook pasta, bring a large pan of lightly salted water to a boil. Add the pasta and 1 tbsp olive oil, but do not cover or the water will boil over. Quickly bring the water back to a rolling boil and avoid overcooking. When the pasta is tender, but still firm to the bite, drain and toss with butter, olive oil, or your prepared sauce. The cooking times given here are guidelines only:

Fresh unfilled pasta:	*2–3 minutes*
Fresh filled pasta:	*8–10 minutes*
Dried unfilled pasta:	*10–12 minutes*
Dried filled pasta:	*15–20 minutes*

BASIC PASTA DOUGH

If you wish to make your own pasta for the dishes in this book, follow this simple recipe.

Serves 4

INGREDIENTS

4 cups durum wheat flour
4 eggs, lightly beaten
1 tbsp olive oil
salt

1 Lightly flour a counter. Sift the flour with a pinch of salt into a mound. Make a well in the center and add the eggs and olive oil.

2 Using a fork or your fingertips, gradually work the mixture until the ingredients are combined. Knead vigorously for 10–15 minutes.

3 Set the dough aside to rest for 25 minutes, before rolling it out as thinly and evenly as possible.

TYPES OF PASTA

There are as many as 200 different pasta shapes and about three times as many names for them. New shapes are being designed—and named—all the time and the same shape may be called a different name in different regions of Italy.

anelli, anellini: *small rings for soup*

bucatini: *long, medium-thick tubes*

cannelloni: *large, thick, round pasta tubes*

capelli d'angelo: *thin strands of 'angel hair'*

conchiglie: *ridged shells*

conchigliette: *little shells*

cresti di gallo: *curved-shaped*

ditali, ditalini: *short tubes*

eliche: *loose spirals*

farfalle: *bows*

fettuccine: *medium ribbons*

fusilli: *spirals*

gemelli: *two pieces wrapped together as 'twins'*

lasagne: *flat, rectangular sheets*

linguini: *long, flat ribbons*

lumache: *snail-shaped shells*

lumaconi: *big shells*

macaroni: *long- or short-cut tubes*

orecchiette: *ear-shaped*

penne: *quill-shaped*

rigatoni: *thick, ridged tubes*

spaghetti: *fine or medium rods*

tagliarini: *thin ribbons*

tagliatelle: *broad ribbons*

vermicelli: *fine pasta, usually folded into skeins*

Cannelloni

Conchigliette

Fusilli

Conchiglie

Orecchiette tricolori

Rigatoni

Lumaconi

Fettuccine

Spaghetti

Each region in Italy has its distinctive culinary style, although in general the north favors the use of milk and butter and the south of olive oil in their cooking.

Piedmont

The food here is substantial, peasant-type fare, although the expensive fragrant white truffle is found in this region. There is an abundance of exotic mushrooms throughout the region. Garlic features strongly in the recipes, and polenta, gnocchi, and rice are eaten in larger quantities than pasta, the former being offered as a first course when soup is not served. A large variety of game is also widely available.

Lombardy

Milan is home to the risotto named after the city and also the Milanese soufflé flavored with lemon. Veal dishes, including *vitello tonnato* and *osso buco*, are specialties of the region, and other excellent meat dishes feature widely. The lakes of the area produce a wealth of fresh fish. Rice and polenta are again popular, but pasta also appears in many guises. The famous sweet cake *panettone* is a product of this region.

Trentino–Alto Adige

The foods are robust and basic here, where fish are plentiful. In the Trentino area particularly, pasta and simple meat dishes are popular, while in the Adige, soups and pot roasts are favored, often with added dumplings and spiced sausages.

Veneto

Polenta is served with almost everything here. The land is intensively farmed, providing mostly cereals and wine. Pasta is less in evidence, with gnocchi and rice more favored. Fish, particularly shellfish, is in abundance and especially good seafood salads are widely available. There are also excellent soups and risottos flavored with the seafood and sausages of the area.

Liguria

All along the Italian Riviera can be found excellent trattorias which produce amazing fish dishes. Pesto sauce comes from this area, along with other excellent sauces. Fresh herbs are widely used in many dishes, including the famous pizza, such as the margherita.

Emilia–Romagna

Tortellini and lasagne feature widely here, along with many other pasta dishes, as do *saltimbocca* and other veal dishes. Parma is famous for its ham, *prosciutto di Parma*, thought to be the best in the world. Balsamic vinegar is also produced in this region,

Tuscany

Tuscany has everything: an excellent coastal area providing splendid fish, hills covered in vineyards, and fertile plains where every conceivable vegetable and fruit grow. There is plenty of game in the region, providing many interesting recipes; tripe cooked in a thick tomato sauce is popular, beans in many guises appear frequently, as well as pot roasts, steaks, and full-bodied soups, all of which are well-flavored. Florence has a wide variety of specialties, while Siena boasts the famous candied fruit cake called *Panforte di Siena*.

Umbria/Marches

Inland Umbria is famous for its pork, and the character of the cuisine is marked by the use of the local fresh ingredients, including lamb, game, and fish. Spit-roasting and broiling is popular, and the local olive oil is used in cooking and to pour over dishes before serving. Black truffles, olives, fruit, and herbs are plentiful and feature in many recipes. First-class sausages and cured pork come from the Marches, particularly on the Umbrian border, and various types of pasta feature all over the region.

Lazio

Here, there are many pasta dishes with delicious sauces, gnocchi in various forms, plenty of dishes featuring lamb and veal (*saltimbocca* being just one), and a variety of meats – all with plenty of herbs and seasonings giving really robust flavors and delicious sauces. Vegetables feature along with fantastic fruits; and beans appear both in soups and many other dishes.

Abruzzi and Molise

The cuisine here is deeply traditional, with local hams and cheeses from the mountain areas, interesting sausages with plenty of garlic and other seasonings, cured meats, and wonderful fish and seafood. Lamb features widely: tender, juicy, and well-flavored with herbs.

Campania

Naples is the home of pasta dishes, served with a splendid tomato sauce. Pizza is said to have been created in Naples. Fish abounds, with *fritto misto* and *fritto pesce* being great favorites. Fish stews are robust and varied, and shellfish in particular is often served with pasta. Cutlets and steaks are excellent, served with strong sauces flavored with garlic, tomatoes, and herbs: pizzaiola steak is one of the favorites. Mozzarella cheese is produced locally and used to create the crispy Mozzarella in Carozza, served with a garlicky tomato sauce. Sweet dishes are popular too, often with flaky pastry and ricotta cheese, and the seasonal fruit salads are laced with wine or liqueur.

Puglia (Apulia)

The ground in this region is stony, but it produces good fruit, olives, vegetables, and herbs, and, of course, there is a large amount of seafood from the sea. Many of the pasta dishes are exclusive to the region. Mushrooms abound and are always added to the local pizzas. Oysters and mussels are plentiful, and so is octopus. Brindisi is famous for its shellfish – both the seafood salads and risottos are memorable. But it is not all fish or pasta: lamb is roasted and stewed to perfection and so is veal, always with plenty of herbs.

Basilicata

Here potent wines are produced to accompany a robust cuisine largely based on pasta, lamb, pork, game, and abundant dairy products. The salami and cured meats are excellent, as are the mountain hams. Lamb is flavored with the herbs and grasses on which it feeds. Wonderful soups – true minestrone – are produced in the mountains, and eels and fish are plentiful in the lakes. Chiles are grown in this region and appear in many of the recipes. The cheeses are excellent, good fruit is grown, and local bread is baked in huge loaves.

Calabria

This is the toe of Italy, where orange and lemon groves flourish, along with olive trees and a profusion of vegetables. Chicken, rabbit, and guinea fowl are often on the menu. Pizzas feature largely, often with a fish topping. Mushrooms grow well in the Calabrian climate and feature in many dishes from sauces and stews to salads. Pasta comes with a great variety of sauces, including baby artichokes, eggs, meat, cheese, mixed vegetables, the large sweet bell peppers of the region, and, of course, garlic. The fish is excellent, too, and fresh tuna and swordfish are available, along with many other varieties. Many desserts and cakes are flavored with aniseed, honey, and almonds and feature the plentiful figs of the region.

Sicily

This is the largest island in the Mediterranean and the cuisine is based mainly on fish and vegetables. Fish soups, stews, and salads appear in unlimited forms, including tuna, swordfish, mussels, and many more; citrus fruits are widely grown, along with almonds and pistachios, and the local wines, including the dark, sweet, dessert wine Marsala, are excellent. Meat is often given a long, slow cooking, or else is ground and shaped before cooking. Game is plentiful and is often cooked in sweet-sour sauces containing the local black olives. Pasta abounds again with more unusual sauces as well as the old favorites. All Sicilians have a love of desserts, cakes, and especially ice cream. *Cassata* and other ice creams from Sicily are famous all over the world.

Sardinia

The national dish of Sardinia is suckling pig or newborn lamb cooked on an open fire or spit, and rabbit, game, and a variety of meat dishes are also very popular. There is fresh fruit of almost every kind in abundance. Fish is also top quality, with excellent sea bass, lobsters, tuna, mullet, eels, and mussels in good supply. Myrtle (*mirto*), a local herb, is added to everything from chicken dishes to the local liqueur; and along with the cakes and breads of Sardinia, myrtle will long remain a fond memory of the island when you have returned home.

7

Starters & *Light Meals*

Pasta is so versatile: it can be used to make
soups more substantial, as a delicious and unusual
starter, or as a quick and easy lunch or light supper.
The recipes in this chapter range from traditional
Italian dishes to new methods of combining pasta
with different ingredients.

Soup recipes include filling winter dishes
that, if served with some crusty bread, make a meal
in themselves. Others are subtle and delicate.
Recipes for snacks and light meals offer something
for every taste—vegetable, cheese, meat, and fish
sauces combined with every pasta shape from
linguine to lumache. You can also try delicious light
meals and roasts, pancakes, and vegetable dishes.

Minestrone

Serves 8-10

INGREDIENTS

3 garlic cloves

3 large onions

2 celery sticks

2 large carrots

2 large potatoes

3 ½ ounces green beans

3 ½ ounces zucchini

4 tbsp butter

½ cup olive oil

2 ounces fatty bacon, finely diced

6 ¼ cups vegetable or chicken stock

1 bunch fresh basil, finely chopped

3 ½ ounces chopped tomatoes

2 tbsp tomato paste

3 ½ ounces Parmesan cheese rind

3 ounces dried spaghetti, broken up

salt and pepper

freshly grated Parmesan cheese, to serve

1 Finely chop the garlic, onions, celery, carrots, potatoes, beans, and zucchini using a sharp knife.

2 Heat the butter and oil together in a large saucepan, add the bacon and cook for 2 minutes. Add the garlic and onion and fry for 2 minutes, then stir in the celery, carrots, and potatoes and fry for 2 minutes longer, stirring the vegetables occasionally.

3 Add the beans to the saucepan and fry for 2 minutes. Stir in the zucchini and cook for 2 minutes longer. Cover and cook all the vegetables, stirring frequently, for about 15 minutes.

4 Add the stock, basil, tomatoes, tomato paste, and cheese rind and season to taste. Bring to a boil, lower the heat and simmer for 1 hour. Remove and discard the cheese rind.

5 Add the spaghetti pieces to the pan and cook for 20 minutes. Serve sprinkled with freshly grated Parmesan cheese.

Italian Cream of Tomato Soup

Serves 4

INGREDIENTS

4 tbsp unsalted butter
1 large onion, chopped
2½ cups vegetable stock
2 pounds Italian plum tomatoes,
    skinned and roughly chopped

pinch of baking soda
2 cups dried fusilli
1 tbsp superfine sugar
⅝ cup heavy cream
salt and pepper

fresh basil leaves, to garnish
deep-fried croutons, to serve

---

1 Melt the butter in a large saucepan, add the onion and sauté for 3 minutes. Add 1¼ cups of the vegetable stock to the saucepan, with the chopped tomatoes and baking soda. Bring the soup to a boil and simmer for 20 minutes.

2 Remove the pan from the heat and set aside to cool slightly. Purée the soup in a blender or food processor and pour through a fine strainer back into the saucepan.

3 Add the remaining vegetable stock and the fusilli to the pan, and season to taste.

4 Add the sugar to the pan, bring to a boil, then lower the heat and simmer for about 15 minutes.

5 Pour the soup into a warm tureen, swirl the heavy cream around the surface of the soup and garnish with fresh basil leaves. Serve immediately with croutons.

VARIATION

To make orange and tomato soup, simply use half the quantity of vegetable stock, topped off with the same amount of fresh orange juice and garnish the soup with orange rind. Or to make tomato and carrot soup, add half the quantity again of vegetable stock with the same amount of carrot juice and 1¼ cups grated carrot to the recipe, cooking the carrot with the onion.

Potato & Parsley Soup with Pesto

Serves 4

INGREDIENTS

3 slices bacon
1 pound mealy potatoes
1 pound onions
2 tbsp butter
2 1/2 cups chicken stock
2 1/2 cups milk

3/4 cup dried conchigliette
5/8 cup heavy cream
chopped fresh parsley
salt and black pepper
freshly grated Parmesan cheese
   and garlic bread, to serve

PESTO SAUCE:
1 cup finely chopped fresh
   parsley
2 garlic cloves, crushed
2/3 cup pine nuts, crushed
2 tbsp chopped fresh basil leaves
2/3 cup freshly grated Parmesan
   cheese
white pepper
5/8 cup olive oil

1 To make the pesto sauce, work all of the ingredients in a blender or food processor for 2 minutes, or blend together by hand (see Cook's Tip).

2 Finely chop the bacon, potatoes, and onions. Fry the bacon in a large pan for 4 minutes. Add the butter, potatoes, and onions and cook for 12 minutes, stirring constantly.

3 Add the stock and milk to the pan, bring to a boil, and simmer for 10 minutes. Add the conchigliette and simmer for 12-14 minutes.

4 Blend in the cream and simmer for 5 minutes. Add the parsley and 2 tbsp pesto sauce. Transfer the soup to serving bowls and serve with Parmesan cheese and fresh garlic bread.

COOK'S TIP

If you are making pesto by hand, it is best to use a mortar and pestle. Thoroughly grind together the parsley, garlic, pine nuts, and basil to make a paste, then mix in the cheese and pepper. Finally, gradually beat in the oil.

Ravioli alla Parmigiana

Serves 4

INGREDIENTS

10 ounces Basic Pasta Dough
5 cups veal stock
freshly grated Parmesan cheese,
    to serve

FILLING:
1 cup freshly grated Parmesan
    cheese
1²/₃ cup fine white breadcrumbs

2 eggs
¹/₂ cup espagnole sauce (see
    Cook's Tip)
1 small onion, finely chopped
1 tsp freshly grated nutmeg

1 Make the basic pasta dough. Carefully roll out 2 sheets of the pasta dough and cover with a damp dish cloth while you prepare the filling for the ravioli.

2 To make the filling, mix together the freshly grated Parmesan cheese, fine white breadcrumbs, eggs, espagnole sauce (see Cook's Tip), finely chopped onion, and the freshly grated nutmeg in a large mixing bowl.

3 Place spoonfuls of the filling at regular intervals on 1 sheet of pasta dough. Cover with the second sheet of pasta dough, then cut into squares and seal the edges.

4 Bring the veal stock to a boil in a large saucepan. Add the ravioli to the pan and cook for about 15 minutes.

5 Transfer the soup and ravioli to warm serving bowls and serve at once, sprinkled with Parmesan.

COOK'S TIP

For espagnole sauce, melt 2 tbsp butter and stir in ¹/₄ cup all-purpose flour. Cook over a low heat, stirring, until lightly colored. Add 1 tsp tomato paste, then stir in 1¹/₄ cups hot veal stock, 1 tbsp Madeira, and 1¹/₂ tsp white wine vinegar. Dice 1 ounce each bacon, carrot, and onion and ¹/₂ ounce each celery, leek, and fennel. Cook with a thyme sprig and a bay leaf in oil until soft. Drain, add to the sauce, and simmer for 4 hours. Strain before using.

Pea & Egg Noodle Soup with Parmesan Cheese Croutons

Serves 4

INGREDIENTS

3 slices bacon, diced
1 large onion, chopped
1 tbsp butter
2¹/₂ cups dried peas, soaked in
cold water for 2 hours and
drained

10 cups chicken stock
8 ounces dried egg noodles
⁵/₈ cup heavy cream
salt and pepper

chopped fresh parsley, to garnish
Parmesan cheese croutons (see
Cook's Tip), to serve

1 Put the bacon, onion, and butter into a large saucepan and cook over a low heat for 6 minutes.

2 Add the peas and the chicken stock to the pan and bring to a boil. Season lightly with salt and pepper, cover, and simmer for 1¹/₂ hours.

3 Add the noodles to the pan and simmer for an additional 15 minutes.

4 Pour in the cream and blend thoroughly. Transfer to a warm tureen, garnish with parsley, and top with Parmesan cheese croutons (see Cook's Tip). Serve immediately.

VARIATION

Use other legumes, such as dried navy beans, borlotti, or pinto beans, instead of the peas.

COOK'S TIP

To make Parmesan cheese croutons, cut a baguette into slices. Coat each slice lightly with olive oil and sprinkle with Parmesan cheese. Broil for about 30 seconds.

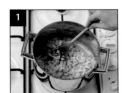

Navy Bean & Pasta Soup

Serves 4

INGREDIENTS

1⅓ cups navy beans, soaked for
    3 hours in cold water and
    drained
4 tbsp olive oil
2 large onions, sliced
3 garlic cloves, chopped

14 ounce can chopped tomatoes
1 tsp dried oregano
1 tsp tomato paste
3½ cups water
¾ cup dried fusilli
    or conchigliette

4 ounces sun-dried tomatoes,
    drained and thinly sliced
1 tbsp chopped fresh cilantro or
    flat leaf parsley
salt and pepper
2 tbsp Parmesan cheese
    shavings, to serve

1 Put the navy beans in a large pan. Cover with cold water and bring to a boil. Boil vigorously for 15 minutes. Drain and keep warm.

2 Heat the oil in a pan over a medium heat and sauté the onions for 2–3 minutes. Stir in the garlic and cook for 1 minute. Stir in the tomatoes, oregano, and tomato paste.

3 Add the water and the reserved beans to the pan. Bring to a boil, cover, then simmer for about 45 minutes, or until the beans are almost tender.

4 Add the pasta to the pan and season to taste. Stir in the sun-dried tomatoes, bring back to a boil, partly cover, and simmer for 10 minutes, or until the pasta is tender, but still firm to the bite.

5 Stir the cilantro or parsley into the soup. Ladle the soup into a warm tureen, sprinkle with the Parmesan and serve.

COOK'S TIP

If desired, place the beans in a pan of cold water and bring to a boil. Remove from the heat and leave the beans to cook in the water. Drain and rinse before using.

Garbanzo Bean & Chicken Soup

Serves 4

INGREDIENTS

2 tbsp butter	5 cups chicken stock	1 cup small dried pasta shapes,
3 scallions, chopped	12 ounce can garbanzo	such as elbow macaroni
2 garlic cloves, crushed	beans, drained	salt and white pepper
1 fresh marjoram sprig,	1 bouquet garni	croutons, to serve
finely chopped	1 red bell pepper, diced	
12 ounces boned chicken	1 green bell pepper, diced	
breasts, diced		

1 Melt the butter in a large saucepan. Add the scallions, garlic, sprig of fresh marjoram, and the diced chicken to the saucepan and cook, stirring frequently, over a medium heat for 5 minutes.

2 Add the chicken stock, garbanzo beans, and bouquet garni to the saucepan and then season to taste with salt and white pepper.

3 Bring the soup to a boil, lower the heat, and then simmer gently for about 2 hours.

4 Add the diced bell peppers and pasta to the pan, then simmer for 20 minutes longer.

5 Transfer the soup to a warm tureen. To serve, ladle the soup into individual serving bowls and serve immediately, garnished with the croutons.

COOK'S TIP

If preferred, use dried garbanzo beans. Cover with cold water and set aside to soak for 5–8 hours. Drain and add the beans to the soup, according to the recipe, and allow an additional 30 minutes—1 hour cooking time.

Cream of Lemon & Chicken Soup with Spaghetti

Serves 4

INGREDIENTS

4 tbsp butter

8 shallots, thinly sliced

2 carrots, thinly sliced

2 celery stalks, thinly sliced

8 ounces boned chicken breasts, finely chopped

3 lemons

5 cups chicken stock

8 ounces dried spaghetti, broken into small pieces

5/8 cup heavy cream

salt and white pepper

TO GARNISH:

fresh parsley sprig

3 lemon slices, halved

1 Melt the butter in a large saucepan. Add the shallots, carrots, celery, and chicken and cook over a low heat, stirring occasionally, for 8 minutes.

2 Thinly pare the lemons and blanch the lemon rind in boiling water for 3 minutes. Squeeze the juice from the lemons.

3 Add the lemon rind and juice to the pan, together with the chicken stock. Slowly bring to a boil and simmer for 40 minutes.

4 Add the spaghetti to the pan and cook for 15 minutes. Season to taste with salt and white pepper and add the cream. Heat through, but do not allow the soup to boil or it will curdle.

5 Pour the soup into a tureen or individual bowls, garnish with the parsley and half slices of lemon, and serve immediately.

COOK'S TIP

You can prepare this soup up to the end of step 3 in advance, so that all you need do before serving is heat it through before adding the pasta and the finishing touches.

Chicken & Corn Soup

Serves 4

INGREDIENTS

1 pound boned chicken breasts,
   cut into strips
5 cups chicken stock

⁵/₈ cup heavy cream
³/₄ cup dried vermicelli
1 tbsp cornstarch

3 tbsp milk
6 ounces corn kernels
salt and pepper

1 Put the chicken, stock, and cream into a large saucepan and slowly bring to a boil. Reduce the heat slightly and simmer for about 20 minutes. Season to taste.

2 Meanwhile, cook the vermicelli in lightly salted boiling water for 10-12 minutes, until just tender. Drain the pasta and keep warm.

3 In a small bowl, mix together the cornstarch and milk to make a smooth paste. Stir the cornstarch paste into the soup until thickened.

4 Add the corn and vermicelli to the saucepan and heat through.

5 Transfer the soup to a warm tureen or individual soup bowls and serve immediately.

COOK'S TIP

If you are short of time, buy ready-cooked chicken, remove any skin, and cut it into slices.

VARIATION

For crab and corn soup, substitute 1 pound cooked crabmeat for the chicken breasts. Flake the crabmeat thoroughly before adding it to the saucepan and reduce the cooking time by 10 minutes. For a Chinese-style soup, substitute egg noodles for the vermicelli and use canned, creamed corn.

Veal & Ham Soup with Sherry

Serves 4

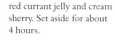

INGREDIENTS

4 tbsp butter	1/2 cup all-purpose flour	5/8 cup cream sherry
1 onion, diced	4 3/8 cups beef stock	3/4 cup dried vermicelli
1 carrot, diced	1 bay leaf	garlic croutons, to serve
1 celery stalk, diced	8 black peppercorns	
1 pound very thinly sliced veal	pinch of salt	
1 pound thinly sliced ham	3 tbsp red currant jelly	

1 Melt the butter in a large saucepan. Cook the onions, carrot, celery, veal, and ham over a low heat for about 6 minutes.

2 Sprinkle in the flour and cook, stirring constantly, for a further 2 minutes. Gradually stir in the stock, then add the bay leaf, peppercorns, and salt. Bring to a boil and simmer for 1 hour.

3 Remove the pan from the heat and add the red currant jelly and cream sherry. Set aside for about 4 hours.

4 Remove and discard the bay leaf. Reheat the soup over a very low heat until warmed through.

5 Meanwhile, cook the vermicelli in a pan of lightly salted boiling water for 10–12 minutes. Stir the vermicelli into the soup and transfer to warm soup bowls. Serve with garlic croutons (see Cook's Tip).

COOK'S TIP

To make garlic croutons, remove the crusts from 3 slices of day-old white bread. Cut the bread into 1/4 inch cubes. Heat 3 tbsp olive oil and stir-fry 1–2 finely chopped garlic cloves for 1–2 minutes. Remove the garlic and add the bread. Cook, tossing the pan and stirring frequently, until golden brown. Remove from the pan with a slotted spoon and drain on paper towels.

Tuscan Veal Broth

Serves 4

INGREDIENTS

1/3 cup dried peas, soaked for 2
hours and drained

2 pounds boned neck of
veal, diced

5 cups beef or brown stock (see
Cook's Tip)

2 1/2 cups water

1/3 cup barley, washed

1 large carrot, diced

1 small turnip (about
6 ounces), diced

1 large leek, thinly sliced

1 red onion, finely chopped

3 1/2 ounces chopped tomatoes

1 fresh basil sprig

3/4 cup dried vermicelli

salt and white pepper

1 Put the peas, veal, stock, and water into a large pan and bring to a boil over a low heat. Skim off any film that rises to the surface of the liquid.

2 When all of the film has been removed, add the barley and a pinch of salt to the mixture. Simmer gently over a low heat for 25 minutes.

3 Add the carrot, turnip, leek, onion, tomatoes, and basil to the pan, and season to taste. Simmer for about 2 hours, skimming the surface with a slotted spoon, from time to time. Remove the pan from the heat and set aside for 2 hours.

4 Set the pan over a medium heat and bring to a boil. Add the vermicelli and cook for 12 minutes. Season with salt and pepper to taste and remove and discard the basil. Ladle the soup into warm bowls and serve immediately.

COOK'S TIP

Brown stock is made with veal bones and shin of beef roasted with drippings in the oven for 40 minutes. Transfer the bones to a large pan and add sliced leeks, onion, celery, and carrots, a bouquet garni, white wine vinegar, and a thyme sprig, and cover with cold water. Simmer over a low heat for 3 hours. Strain and blot the fat from the surface of the stock with paper towels.

Veal & Mushroom Soup with Vermicelli

Serves 4

INGREDIENTS

1 pound veal, thinly sliced	pinch of mace	³/₄ cup dried vermicelli
1 pound veal bones	5 ounces oyster and shiitake	1 tbsp cornstarch
5 cups water	mushrooms, roughly	3 tbsp milk
1 small onion	chopped	salt and pepper
6 peppercorns	⁵/₈ cup heavy cream	
1 tsp cloves		

1 Put the veal, bones, and water into a large saucepan. Bring to a boil and lower the heat. Add the onion, peppercorns, cloves, and mace and simmer for about 3 hours, until the veal stock is reduced by one-third.

2 Strain the stock, skim off any fat on the surface with a slotted spoon, and pour the stock into a clean saucepan. Add the veal meat to the pan.

3 Add the mushrooms and cream, bring to a boil over a low heat, and simmer for 12 minutes. Meanwhile, cook the vermicelli in lightly salted boiling water until tender, but still firm to the bite. Drain and keep warm.

4 Mix together the cornstarch and milk to form a smooth paste. Stir the cornstarch paste into the soup to thicken. Season to taste and just before serving, add the vermicelli. Transfer the soup to a warm tureen and serve immediately.

COOK'S TIP

You can make this soup with the more inexpensive cuts of veal, such as breast or neck slices. These are lean and the long cooking time ensures that the meat is really tender.

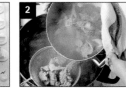

Mussel & Potato Soup

Serves 4

INGREDIENTS

1 pound 10 ounces mussels	1 pound potatoes, thinly sliced	TO GARNISH:
2 tbsp olive oil	³/₄ cup dried conchigliette	2 tbsp finely chopped fresh
7 tbsp unsalted butter	1¼ cups heavy cream	parsley
2 slices bacon, chopped	1 tbsp lemon juice	lemon wedges
1 onion, chopped	2 egg yolks	
2 garlic cloves, crushed	salt and pepper	
½ cup all-purpose flour		

1 Debeard the mussels and scrub them under cold water for 5 minutes. Discard any mussels that do not close immediately when sharply tapped.

2 Bring a large pan of water to a boil, add the mussels, oil, and a little pepper and cook until the mussels open.

3 Drain the mussels, reserving the cooking liquid. Discard any mussels that are closed. Remove the mussels from their shells.

4 Melt the butter in a large saucepan and cook the bacon, onion, and garlic for 4 minutes. Carefully stir in the flour and then 5 cups of the reserved cooking liquid.

5 Add the potatoes to the pan and simmer for 5 minutes. Add the conchigliette and simmer for a further 10 minutes.

6 Add the cream and lemon juice, season to taste, then add the mussels to the pan.

7 Blend the egg yolks with 1-2 tbsp of the remaining cooking liquid, stir into the pan, and cook for 4 minutes.

8 Ladle the soup into warm soup bowls, garnish with the chopped fresh parsley and lemon wedges, and serve.

Italian Fish Soup

Serves 4

INGREDIENTS

4 tbsp butter

1 pound assorted fish fillets,
such as red mullet and
snapper

1 pound prepared seafood, such
as squid and shrimp

8 ounces fresh crabmeat

1 large onion, sliced

1/4 cup all-purpose flour

5 cups fish stock (see Cook's Tip)

3/4 cup dried pasta shapes, such
as ditalini or elbow macaroni

1 tbsp anchovy extract

grated rind and juice of
1 orange

1/4 cup dry sherry

1 1/4 cups heavy cream

salt and black pepper

crusty brown bread, to serve

1 Melt the butter in a large saucepan and cook the fish fillets, seafood, crabmeat, and onion over a low heat for 6 minutes.

2 Stir the flour into the mixture.

3 Gradually stir in the fish stock until the soup comes to a boil. Reduce the heat and simmer for 30 minutes.

4 Add the pasta to the saucepan and cook for a further 10 minutes.

5 Stir in the anchovy extract, orange rind, orange juice, sherry, and heavy cream. Season to taste with salt and pepper.

6 Heat the soup until completely warmed through then transfer to warm soup bowls and serve with crusty brown bread.

COOK'S TIP

The heads, tails, trimmings and bones of most non-oily fish can be used to make fish stock. Simmer 2 pounds fish pieces, including heads, in a large saucepan with 5/8 cup white wine, 1 chopped onion, 1 sliced carrot, 1 sliced celery stalk, 4 black peppercorns, 1 bouquet garni, and 7 1/2 cups water for 30 minutes, then strain.

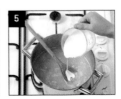

Chicken & Pasta Broth

Serves 6

INGREDIENTS

12 ounces boneless chicken breasts	1 1/2 cups diced carrots	1 cup small pasta shapes
2 tablespoons sunflower oil	9 ounces cauliflower flowerets	salt and pepper
1 medium onion, diced	3 3/4 cups chicken stock	Parmesan cheese (optional)
	2 teaspoons dried mixed herbs	and crusty bread, to serve

1 Using a sharp knife, finely dice the chicken, discarding any skin.

2 Heat the oil in a large saucepan and quickly sauté the chicken and vegetables until they are lightly colored.

3 Stir in the stock and herbs. Bring to a boil and add the pasta. Return to a boil, cover, and simmer for 10 minutes, stirring occasionally to prevent the pasta shapes from sticking together.

4 Season with salt and pepper to taste and sprinkle with Parmesan cheese, if using. Serve with fresh crusty bread.

COOK'S TIP

You can use any small pasta shapes for this soup—try conchigliette or ditalini, or even spaghetti broken up into small pieces. To make a fun soup for children, you could add animal-shaped or alphabet pasta.

VARIATION

Broccoli flowerets can be used to replace the cauliflower flowerets. Substitute 2 tablespoons chopped fresh mixed herbs for the dried mixed herbs.

Chicken, Guinea Fowl, & Spaghetti Soup

Serves 6

INGREDIENTS

1 pound 2 ounces skinless chicken, chopped	1 small onion	2 teaspoons butter
1 pound 2 ounces skinless guinea fowl meat	6 peppercorns	2 teaspoons all-purpose flour
	1 teaspoon cloves	1 cup quick-cook spaghetti, broken into short lengths and cooked
2½ cups chicken stock	pinch of mace	
	⅔ cup heavy cream	2 tablespoons chopped fresh parsley, to garnish

1 Put the chicken and guinea fowl meat into a large saucepan with the chicken stock.

2 Bring to a boil and add the onion, peppercorns, cloves, and mace. Simmer gently for about 2 hours, until the stock is reduced by one third.

3 Strain the soup, skim off any fat, and remove any bones from the chicken and guinea fowl.

4 Return the soup and the chicken and guinea fowl meat to a clean saucepan. Add the heavy cream and bring to a boil slowly.

5 To make a roux, melt the butter and stir in the flour until it has a paste-like consistency. Add to the soup, stirring until slightly thickened.

6 Just before serving, add the cooked spaghetti.

7 Transfer the soup to individual serving bowls, garnish with parsley, and serve.

VARIATION

Guinea fowl is available from specialty grocers, but you could use quail or other game bird.

Tuscan Bean Soup

Serves 4

INGREDIENTS

1¼ cups dried lima beans soaked
    overnight or 2 x 14½ ounce cans
    lima beans
1 tbsp olive oil

2 garlic cloves, crushed
1 vegetable or chicken stock cube,
    crumbled

⅔ cup milk
2 tbsp chopped fresh oregano
salt and pepper

1 If you are using dried beans that have been soaked overnight, drain them thoroughly. Bring a large pan of water to a boil, add the beans, and boil for 10 minutes. Cover the pan and simmer for a further 30 minutes or until tender. Drain the beans, reserving the cooking liquid. If you are using canned beans, drain them thoroughly and reserve the liquid.

2 Heat the oil in a large skillet and sauté the garlic for 2–3 minutes or until just beginning to brown.

3 Add the beans and 1⅔ cups of the reserved liquid to the skillet, stirring constantly. You may need to add a little water if there is insufficient liquid. Stir in the crumbled stock cube. Bring the mixture to a boil, stirring, and then remove the skillet from the heat.

4 Place the bean mixture in a food processor and blend to form a smooth purée. Alternatively, mash the bean mixture to a smooth consistency. Season to taste with salt and pepper, and stir in the milk.

5 Pour the soup back into the skillet and gently heat to just below boiling point. Stir in the chopped oregano just before serving.

VARIATION

If you prefer, use 3 teaspoons of dried oregano instead of fresh, but add with the beans in step 2. This soup can also be made with cannellini or borlotti beans following the same method.

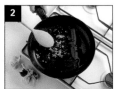

Brown Lentil Soup with Pasta

Serves 4

INGREDIENTS

4 slices bacon, cut into small squares	2 celery stalks, chopped	5 cups hot ham or vegetable stock
1 onion, chopped	$1/4$ cup farfalline or spaghetti broken into small pieces	2 tbsp chopped, fresh mint
2 garlic cloves, crushed	$14^1/2$ ounce can brown lentils, drained	

1 Place the bacon in a large skillet together with the onions, garlic, and celery. Dry fry for 4–5 minutes, stirring, until the onion is tender and the bacon is just beginning to brown.

2 Add the farfalline or spaghetti pieces to the skillet and cook, stirring, for about 1 minute to coat the pasta in the oil.

3 Add the lentils and the stock and bring to a boil. Reduce the heat and simmer for 12–15 minutes or until the pasta is tender.

4 Remove the skillet from the heat and stir in the chopped fresh mint.

5 Transfer the soup to warm soup bowls and serve immediately.

COOK'S TIP

If you prefer to use dried lentils, add the stock before the pasta and cook for 1–1¼ hours, until the lentils are tender. Add the pasta and cook for a further 12–15 minutes.

VARIATION

Any type of pasta can be used in this recipe. Try fusilli, conchiglie, or rigatoni, if you wish.

Vegetable Soup with Cannellini Beans

Serves 4

INGREDIENTS

1 small eggplant

2 large tomatoes

1 potato, peeled

1 carrot, peeled

1 leek

14½ ounce can cannellini beans

3¾ cups hot vegetable or chicken
stock

2 tsp dried basil

½ ounce dried porcini mushrooms,
soaked for 10 minutes in
enough warm water to cover

¼ cup vermicelli

3 tbsp pesto (see

freshly grated Parmesan cheese, to
serve (optional)

1 Using a sharp knife, slice the eggplant into rings about ½ inch thick, then cut each ring into 4.

2 Cut the tomatoes and potato into small dice. Cut the carrot into sticks, about 1 inch long and cut the leek into rings.

3 Place the cannellini beans and their liquid in a large saucepan. Add the eggplant, tomatoes, potatoes, carrot, and leek, stirring to mix.

4 Add the stock to the pan and bring to a boil. Reduce the heat and simmer for 15 minutes.

5 Add the basil, dried mushrooms, their soaking liquid, and the vermicelli and simmer for 5 minutes or until all the vegetables are tender.

6 Remove the pan from the heat and stir in the pesto.

7 Ladle into bowls and serve with freshly grated Parmesan cheese, if using.

COOK'S TIP

Porcini mushrooms are grown in southern Italy. When dried and rehydrated they have a very intense flavor, so although they are expensive to buy, only a small amount is required to add flavor to soups or risottos.

Tucsan Onion Soup

Serves 4

INGREDIENTS

$^1/_3$ cup diced pancetta	3 garlic cloves, chopped	3 tbsp butter
1 tbsp olive oil	3$^3/_4$ cups hot chicken or ham stock	2$^3/_4$ ounces Swiss or cheddar
4 large white onions, thinly sliced in rings	4 slices ciabatta or other Italian bread	cheese
		salt and pepper

1 Dry fry the pancetta in a large saucepan for 3–4 minutes, until it just begins to brown. Remove the pancetta from the saucepan and set aside until required.

2 Add the oil to the pan and sauté the onions and garlic over a high heat for 4 minutes. Reduce the heat, cover, and cook for 15 minutes, until lightly caramelized.

3 Add the stock to the saucepan and bring to a boil. Reduce the heat and simmer, covered, for about 10 minutes.

4 Toast the slices of ciabatta on both sides, under a preheated broiler, for 2–3 minutes, or until golden. Spread the ciabatta with butter and top with the Swiss or cheddar cheese. Cut the bread into bite-size pieces.

5 Add the reserved pancetta to the soup and season to taste with salt and pepper. Pour into 4 soup bowls and top with the toasted bread.

COOK'S TIP

Pancetta is similar to bacon, but it is air- and salt-cured for about 6 months. Pancetta is available from most delicatessens and some large supermarkets. If you cannot obtain pancetta, use unsmoked bacon instead.

Green Soup

Serves 4

INGREDIENTS

1 tbsp olive oil

1 onion, chopped

1 garlic clove, chopped

7 ounces potatoes, peeled and cut
into 1-inch cubes

3 cups vegetable or chicken stock

1 small cucumber or ¹/₂ large
cucumber, cut into chunks

3 ounce bunch watercress

4¹/₂ ounces green beans, trimmed

and halved lengthwise

salt and pepper

1 Heat the oil in a large pan and sauté the onion and garlic for 3–4 minutes, or until softened. Add the cubed potatoes and cook for a further 2–3 minutes.

2 Stir in the stock, bring to a boil, and simmer for 5 minutes.

3 Add the cucumber to the pan and cook for a further 3 minutes, or until the potatoes are tender. Test by inserting the tip of a knife into the potato cubes—it should pass through easily.

4 Add the watercress and allow to wilt. Then place the soup in a food processor and blend until smooth. Alternatively, before adding the watercress, mash the soup with a potato masher and push through a strainer, then chop the watercress finely and stir into the soup.

5 Bring a small pan of water to a boil and steam the beans for 3–4 minutes, or until tender.

6 Add the beans to the soup, season, and warm through.

VARIATION

Try using 4¹/₂ ounces of snow peas instead of the beans, if you prefer.

Artichoke Soup

Serves 4

INGREDIENTS

1 tbsp olive oil
1 onion, chopped
1 garlic clove, crushed

2 x 14 ounce cans artichoke hearts, drained
2½ cups hot vegetable stock
⅔ cup light cream

2 tbsp fresh thyme, stalks removed
2 sun-dried tomatoes, cut into strips
crusty bread, to serve

1 Heat the oil in a large saucepan and sauté the chopped onion and crushed garlic until just softened.

2 Using a sharp knife, roughly chop the artichoke hearts. Add the artichoke pieces to the onion and garlic mixture in the pan. Pour in the hot vegetable stock, stirring.

3 Bring the mixture to a boil, then reduce the heat, and simmer, covered, for about 3 minutes.

4 Place the mixture into a food processor and blend until smooth. Alternatively, push the mixture through a strainer to remove any lumps.

5 Return the soup to the saucepan. Stir the light cream and fresh thyme into the soup, mixing well.

6 Transfer the soup to a large bowl, cover, cool, and chill in the refrigerator for about 3–4 hours.

7 Transfer the chilled soup to individual soup bowls and garnish with strips of sun-dried tomato. Serve with lots of fresh, crusty bread.

VARIATION

Try adding 2 tablespoons of dry vermouth, such as Martini, to the soup in step 5 if you wish.

Orange, Thyme, & Pumpkin Soup

Serves 4

INGREDIENTS

2 tbsp olive oil	6¼ cups boiling vegetable or	3 tbsp fresh thyme, stalks removed
2 medium onions, chopped	chicken stock	⅔ cup milk
2 cloves garlic, chopped	finely grated rind and juice of	salt and pepper
7 cups diced pumpkin	1 orange	crusty bread, to serve

1 Heat the olive oil in a large saucepan. Add the onions to the pan and sauté for 3–4 minutes, or until softened. Add the garlic and pumpkin and cook for a further 2 minutes, stirring well.

2 Add the boiling vegetable or chicken stock, orange rind and juice, and 2 tablespoons of the thyme to the pan. Simmer, covered, for 20 minutes, or until the pumpkin is tender.

3 Place the mixture in a food processor and blend until smooth. Alternatively, mash the mixture with a potato masher until smooth. Season to taste with salt and pepper.

4 Return the soup to the saucepan and add the milk. Reheat the soup for 3–4 minutes, or until it is piping hot, but not boiling. Sprinkle with the remaining fresh thyme just before serving.

5 Divide the soup between 4 warm soup bowls and serve with lots of fresh crusty bread.

COOK'S TIP

Pumpkins are usually large vegetables. To make things a little easier, buy a piece weighing about 2 pounds. Alternatively, make double the quantity and freeze the soup for up to 3 months.

Calabrian Mushroom Soup

Serves 4

INGREDIENTS

2 tbsp olive oil	1¼ cups milk	3 tbsp butter, melted
1 onion, chopped	3¾ cups hot vegetable stock	2 garlic cloves, crushed
1 pound mixed mushrooms, such as ceps, oyster, and button	8 slices of rustic bread or French bread	¾ cup finely grated Swiss cheese salt and pepper

1 Heat the oil in a large skillet and sauté the onion for 3–4 minutes, or until soft and golden.

2 Wipe each mushroom with a damp cloth and cut any large mushrooms into smaller, bite-size pieces.

3 Add the mushrooms to the pan, stirring quickly to coat them in the oil.

4 Add the milk to the pan, bring to a boil, cover, lower the heat, and simmer for about 5 minutes. Gradually stir in the hot vegetable stock.

5 Under a preheated broiler, toast the bread on both sides until golden.

6 Mix together the garlic and butter and spoon generously over the toast.

7 Place the toast in the bottom of a large tureen or divide it between 4 individual serving bowls and pour in the hot soup. Top with the grated Swiss cheese and serve at once.

COOK'S TIP

Mushrooms absorb liquid, which can lessen the flavor and affect cooking properties. Wipe them with a damp cloth rather than rinsing them in water.

VARIATION

Supermarkets stock a wide variety of exotic mushrooms. If you prefer, use a combination of cultivated and exotic mushrooms.

Tomatoes Stuffed with Tuna Mayonnaise

Serves 4

INGREDIENTS

4 plum tomatoes	4 tbsp olive oil	TO GARNISH:
2 tbsp sun-dried tomato paste	4 ounce can tuna, drained	2 sun-dried tomatoes, cut
2 egg yolks	2 tbsp capers, rinsed	into strips
2 tsp lemon juice	salt and pepper	fresh basil leaves
finely grated rind of 1 lemon		

1 Halve the tomatoes and scoop out the seeds. Divide the sun-dried tomato paste among the tomato halves and spread carefully around the inside of the skin.

2 Place on a cookie sheet and roast in a preheated oven at 400°F for 12–15 minutes. Cool slightly.

3 Meanwhile, make the mayonnaise. In a food processor, blend the egg yolks and lemon juice with the lemon rind until smooth. Once mixed and with the motor still running, slowly add the olive oil. Stop the processor as soon as the mayonnaise has thickened. Alternatively, use a hand whisk, beating the mixture continuously until it thickens.

4 Add the tuna and capers to the mayonnaise and season with salt and pepper to taste.

5 Spoon the tuna mayonnaise mixture into the tomato shells and garnish with sun-dried tomato strips and basil leaves. Return to the oven or serve chilled.

COOK'S TIP

For a picnic, do not roast the tomatoes, just scoop out the seeds, drain, cut-side down, on absorbent paper towels for 1 hour, and fill with the mayonnaise mixture. They are firmer to handle and easier to eat with the fingers this way. If you prefer, ready-made mayonnaise may be used instead — just stir in the lemon rind.

Deep-Fried Risotto Balls

Serves 4

INGREDIENTS

2 tbsp olive oil	³/₄ cup risotto rice, washed	¹/₂ cup dry white wine
1 medium onion, finely chopped	1 tsp dried oregano	2³/₄ ounces mozzarella cheese
1 garlic clove, chopped	1²/₃ cup hot vegetable or chicken	oil, for deep-frying
¹/₂ red bell pepper, diced	stock	fresh basil sprig, to garnish

1 Heat the oil in a skillet and sauté the onion and garlic for 3–4 minutes, or until just softened.

2 Add the bell pepper, rice, and oregano to the pan. Cook for 2–3 minutes, stirring to coat the rice in the oil.

3 Mix the stock together with the wine and add to the pan a ladleful at a time, waiting for the liquid to be absorbed by the rice before you add the next ladleful of liquid.

4 Once all the liquid has been absorbed and the rice is tender (about 15 minutes total), remove the pan from the heat and leave until the mixture is cool enough to handle.

5 Cut the cheese into 12 pieces. Taking about a tablespoon of risotto, shape the mixture around the cheese pieces to make 12 balls.

6 Heat the oil until a piece of bread browns in 30 seconds. Cook the risotto balls in batches of 4 for 2 minutes, until golden.

7 Remove the risotto balls with a slotted spoon and drain thoroughly on absorbent paper towels. Garnish with a sprig of basil and serve hot.

VARIATION

Although mozzarella is the traditional cheese for this recipe and creates the stringy "telephone wire" effect, other cheeses, such as cheddar, may be used if desired.

Black Olive Pâté

Serves 4

INGREDIENTS

1½ cups pitted black olives, chopped	3 tbsp sweet butter	2 tbsp extra-virgin olive oil
finely grated rind and juice of 1 lemon	4 canned anchovy fillets, drained and rinsed	2 tbsp ground almonds

1 If you are making the pâté by hand, chop the olives very finely and then mash them, together with the lemon rind, juice, and butter, using a fork or potato masher. Alternatively, place the olives, lemon rind, juice, and butter in a food processor and blend until all the ingredients are finely chopped.

2 Using a sharp knife, chop the drained anchovies and add them to the olive and lemon mixture. Mash the pâté by hand or blend it in a food processor for about 20 seconds.

3 Gradually beat in the olive oil and stir in the ground almonds. Place the black olive pâté in a serving bowl.

4 Chill the pâté in the refrigerator for about 30 minutes. Serve accompanied by thin pieces of toast.

COOK'S TIP

Extra-virgin olive oil is the finest grade of olive oil. It is made from the first, cold pressing of hand-gathered olives.

COOK'S TIP

The pâté will keep for up to 5 days in a serving bowl in the refrigerator if you pour a thin layer of extra-virgin olive oil over the top to seal it. Then use the oil to brush on the toast before spreading the pâté.

Fresh Figs with Parma Ham (Prosciutto)

Serves 4

INGREDIENTS

1½ ounces arugula	4 tbsp olive oil	1 small red chili
4 fresh figs	1 tbsp fresh orange juice	
4 slices prosciutto	1 tbsp clear honey	

1 Tear the arugula into fairly small pieces and arrange on 4 serving plates.

2 Using a sharp knife, cut each of the figs into quarters and place them on top of the arugula leaves.

3 Using a sharp knife, cut the prosciutto into strips and scatter over the arugula and figs.

4 Place the oil, orange juice, and honey in a screw-top jar. Shake the jar vigorously until the mixture emulsifies and forms a thick dressing. Transfer to a serving bowl.

5 Using a sharp knife, dice the chili, remembering not to touch your face before you have washed your hands (see Cook's Tip, right). Add the chopped chili to the dressing and mix well.

6 Drizzle the dressing over the prosciutto, arugula, and figs, tossing to mix well. Serve the salad at once.

COOK'S TIP

Chiles can burn the skin for several hours after chopping, so it is advisable to wear gloves when you are handling the very hot varieties.

COOK'S TIP

Parma, in the Emilia-Romagna region of Italy, is famous for its ham, prosciutto di Parma, thought to be the best in the world.

Roasted Bell Peppers

Serves 4

INGREDIENTS

2 each, red, yellow, and orange bell peppers	1 tbsp olive oil	2 tbsp fresh thyme
4 tomatoes, halved	3 garlic cloves, chopped	salt and pepper
	1 onion, sliced in rings	

1 Halve and seed the bell peppers. Place them, cut-side down, on a cookie sheet and cook under a preheated broiler for 10 minutes.

2 Add the tomatoes to the cookie sheet and broil for 5 minutes, until the skins of the bell peppers and tomatoes are charred.

3 Put the bell peppers into a plastic bag for 10 minutes to sweat, which will make the skin easier to peel. Remove the tomato skins and roughly chop the flesh.

4 Peel the skins from the bell peppers and slice the flesh into strips.

5 Heat the oil in a large skillet and sauté the garlic and onion for 3–4 minutes, or until softened.

6 Add the bell peppers and tomatoes to the skillet and cook for 5 minutes. Stir in the fresh thyme and season to taste with salt and pepper.

7 Transfer to serving bowls and serve warm. Alternatively, chill before serving.

COOK'S TIP

You can preserve the bell peppers in the refrigerator by placing them in a sterilized jar and pouring olive oil over the top to seal. Alternatively, heat ¼ cup white wine vinegar with a bay leaf and 4 juniper berries and bring to a boiling point. Pour over the bell peppers and set aside until completely cold. Pack into sterilized jars — they will keep for up to one month.

Baked Eggplant & Tomatoes

Serves 4

INGREDIENTS

3-4 tbsp olive oil
2 garlic cloves, crushed
2 large eggplant

$3^{1}/_{2}$ ounces mozzarella cheese,
    thinly sliced
7 ounces tomato sauce

$^{2}/_{3}$ cup grated Parmesan cheese

1 Heat 2 tablespoons of the olive oil in a large skillet. Add the garlic to the skillet and sauté for 30 seconds.

2 Slice the eggplant lengthwise. Add the slices to the skillet and cook them in the oil for about 3–4 minutes on each side, or until just tender. (You will probably have to cook them in batches, so add the remaining olive oil as necessary.)

3 Remove the eggplant slices with a slotted spoon and drain thoroughly on absorbent paper towels.

4 Place a layer of eggplant slices in a shallow ovenproof dish. Cover the eggplant with a layer of mozzarella cheese and then pour a third of the tomato sauce on top. Continue layering in the same order, finishing with a layer of tomato sauce on top.

5 Generously sprinkle the grated Parmesan cheese over the top and then bake in a preheated oven at 400°F for 25–30 minutes.

6 Transfer the baked eggplant and tomatoes to serving plates and serve warm or chilled.

COOK'S TIP

Passata is a simple tomato sauce, which can be bought from most supermarkets. Alternatively, you can purée and sieve a can of tomatoes and season with salt and pepper to taste.

Zucchini & Thyme Fritters

Makes 16

INGREDIENTS

³/₄ cup self–rising flour	10¹/₂ ounces zucchini	1 tbsp oil
2 eggs, beaten	2 tbsp fresh thyme	salt and pepper
¹/₄ cup milk		

1 Sift the self-rising flour into a large bowl and make a well in the center. Add the eggs to the well, and using a wooden spoon, gradually fold in the flour.

2 Slowly add the milk to the mixture of flour and eggs, stirring constantly to form a thick batter.

3 Wash the zucchini. Grate the zucchini over a paper towel placed in a bowl to absorb some of the juices.

4 Add the zucchini, thyme, salt, and pepper to taste to the batter, and mix thoroughly.

5 Heat the oil in a large, heavy-based skillet. Taking a tablespoon of the batter for a medium-size fritter or half a tablespoon of batter for a smaller-size fritter, spoon the mixture into the hot oil and cook, in batches, for 3–4 minutes on each side.

6 Remove the fritters with a slotted spoon and drain thoroughly on absorbent paper towels. Keep each batch of fritters warm in the oven while making the rest. Serve hot.

VARIATION

Try adding ¹/₂ teaspoon dried, crushed chiles in step 4 for spicier tasting fritters.

Cured Meats with Olives & Tomatoes

Serves 4

INGREDIENTS

4 plum tomatoes	2 tbsp capers, drained and rinsed	1 tbsp extra-virgin olive oil
1 tbsp balsamic vinegar	1 cup pitted green olives	salt and pepper
6 canned anchovy fillets, drained and rinsed	6 ounces mixed, cured meats, sliced	crusty bread, to serve
	8 fresh basil leaves	

1 Using a sharp knife, cut the tomatoes into evenly sized slices. Sprinkle the tomato slices with the balsamic vinegar and a little salt and pepper to taste and set aside.

2 Chop the anchovy fillets into pieces measuring about the same length as the olives.

3 Push a piece of anchovy and a caper into each olive.

4 Arrange the sliced meat on 4 individual serving plates together with the tomatoes, filled olives, and basil leaves.

5 Lightly drizzle the olive oil over the sliced meat, tomatoes, and olives.

6 Serve the cured meats, olives, and tomatoes with lots of fresh crusty bread.

COOK'S TIP

Fill a screw-top jar with the stuffed olives, cover with olive oil, and use when required — they will keep for one month in the refrigerator.

COOK'S TIP

The cured meats for this recipe are up to your individual taste. They can include a selection of prosciutto, pancetta, bresaola (dried salt beef), and salame di Milano (pork and beef sausage).

Spinach & Ricotta Patties

Serves 4

INGREDIENTS

1 pound fresh spinach
1¹/₈ cups ricotta cheese
1 egg, beaten
2 tsp fennel seeds, lightly crushed

²/₃ cup finely grated pecorino or
    Parmesan cheese
¹/₄ cup all-purpose flour, mixed
    with 1 tsp dried thyme

5 tbsp butter
2 garlic cloves, crushed
salt and pepper

---

1 Wash the spinach and trim off any long stalks. Place in a pan, cover, and cook for 4–5 minutes, until wilted. This will probably have to be done in batches as the volume of spinach is quite large. Place in a colander to drain, and cool.

2 Mash the ricotta and beat in the egg and the fennel seeds. Season with plenty of salt and pepper, then stir in the pecorino or Parmesan cheese.

3 Squeeze as much excess water as possible from the spinach and finely chop the leaves. Stir into the cheese mixture.

4 Taking about 1 tablespoon of the spinach and cheese mixture, shape it into a ball and flatten it slightly to form a patty. Gently roll in the seasoned flour. Continue this process until all the mixture has been used up.

5 Half fill a large saucepan with water and bring to a boil. Carefully add the patties and cook for 3–4 minutes, or until they rise to the surface. Remove with a slotted spoon.

6 Melt the butter in a pan. Add the garlic and sauté for 2–3 minutes. Pour the garlic butter over the patties, season with freshly ground black pepper, and serve at once.

COOK'S TIP

Once it is washed, spinach holds enough water on the leaves to cook without adding any extra liquid. If you use frozen spinach instead of fresh, simply thaw it and squeeze out the excess water.

Sweet & Sour Baby Onions

Serves 4

INGREDIENTS

12 ounces baby or pickling onions	thinly pared rind of 1 lemon	4 tbsp red wine vinegar
2 tbsp olive oil	1 tbsp brown sugar	
2 fresh bay leaves, torn into strips	1 tbsp clear honey	

1 Soak the onions in a bowl of boiling water–this will make them easier to peel. Using a sharp knife, peel and halve the onions.

2 Heat the oil in a large skillet. Add the bay leaves and onions to the pan and cook over a medium-high heat for 5–6 minutes, or until browned all over.

3 Cut the lemon rind into thin matchsticks. Add to the skillet with the sugar and honey. Cook for 2-3 minutes, stirring occasionally, until the onions are lightly caramelized.

4 Add the red wine vinegar to the skillet, being careful because it will spit. Cook for about 5 minutes, stirring, or until the onions are tender and the liquid has all but disappeared.

5 Transfer the onions to a serving dish and serve them at once.

COOK'S TIP

Adjust the piquancy of this dish to your liking by adding more sugar for a sweeter, more caramelized taste, or extra red wine vinegar for a sharper, tarter flavor.

COOK'S TIP

To make the onions easier to peel, place them in a large saucepan, add boiling water, and set aside for 10 minutes. Drain the onions thoroughly, and when they are cold enough to handle, peel them.

Stewed Artichokes

Serves 4

INGREDIENTS

4 small globe artichokes	2 bay leaves	olive oil
4 garlic cloves, peeled	finely grated rind and juice of	2 tbsp fresh marjoram
	1 lemon	lemon wedges, to serve

---

1 Using a sharp knife, carefully peel away the tough outer leaves surrounding the artichokes. Trim the artichoke stems to about 1 inch.

2 Using a knife, cut each artichoke in half and scoop out the choke.

3 Place the artichokes in a large heavy-based pan. Add enough olive oil to half cover the artichokes in the pan.

4 Add the garlic cloves, bay leaves, and half of the grated lemon rind to the artichoke mixture.

5 Start to heat the artichokes gently, cover the pan, and continue to cook over a low heat for about 40 minutes. The artichokes should be stewed in the oil, not fried.

6 Once the artichokes are tender, remove them with a slotted spoon and drain thoroughly. Remove the bay leaves.

7 Transfer the artichokes to warm serving plates. Serve the artichokes sprinkled with the remaining grated lemon rind, fresh marjoram, and a little lemon juice.

COOK'S TIP

To prevent the artichokes from oxidizing and turning brown before cooking, brush them with a little lemon juice. In addition, use the oil used for cooking the artichokes for salad dressings — it will impart a lovely lemon and herb flavor.

Garbanzo Beans with Prosciutto

Serves 4

INGREDIENTS

1 tbsp olive oil
1 medium onion, thinly sliced
1 garlic clove, chopped

1 small red bell pepper, seeded and
cut into thin strips
1¼ cups chopped prosciutto

14 ounce can garbanzo beans,
drained and rinsed
1 tbsp chopped parsley, to garnish
crusty bread, to serve

1 Heat the oil in a large skillet. Add the sliced onion, chopped garlic, and sliced bell pepper and sauté for 3–4 minutes, or until the vegetables have softened.

2 Add the prosciutto to the skillet and fry with the vegetables for 5 minutes, or until the prosciutto is just beginning to brown.

3 Add the garbanzo beans to the skillet and cook, stirring, for 2–3 minutes, until warmed through.

4 Sprinkle with chopped parsley and transfer to warm serving plates. Serve with lots of fresh crusty bread.

COOK'S TIP

Whenever possible, use fresh herbs when cooking. They are becoming more readily available, especially since the introduction of "growing" herbs, small pots of herbs that you can buy from the supermarket and grow at home. This ensures the herbs are fresh and also provides a continuous supply.

VARIATION

Try adding a small finely diced chili in step 1 for a spicier taste, if desired.

Deep-Fried Seafood

Serves 4

INGREDIENTS

7 ounces prepared squid	⅓ cup all-purpose flour	TO SERVE:
7 ounces raw tiger shrimp, peeled	1 tsp dried basil	garlic mayonnaise (see Cook's Tip)
5½ ounces whitebait	salt and pepper	lemon wedges
oil, for deep-frying		

1 Carefully rinse the squid, shrimp, and whitebait under cold running water, in order to completely removing any dirt or grit.

2 Using a very sharp knife, slice the squid into rings, leaving the tentacles whole.

3 Heat the oil in a large pan until a cube of bread browns in 30 seconds – the oil will then be hot enough for deep-frying.

4 Place the flour in a bowl and season with the salt, pepper, and basil.

5 Roll the squid, shrimp, and whitebait in the seasoned flour until coated all over. Carefully shake off any excess flour.

6 Cook the seafood in the hot oil in batches for 2–3 minutes, or until crispy and golden all over. Remove the seafood with a slotted spoon and drain thoroughly on paper towels. Keep warm while you cook the remaining batches of seafood.

7 Transfer the deep-fried seafood to serving plates and serve with garlic mayonnaise (see Cook's Tip) and lemon wedges.

COOK'S TIP

To make garlic mayonnaise for serving with the deep-fried seafood, crush 2 garlic cloves, stir into 8 tablespoons of mayonnaise, and season with salt and pepper and a little chopped parsley.

Tuscan Bean Salad with Tuna

Serves 4

INGREDIENTS

1 small white onion or 2 scallions, finely chopped

2 x 14 ounce cans dried lima beans, drained

2 medium tomatoes

6½ ounce can tuna, drained

2 tbsp flat leaf parsley, chopped

2 tbsp olive oil

1 tbsp lemon juice

2 tsp clear honey

1 garlic clove, crushed

1 Place the chopped onion or scallions and lima beans in a bowl and mix well to combine.

2 Using a sharp knife, cut the tomatoes into wedges. Add the tomatoes to the onion and bean mixture.

3 Flake the tuna with a fork and add it to the onion and bean mixture, together with the parsley.

4 In a screw-top jar, mix together the olive oil, lemon juice, honey, and garlic. Shake the jar vigorously until the dressing emulsifies and thickens.

5 Pour the dressing over the bean salad. Toss the ingredients together using 2 spoons and serve.

COOK'S TIP

This salad will keep for several days in a covered container in the refrigerator. Make up the dressing just before serving and toss the ingredients together to mix well.

VARIATION

Substitute fresh salmon for the tuna if you wish to create a luxurious version of this recipe for a special occasion.

Italian Potato Salad

Serves 4

INGREDIENTS

1 pound baby potatoes, unpeeled,
    or larger potatoes, halved
4 tbsp unsweetened yogurt

4 tbsp mayonnaise
8 sun-dried tomatoes

2 tbsp flat leaf parsley, chopped
salt and pepper

1 Rinse and clean the potatoes and place them in a large pan of water. Bring to a boil and cook for 8–12 minutes, or until just tender. (The cooking time will vary according to the size of your potatoes.)

2 Using a sharp knife, cut the sun-dried tomatoes into thin slices.

3 To make the dressing, mix together the yogurt and mayonnaise in a bowl and season to taste with a little salt and pepper. Stir in the sun-dried tomato slices and the chopped flat leaf parsley.

4 Remove the potatoes with a slotted spoon, drain them thoroughly, and then set them aside to cool. If you are using larger potatoes, cut them into 2-inch chunks.

5 Pour the dressing over the potatoes and toss to mix.

6 Chill the potato salad in the refrigerator for about 20 minutes, then serve as a starter or as an accompaniment.

COOK'S TIP

It is easier to cut the larger potatoes once they are cooked. Although smaller pieces of potato will cook more quickly, they tend to disintegrate and become mushy.

Green Salad

Serves 4

INGREDIENTS

¹/₄ cup pistachios	4 slices rustic bread	1 ounce arugula
5 tbsp extra-virgin olive oil	1 tbsp red wine vinegar	1 ounce red chard
1 tbsp rosemary, chopped	1 tsp wholegrain mustard	¹/₂ cup pitted green olives
2 garlic cloves, chopped	1 tsp sugar	2 tbsp fresh basil, shredded

1 Shell the pistachios and roughly chop them, using a sharp knife.

2 Heat 2 tablespoons of the extra-virgin olive oil in a skillet. Add the rosemary and garlic and cook over a medium heat for 2 minutes.

3 Add the slices of bread to the skillet and fry for 2–3 minutes on both sides, until golden. Remove the bread from the pan and drain on absorbent paper towels.

4 To make the dressing, mix together the remaining olive oil, the red wine vinegar, mustard, and sugar.

5 Place a slice of bread onto 4 serving plates and top with the arugula and red chard. Sprinkle with the olives.

6 Drizzle the dressing over the top of the salad greens. Sprinkle with the chopped pistachios and shredded basil leaves and serve the salad immediately.

COOK'S TIP

If you cannot find red chard, try slicing a tomato into very thin wedges to add a splash of vibrant red color to the salad.

VARIATION

Watercress may be used instead of the arugula, if desired.

Minted Fennel Salad

Serves 4

INGREDIENTS

1 bulb fennel	1 small or ½ a large cucumber	1 tbsp virgin olive oil
2 small oranges	1 tbsp chopped mint	2 eggs, hard-boiled

1 Using a sharp knife, trim the outer leaves from the fennel bulb. Slice the fennel bulb thinly into a bowl of water and sprinkle with lemon juice (see Cook's Tip).

2 Grate the rind of the oranges over a bowl. Using a sharp knife, pare away the orange pith, then segment the oranges by carefully slicing between each line of pith. Do this over the bowl in order to retain the juice.

3 Using a sharp knife, cut the cucumber into ½-inch slices and then cut each slice into quarters. Add the cucumber to the fennel and orange mixture together with the mint.

4 Pour the olive oil over the fennel and cucumber salad and toss well.

5 Peel and quarter the eggs and use them to decorate the top of the salad. Serve at once.

COOK'S TIP

Virgin olive oil, which has a fine aroma and flavor, is made by the cold pressing of olives. However, it may have a slightly higher acidity level than extra-virgin oil.

COOK'S TIP

Fennel will discolor if it is left for any length of time without a dressing. To prevent any discoloration, place it in a bowl of water and sprinkle with lemon juice.

Capri Salad

Serves 4

INGREDIENTS

2 beef tomatoes	8 basil leaves	salt and pepper
4½ ounces mozzarella cheese	1 tbsp balsamic vinegar	basil leaves, to garnish
12 black olives	1 tbsp olive oil	

1 Using a sharp knife, cut the tomatoes into thin slices.

2 Using a sharp knife, cut the mozzarella into slices.

3 Pit the olives and slice them into rings.

4 Layer the tomato, mozzarella cheese, and olives in a stack, finishing with a layer of cheese on top.

5 Place each stack under a preheated hot broiler for 2–3 minutes, or just long enough to melt the mozzarella.

6 Drizzle with the vinegar and olive oil, and season to taste with salt and pepper.

7 Transfer to serving plates and garnish with basil leaves. Serve immediately.

COOK'S TIP

Balsamic vinegar, which has grown in popularity over the past decade, is produced in the Emilia-Romagna region of Italy. It is made from wine that is distilled until it is dark brown and extremely strongly flavored.

COOK'S TIP

Buffalo mozzarella cheese, although it is usually more expensive because of the comparative rarity of buffalo, does have a better flavor than the cow's milk variety. It is popular in salads, but also provides a tangy layer in baked dishes.

Mushroom Salad

Serves 4

INGREDIENTS

5¹/₂ ounces firm white mushrooms
4 tbsp virgin olive oil

1 tbsp lemon juice
5 anchovy fillets, drained and
    chopped

1 tbsp fresh marjoram
salt and pepper

1 Gently wipe each mushroom with a damp cloth to remove any excess dirt. Slice the mushrooms thinly, using a sharp knife.

2 Mix together the olive oil and lemon juice and pour the mixture over the mushrooms. Toss together so that the mushrooms are completely coated with the lemon juice and oil.

3 Stir the chopped anchovy fillets into the mushrooms. Season the mushroom mixture with black pepper and garnish with the fresh marjoram.

4 Let the mushroom salad stand for 5 minutes before serving in order for all the flavors to be absorbed. Season with a little salt (see Cook's Tip, below) and then serve.

COOK'S TIP

Do not season the mushroom salad with salt until the very last minute as it will cause the mushrooms to blacken and the juices to leak. The result will not be as tasty as it should be as the full flavors will not be absorbed and it will look very unattractive.

COOK'S TIP

If you use dried herbs rather than fresh, remember that you need only about one-third of dried to fresh.

Yellow Bell Pepper Salad

Serves 4

INGREDIENTS

4 slices bacon, chopped

2 yellow bell peppers

8 radishes, washed and trimmed

1 celery stalk, finely chopped

3 plum tomatoes, cut into wedges

3 tbsp olive oil

1 tbsp fresh thyme

1 Dry fry the chopped bacon in a skillet for 4–5 minutes, or until crispy. Remove the bacon from the skillet, set aside, and cool until required.

2 Using a sharp knife, halve and seed the bell peppers. Slice the bell peppers into long strips.

3 Using a sharp knife, halve the radishes and cut them into wedges.

4 Mix together the bell peppers, radishes, celery, and tomatoes, and toss the mixture in the olive oil and fresh thyme. Season to taste with a little salt and pepper.

5 Transfer the salad to serving plates and garnish with the reserved crispy bacon.

COOK'S TIP

Tomatoes are actually berries and are related to potatoes. There are many different shapes and sizes of this versatile fruit. The one most used in Italian cooking is the plum tomato, which is very flavorsome.

COOK'S TIP

Pre-packaged diced bacon can be purchased from most supermarkets, which helps to save on preparation time.

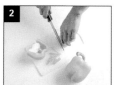

Spinach Salad

Serves 4

INGREDIENTS

1³/₄ ounces mushrooms

3¹/₂ ounces baby spinach, washed

2³/₄ ounces radicchio leaves,
    shredded

3¹/₂ ounces cooked chicken,
    preferably breast

1³/₄ ounces prosciutto

2 tbsp olive oil

finely grated rind of ¹/₂ orange and
    juice of 1 orange

1 tbsp unsweetened yogurt

1 Wipe the mushrooms with a damp cloth to remove any excess dirt.

2 Gently mix together the spinach and radicchio in a large salad bowl.

3 Thinly slice the wiped mushrooms and add them to the bowl containing the spinach and radicchio.

4 Tear the cooked chicken breast and prosciutto into strips and mix them into the salad.

5 To make the dressing, place the olive oil, orange rind, juice, and yogurt into a screw-top jar. Shake the jar until the mixture is well combined. Season to taste with salt and pepper.

6 Drizzle the dressing over the spinach salad and toss to mix well. Serve immediately.

COOK'S TIP

Radiccio is a variety of endive originating in Italy. It has a slightly bitter flavor.

VARIATION

Spinach is delicious when served raw. Try raw spinach in a salad garnished with bacon or garlicky croutons. The young leaves have a wonderfully sharp flavor.

Sweet & Sour Eggplant Salad

Serves 4

INGREDIENTS

6 tbsp olive oil
1 onion, chopped
2 garlic cloves, chopped
2 celery stalks, chopped
1 pound eggplant

14 ounce can tomatoes, chopped
1/2 cup pitted green olives, chopped
2 tbsp sugar
2 1/3 cup red wine vinegar
1 ounce capers, drained

salt and pepper
1 tbsp flat leaf parsley, roughly
    chopped, to garnish

1 Heat 2 tablespoons of the oil in a large skillet. Add the prepared onions, garlic, and celery to the skillet and cook, stirring, for 3–4 minutes.

2 Using a sharp knife, slice the eggplant into thick rounds, then cut each round into 4 pieces.

3 Add the eggplant pieces to the skillet with the remaining olive oil and fry for 5 minutes, or until golden.

4 Add the tomatoes, olives, and sugar to the skillet, stirring until the sugar has completely dissolved.

5 Add the red wine vinegar, reduce the heat, and simmer for 10–15 minutes or until the sauce is thick and the eggplant slices are tender.

6 While the skillet is still on the heat, carefully stir in the capers. Season to taste with a little salt and pepper.

7 Transfer to serving plates and garnish with the chopped fresh parsley.

COOK'S TIP

This salad is best served cold the day after it is made, which allows the flavors to mingle and be fully absorbed.

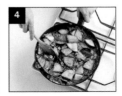

Lentil & Tuna Salad

Serves 4

INGREDIENTS

3 tbsp virgin olive oil	½ tsp ground cumin	14 ounce can lentils, drained
1 tbsp lemon juice	½ tsp ground cilantro	6½ can tuna, drained
1 tsp wholegrain mustard	1 small red onion	2 tbsp fresh cilantro, chopped
1 garlic clove, crushed	2 ripe tomatoes	pepper

1 Using a sharp knife, seed and dice the tomatoes into pieces.

2 Using a very sharp knife, finely chop the red onion.

3 To make the dressing, beat together the virgin olive oil, lemon juice, mustard, garlic, ground cumin, and ground cilantro in a small bowl. Set aside until required.

4 Carefully mix together the chopped onion, diced tomatoes, and drained lentils in a large bowl.

5 Flake the tuna and stir it into the onion, tomato, and lentil mixture.

6 Stir in the chopped fresh cilantro.

7 Pour the dressing over the lentil and tuna salad and season with freshly ground black pepper. Serve at once.

COOK'S TIP

Lentils are a good source of protein and contain important vitamins and minerals. Buy them dried for soaking and cooking yourself, or buy canned varieties for speed and convenience.

VARIATION

Nuts would add extra flavor and texture to this salad.

Bruschetta with Tomatoes

Serves 4

INGREDIENTS

10½ ounces cherry tomatoes	16 fresh basil leaves, shredded	salt and pepper
4 sun-dried tomatoes	2 garlic cloves, peeled	
4 tbsp extra-virgin olive oil	8 slices ciabatta	

1 Using a sharp knife, cut the cherry tomatoes in half.

2 Using a sharp knife, slice the sun-dried tomatoes into strips.

3 Place the cherry tomatoes and sun-dried tomatoes in a bowl. Add the olive oil and the shredded basil leaves and toss to mix well. Season to taste with a little salt and pepper.

4 Using a sharp knife, cut the garlic cloves in half. Lightly toast the ciabatta bread.

5 Rub the garlic, cut-side down, over both sides of the toasted ciabatta bread.

6 Top the ciabatta bread with the tomato mixture and serve immediately.

COOK'S TIP

Ciabatta is an Italian rustic bread which is slightly holed and quite chewy. It is very good in this recipe as it absorbs the full flavor of the garlic and extra-virgin olive oil.

VARIATION

Plum tomatoes are also good in this recipe. Halve them, then cut them into wedges. Mix them with the sun-dried tomatoes in step 3.

Italian Omelette

Serves 4

INGREDIENTS

2 pounds potatoes
1 tbsp oil
1 large onion, sliced
2 garlic cloves, chopped

6 sun-dried tomatoes, cut into
    strips
14 ounce can artichoke hearts,
    drained and halved
1 1/8 cups ricotta cheese

4 large eggs, beaten
2 tbsp milk
2/3 cup grated Parmesan cheese
3 tbsp chopped thyme

1 Peel the potatoes and place them in a bowl of cold water (see Cook's Tip). Cut the potatoes into thin slices.

2 Bring a large saucepan of water to a boil and add the potato slices. Lower the heat and simmer for 5–6 minutes, or until just tender.

3 Heat the oil in a large skillet. Add the onion slices and garlic to the pan and sauté, stirring occasionally, for about 3–4 minutes.

4 Add the sun-dried tomatoes and continue cooking for a further 2 minutes.

5 Place a layer of potatoes at the bottom of a deep, ovenproof dish. Top with a layer of the onion mixture, artichokes, and ricotta cheese. Repeat the layers in the same order, finishing with a layer of potatoes on top.

6 Beat together the eggs, milk, half the Parmesan, thyme, and salt and pepper to taste and pour over the potatoes.

7 Top with the remaining Parmesan cheese and bake in a preheated oven at 375°F for 20–25 minutes, or until cooked through and golden brown. Cut into slices and serve.

COOK'S TIP

Placing the potatoes in a bowl of cold water will prevent them from turning brown while you cut the rest into slices.

Casserole of Beans in Tomato Sauce

Serves 4

INGREDIENTS

14 ounce can cannellini beans	1 celery stalk	1 pound tomatoes
14 ounce can borlotti beans	2 garlic cloves, chopped	2¾ ounces arugula
2 tbsp olive oil	6 ounces baby onions, halved	

1 Drain both cans of beans and reserve 6 tbsp of the liquid.

2 Heat the oil in a large pan. Add the celery, garlic, and onions and sauté for 5 minutes, or until the onions are golden.

3 Cut a cross in the base of each tomato and plunge them into a bowl of boiling water for 30 seconds, until the skins split. Remove them with a slotted spoon and leave until cool enough to handle. Peel off the skin and chop the flesh. Add the tomato flesh and the reserved bean liquid to the pan and cook for 5 minutes.

4 Add the beans to the pan and cook for a further 3–4 minutes, or until the beans are hot.

5 Stir in the arugula and allow to wilt slightly before serving.

VARIATION

For a spicier-tasting dish, add 1–2 teaspoons hot pepper sauce with the beans in step 4.

COOK'S TIP

Another way to peel tomatoes is to cut a cross in the base, then push it onto a fork, and hold it over a flame, turning it slowly so that the skin heats evenly all over. The skin will start to bubble and split, and should then slide off easily.

Small Crêpes with Smoked Fish

Makes 12 Pancakes

INGREDIENTS

CRÊPES:
¾ cup all-purpose flour
½ tsp salt
1 egg, beaten
1¼ cups milk
1 tbsp oil, for frying

SAUCE:
1 pound smoked haddock, skinned
1¼ cups milk
3 tbsp butter or margarine
⅓ cup all-purpose flour
1¼ cups fish stock

1 cup grated Parmesan cheese
1 cup frozen peas, thawed
3½ ounces cooked, peeled shrimp
½ grated Swiss cheese
salt and pepper

1 To make the crêpe batter, sift the flour and salt into a large bowl and make a well in the center. Add the egg and, using a wooden spoon, begin to draw in the flour. Slowly add the milk and beat to form a smooth batter. Set aside until required.

2 Place the fish in a skillet, add the milk, and bring to a boil. Simmer for 10 minutes, or until the fish begins to flake. Drain, reserving the milk.

3 Melt the butter in a saucepan. Add the flour, mix to a paste, and cook for 2–3 minutes. Remove the pan from the heat and add the reserved milk a little at a time, stirring to make a smooth sauce. Repeat with the fish stock. Return to the heat and bring to a boil, stirring. Stir in the Parmesan and season with salt and pepper.

4 Grease a skillet with oil. Add 2 tablespoons of the crêpe batter, swirling it around, and cook for 2–3 minutes. Loosen the sides with a spatula and flip the crêpe over. Cook for 2–3 minutes, until golden. Repeat with the remaining batter. Stack the crêpes with sheets of baking parchment between them and keep warm in the oven.

5 Stir the fish, peas, and shrimp into half the sauce and use to fill each crêpe. Pour the remaining sauce over the crêpes, top with the Swiss cheese, and bake at 375°F for 20 minutes, until golden.

Roasted Seafood

Serves 4

INGREDIENTS

1 pound 5 ounces new potatoes	2 lemons, cut into wedges	2 small squid, chopped into rings
3 red onions, cut into wedges	4 sprigs rosemary	4 tomatoes, quartered
2 zucchini, sliced into chunks	4 tbsp olive oil	
8 garlic cloves, peeled	12 ounces raw shrimp	

1 Scrub the potatoes to remove any dirt. Cut any large potatoes in half. Place the potatoes in a large roasting pan, together with the onion wedges, sliced zucchini, garlic, lemon wedges, and rosemary.

2 Pour the oil over the vegetables and toss to coat all of them in the oil.

3 Cook in a preheated oven at 400°F for about 40 minutes, turning occasionally, until the potatoes are cooked through and tender.

4 Once the potatoes are tender, add the shrimp, squid, and tomatoes, tossing to coat them in the oil, and roast for 10 minutes. All the vegetables should be cooked through and slightly charred for full flavor.

5 Transfer to serving plates and serve hot.

COOK'S TIP

Squid and octopus are great favorites in Italy and all around the Mediterranean.

VARIATION

Most vegetables are suitable for roasting in the oven. Try adding 1 pound pumpkin, squash, or eggplant, if you prefer.

Omelet Strips in Tomato Sauce

Serves 4

INGREDIENTS

2 tbsp butter
1 onion, finely chopped
2 garlic cloves, chopped
4 eggs, beaten

²/₃ cup milk
³/₄ cup diced Swiss cheese
14 ounce can tomatoes, chopped
1 tbsp rosemary, stalks removed

²/₃ cup vegetable stock
freshly grated Parmesan cheese, for
    sprinkling
crusty bread, to serve

1 Melt the butter in a large skillet. Add the onion and garlic and sauté for 4–5 minutes, until softened.

2 Beat together the eggs and milk and add to the skillet.

3 Using a spatula, gently raise the cooked edges of the omelet and tip any uncooked egg around the edge of the skillet.

4 Scatter the Swiss cheese over the omelet. Cook for 5 minutes, turning once, until golden on both sides. Remove from the skillet and roll up.

5 Add the chopped tomatoes, rosemary, and vegetable stock to the skillet, stirring, and bring to a boil.

6 Simmer for about 10 minutes, until reduced and thickened.

7 Slice the omelet into strips and add to the tomato sauce in the skillet. Cook for 3–4 minutes, until piping hot.

8 Sprinkle the freshly grated Parmesan cheese over the omelet strips in tomato sauce and serve with fresh crusty bread.

VARIATION

Try adding ²/₃ cup diced pancetta or unsmoked bacon in step 1 and cooking the meat with the onions.

Mozzarella in Carriages

Serves 4

INGREDIENTS

8 slices day-old bread, crusts removed	8 canned anchovy fillets, drained and chopped	4 eggs, beaten
3¹/₂ ounces mozzarella cheese, thickly sliced	16 fresh basil leaves	²/₃ cup milk
	¹/₂ cup pitted black olives, chopped	oil, for deep-frying
		salt and pepper

1 Cut each slice of bread into 2 triangles. Top 8 of the bread triangles with the mozzarella slices and chopped anchovies.

2 Place the basil leaves and olives on top and season with salt and pepper to taste.

3 Lay the other 8 triangles of bread over the top and press down around the edges to seal.

4 Mix the eggs and milk and pour into an ovenproof dish. Add the sandwiches and leave to soak for 5 minutes.

5 Heat the oil in a large pan until a cube of bread browns in 30 seconds — the oil will then be hot enough for deep-frying.

6 Before cooking the sandwiches, squeeze the edges together again.

7 Carefully place the sandwiches in the oil and deep-fry for 2 minutes, or until golden, turning once. Remove the sandwiches with a slotted spoon and drain on absorbent paper towels. Serve immediately while still hot.

COOK'S TIP

If desired, try adding a peeled, cooked shrimp to each triangle. For smaller sandwiches, cut the bread into 4 triangles.

Baked Fennel

Serves 4

INGREDIENTS

2 fennel bulbs	6 sun-dried tomatoes, halved	2 tsp dried oregano
2 celery stalks cut into 3-inch sticks	7 ounces tomato sauce	²/₃ cup grated Parmesan cheese

1 Using a sharp knife, trim the fennel, discarding any tough outer leaves, and cut the bulb into quarters.

2 Bring a large pan of water to a boil, add the fennel and celery, and cook for 8–10 minutes, or until just tender. Remove with a slotted spoon and drain.

3 Place the fennel pieces, celery, and sun-dried tomatoes in an ovenproof dish.

4 Mix the tomato sauce and oregano and pour the mixture over the fennel.

5 Sprinkle the Parmesan cheese on top and bake in a preheated oven at 375°F for 20 minutes or until hot.

6 Serve as a starter with fresh, crusty bread or as a vegetable side dish.

VARIATION

If you cannot find any fennel in the shops, leeks make a delicious alternative. Use about 1 lb 10 oz, chopped, making sure that they are washed thoroughly to remove all traces of soil.

VARIATION

Add a 14 ounce can of lima beans, drained, in step 3 for a substantial vegetarian supper dish.

Garlic & Pine Nut Tarts

Serves 4

INGREDIENTS

4 slices whole-wheat or granary bread	$^2/_3$ cup butter	4 black olives, halved
$^1/_2$ cup pine nuts	5 garlic cloves, peeled and halved	oregano leaves, to garnish
	2 tbsp fresh oregano	

1 Using a rolling pin, flatten the bread slightly. Using a pastry cutter, cut out 4 rounds to fit your individual tart pans—they should measure about 4 inches across. Reserve the trimmings of bread and put in the refrigerator for 10 minutes, or until required.

2 Meanwhile, spread out the pine nuts on a cookie sheet. Toast the pine nuts under a preheated broiler for 2–3 minutes, or until golden.

3 Put the bread trimmings, pine nuts, butter, garlic, and oregano into a food processor and blend for about 20 seconds. Alternatively, pound the ingredients by hand in a mortar with a pestle. The mixture should have a rough texture.

4 Spoon the pine nut butter mixture into the lined pan and top with the olives. Bake in a preheated oven at 400°F for 10–15 minutes, or until a golden brown color.

5 Transfer the tarts to serving plates and serve warm, garnished with the fresh oregano leaves.

VARIATION

Puff pastry can be used instead of the bread for the tart shells. Use 7 ounces puff pastry dough to line 4 tart pans. Chill the puff pastry dough in the refrigerator for 20 minutes. Line the tart pans with the dough and foil and bake for 10 minutes. Remove the foil and bake for a further 3–4 minutes, or until the pastry is just set. Cool, then continue from step 2, adding 2 tablespoons of bread crumbs to the mixture.

Potatoes with Olives & Anchovies

Serves 4

INGREDIENTS

1 pound baby new potatoes, scrubbed	2 fennel bulbs, trimmed and sliced	½ cup mixed olives
2 tbsp olive oil	2 sprigs rosemary, stalks removed	8 canned anchovy fillets, drained

1 Bring a large saucepan of water to a boil and cook the potatoes for 8–10 minutes, or until just tender. Remove the potatoes from the saucepan using a slotted spoon and set aside to cool slightly.

2 Once the potatoes are just cool enough to handle, cut them into wedges, using a sharp knife.

3 Pit the mixed olives and cut them in half, using a sharp knife.

4 Using a sharp knife, chop the anchovy fillets into small strips.

5 Heat the oil in a large skillet. Add the potato wedges, sliced fennel, and rosemary. Cook for 7–8 minutes, or until the potatoes are golden.

6 Stir in the olives and anchovies and cook for 1 minute, or until warmed through.

7 Transfer to serving plates and serve immediately.

COOK'S TIP

Fresh rosemary is a particular favorite with Italians, but you can experiment with your own favorite herbs in this recipe.

Tuscan Chicken Livers on Toast

Serves 4

INGREDIENTS

2 tbsp olive oil

1 garlic clove, finely chopped

8 ounces fresh or frozen chicken livers, thawed

2 tbsp white wine

2 tbsp lemon juice

4 fresh sage leaves, finely chopped or 1 tsp dried, crumbled sage

salt and pepper

4 slices ciabatta or other Italian bread

wedges of lemon, to garnish

1 Heat the olive oil in a skillet and sauté the garlic for 1 minute.

2 Rinse and roughly chop the chicken livers, using a sharp knife.

3 Add the chicken livers to the skillet, together with the white wine and lemon juice. Cook for 3–4 minutes, or until the juices from the chicken livers run clear.

4 Stir in the sage and season to taste with salt and pepper.

5 Toast the bread under a preheated broiler for 2 minutes on both sides, or until golden brown.

6 Spoon the hot chicken livers on top of the toasted bread and serve garnished with a wedge of lemon.

COOK'S TIP

Overcooked liver is dry and tasteless. Cook the chopped liver for only 3–4 minutes — it should be soft and tender.

VARIATION

Another way to make crostini is to slice a crusty loaf or a French loaf into small rounds or squares. Heat the olive oil in a skillet and fry the slices of bread until golden brown and crisp on both sides. Remove the crostini from the pan with a slotted spoon and drain thoroughly on paper towels. Top with the chicken livers.

Onion & Mozzarella Tarts

Serves 4

INGREDIENTS

9 ounces ready-made puff pastry
dough, defrosted if frozen
2 medium red onions

1 red bell pepper
8 cherry tomatoes, halved
8 sprigs thyme

3 3/4 ounces mozzarella cheese, cut
into chunks

1 Roll out the dough to make 4 x 3-inch squares. Using a sharp knife, trim the edges of the dough, reserving the trimmings. Chill the dough in the refrigerator for 30 minutes.

2 Place the dough squares on a cookie sheet. Brush a little water along each edge of the dough squares and use the reserved dough trimmings to make a rim around each tart.

3 Using a sharp knife, cut the red onions into wedges and halve and seed the red bell pepper.

4 Place the onions and bell pepper in a roasting pan. Cook under a preheated broiler for 15 minutes or until charred.

5 Place the roasted bell pepper halves in a plastic bag and set aside to sweat for 10 minutes. Carefully peel off the skin from the bell pepper and cut the flesh into strips.

6 Line the dough squares with squares of foil.

Bake in a preheated oven at 400°F for 10 minutes. Remove the foil squares and bake for a further 5 minutes.

7 Place the onions, bell pepper strips, tomatoes, and cheese in each tart and sprinkle with the fresh thyme.

8 Bake in the oven for 15 minutes, or until the pastry is golden. Serve hot.

Spaghetti alla Carbonara

Serves 4

INGREDIENTS

15 ounces dried spaghetti
2 tbsp olive oil
1 large onion, thinly sliced
2 garlic cloves, chopped
6 slices bacon
2 tbsp butter

6 ounces mushrooms, thinly
  sliced
1¼ cups heavy cream
3 eggs, beaten

1 cup freshly grated Parmesan
  cheese, plus extra to serve
  (optional)
salt and pepper
fresh sage sprigs, to garnish

1 Warm a large serving dish or bowl. Bring a large pan of lightly salted water to a boil. Add the spaghetti and 1 tbsp of the oil and cook until tender, but still firm to the bite. Drain, return to the pan, and keep warm.

2 Meanwhile, heat the remaining oil in a skillet over a medium heat. Add the onion and sauté until it is transparent. Add the garlic and bacon and fry until the bacon is crisp. Transfer to the warm plate.

3 Melt the butter in the skillet. Add the mushrooms and sauté, stirring occasionally, for 3-4 minutes. Return the bacon mixture to the pan. Cover and keep warm.

4 Mix together the cream, eggs, and cheese in a large bowl and then season to taste.

5 Working very quickly, tip the spaghetti into the bacon and mushroom mixture and pour in the eggs. Toss the spaghetti

quickly into the egg and cream mixture, using 2 forks, and serve immediately. If you wish, serve with extra grated Parmesan cheese.

COOK'S TIP

The key to success with this recipe is not to overcook the egg. That is why it is important to keep all the ingredients hot enough just to cook the egg and to work rapidly to avoid scrambling it.

Smoked Ham Linguini

Serves 4

INGREDIENTS
---

1 pound dried linguini

1 pound broccoli, broken into florets

⅝ cup Italian cheese sauce (see Cook's Tip)

8 ounces Italian smoked ham

salt and pepper

Italian bread, to serve

---

1 Bring a large pan of lightly salted water to a boil. Add the linguini and broccoli florets and cook for 10 minutes, until the linguini is tender, but still firm to the bite.

2 Drain the linguini and broccoli thoroughly, set aside, and keep warm.

3 Meanwhile, make the Italian cheese sauce (see Cook's Tip, right).

4 Using a sharp knife, cut the Italian smoked ham into thin strips. Toss the linguini, broccoli, and ham into the Italian cheese sauce and gently warm through over a very low heat.

5 Transfer the pasta mixture to a warm serving dish. Sprinkle with black pepper and serve with Italian bread.

COOK'S TIP

There are many types of Italian bread which would be suitable to serve with this dish. Ciabatta is made with olive oil and is available plain and with different ingredients, such as olives or sun-dried tomatoes.

COOK'S TIP

For Italian cheese sauce, melt 2 tbsp butter in a pan and stir in ¼ cup all-purpose flour. Cook, stirring, over a low heat until the roux is light in color and crumbly in texture. Stir in 1¼ cups hot milk. Cook, stirring, for 15 minutes until thick and smooth. Add a pinch of nutmeg, a pinch of dried thyme, 2 tbsp white wine vinegar, and season to taste. Stir in 3 tbsp heavy cream and mix. Stir in ½ cup grated Mozzarella cheese, ⅔ cup grated Parmesan cheese, 1 tsp English mustard, and 2 tbsp sour cream.

Chorizo & Mushrooms
with a Spicy Vermicelli

Serves 6

INGREDIENTS

1½ pounds dried vermicelli	8 ounces exotic mushrooms	salt and pepper
½ cup olive oil	3 fresh chilies, chopped	10 anchovy fillets, to garnish
2 garlic cloves	2 tbsp freshly grated	
4½ ounces chorizo, sliced	Parmesan cheese	

1 Bring a large saucepan of lightly salted water to a boil. Add the pasta and 1 tablespoon of the oil and cook until just tender, but still firm to the bite. Drain, transfer to a serving plate and keep warm.

2 Meanwhile heat the remaining oil in a large skillet. Add the garlic and fry for 1 minute. Add the chorizo and mushrooms and cook for about 4 minutes, then add the chopped chilies, and cook for 1 minute.

3 Pour the chorizo and mushroom mixture over the vermicelli and season with a little salt and pepper. Sprinkle with Parmesan, garnish with a lattice of anchovy fillets, and serve immediately.

VARIATION

Fresh sardines may be used instead of the chorizo. However, ensure that you gut and clean the sardines, removing the backbone, before using them.

COOK'S TIP

Always obtain exotic mushrooms from a reliable source and never pick them yourself. Many varieties of mushroom are now cultivated and most are indistinguishable from the exotic varieties. Mixed color oyster mushrooms have been used here, but you could also use chanterelles. However, remember that chanterelles tend to shrink during cooking, so you may need a larger quantity.

Pancetta & Pecorino Cakes on a Bed of Farfalle

Serves 4

INGREDIENTS

2 tbsp butter, plus extra
    for greasing
3½ ounces pancetta, rind
    removed
2 cups self-rising flour
⅞ cup grated pecorino cheese

⅝ cup milk, plus extra for
    glazing
1 tsp Worcestershire sauce
1 tbsp ketchup
3½ cups dried farfalle
1 tbsp olive oil

salt and black pepper
3 tbsp pesto or anchovy sauce
    (optional)
salad greens, to serve

1 Grease a cookie sheet with a little butter. Broil the pancetta until it is cooked. Allow the pancetta to cool, then chop it finely.

2 Sift together the flour and a pinch of salt into a mixing bowl. Add the butter and rub in with your fingertips. When the butter and flour have been thoroughly incorporated, add the pancetta and one-third of the grated cheese.

3 Mix together the milk, Worcestershire sauce, and ketchup and add to the dry ingredients, mixing to make a soft dough.

4 Roll out the dough on a lightly floured board to make a 7-inch round. Brush with a little milk to glaze and cut into 8 wedges.

5 Arrange the dough wedges on the prepared cookie sheet and

sprinkle with the remaining cheese. Bake in a preheated oven at 400°F for 20 minutes.

6 Bring a pan of salted water to a boil. Add the farfalle and the oil and cook until just tender. Drain and transfer to a large serving dish. Top with the pancetta and pecorino cakes. Serve with the sauce of your choice and salad greens.

Orecchiette with Bacon & Tomatoes

Serves 4

INGREDIENTS

2 pounds small, sweet tomatoes
6 slices smoked bacon
4 tbsp butter
1 onion, chopped
1 garlic clove, crushed

4 fresh oregano sprigs,
   finely chopped
4 cups dried orecchiette
1 tbsp olive oil
salt and pepper

freshly grated Pecorino cheese,
   to serve

1 Blanch the tomatoes in boiling water. Drain, skin, and seed the tomatoes, then roughly chop the flesh. Chop the bacon into small pieces.

2 Melt the butter in a saucepan and fry the bacon until it is golden. Add the onion and garlic and fry over a medium heat until softened.

3 Add the tomatoes and oregano to the saucepan and season to taste. Lower the heat and simmer for 10-12 minutes.

4 Bring a pan of salted water to a boil. Add the orecchiette and oil and cook for 12 minutes, until just tender. Drain the pasta and transfer to a warm serving dish. Spoon the bacon and tomato sauce over the pasta, toss to coat, and serve with the cheese.

VARIATION

You could also use 1 pound spicy Italian sausages. Squeeze the meat out of the skins and add to the pan in step 2 instead of the bacon.

COOK'S TIP

For an authentic Italian flavor use pancetta, rather than ordinary bacon. This kind of bacon is streaked with fat and adds rich undertones of flavor to many traditional dishes. It is available both smoked and unsmoked, and can be bought in a single, large piece or cut into slices. You can buy it in some supermarkets and all Italian delicatessens.

Creamed Veal Kidneys with Penne & Pesto Sauce

Serves 4

INGREDIENTS

5 tbsp butter

12 veal kidneys, trimmed and thinly sliced

6 ounces button mushrooms, sliced

1 tsp English mustard

pinch of freshly grated ginger root

2 tbsp dry sherry

5/8 cup heavy cream

2 tbsp pesto sauce

14 ounces dried penne

1 tbsp olive oil

salt and pepper

4 slices of hot toast cut into triangles

fresh parsley sprigs, to garnish

1 Melt the butter in a large skillet and fry the kidneys over a low heat for 4 minutes. Transfer the kidneys to an ovenproof dish and keep warm.

2 Add the mushrooms to the skillet, and cook for about 2 minutes.

3 Add the mustard and ginger to the pan and season to taste. Cook for 2 minutes, then add the sherry, cream, and pesto sauce. Cook for an additional 3 minutes, then pour the sauce over the kidneys. Bake in a preheated oven at 375°F for 10 minutes.

4 Meanwhile, bring a large pan of lightly salted water to a boil. Add the penne and the oil and cook until just tender, but still firm to the bite. Drain the pasta and transfer to a warm serving dish.

5 Top the pasta with the kidneys in the pesto sauce. Place triangles of warm toast around the kidneys, garnish with fresh parsley and serve.

COOK'S TIP

Store the pesto sauce in an airtight container for up to a week in the refrigerator, or freeze (before adding the Parmesan) for 3 months.

Marinated Eggplant on a Bed of Linguine

Serves 4

INGREDIENTS

⁵/₈ cup vegetable stock
⁵/₈ cup white wine vinegar
2 tsp balsamic vinegar
3 tbsp olive oil
fresh oregano sprig
1 pound eggplant, peeled and
    thinly sliced
14 ounces dried linguine

MARINADE:
2 tbsp extra virgin oil
2 garlic cloves, crushed
2 tbsp chopped fresh oregano
2 tbsp finely chopped
    roasted almonds
2 tbsp diced red bell pepper
2 tbsp lime juice

grated rind and juice of
    1 orange
salt and pepper

1 Put the vegetable stock, wine vinegar, and balsamic vinegar into a saucepan and bring to a boil over a low heat. Add 2 tsp of the olive oil and the sprig of oregano and simmer gently for about 1 minute.

2 Add the eggplant slices to the saucepan, remove from the heat and set aside for 10 minutes.

3 Meanwhile, make the marinade. Combine the olive oil, garlic, fresh oregano, almonds, bell pepper, lime juice, orange rind, and juice in a large bowl and season to taste with salt and pepper.

4 Remove the eggplant from the saucepan and drain well. Add the eggplant slices to the marinade, mixing well, and

set aside in the refrigerator for about 12 hours.

5 Bring a pan of lightly salted water to a boil. Add half the remaining oil and the linguine and cook until just tender. Drain the pasta and toss with the remaining oil. Arrange the pasta on a serving plate with the eggplant slices and the marinade and serve.

Spinach & Ricotta Shells

Serves 4

INGREDIENTS

14 ounces dried lumache rigate grande	10½ ounces frozen spinach, thawed and drained	14 ounce can chopped tomatoes, drained
5 tbsp olive oil	1 cup ricotta cheese	1 garlic clove, crushed
1 cup fresh white breadcrumbs	pinch of freshly grated nutmeg	salt and pepper
½ cup milk		

1 Bring a large saucepan of lightly salted water to a boil. Add the lumache and 1 tbsp of the olive oil and cook until just tender, but still firm to the bite. Drain the pasta, rinse under cold water, and set aside.

2 Put the breadcrumbs, milk, and 3 tbsp of the remaining olive oil in a food processor and work to combine.

3 Add the spinach and ricotta cheese to the food processor and work to a smooth mixture. Transfer to a bowl, stir in the nutmeg, and season with salt and pepper to taste.

4 Mix together the tomatoes, garlic, and remaining oil and spoon the mixture into the base of an ovenproof dish.

5 Using a teaspoon, fill the lumache with the spinach and ricotta mixture and arrange on top of the tomato mixture in the dish. Cover and bake in a preheated oven at 350°F for 20 minutes. Serve hot.

COOK'S TIP

Ricotta is a creamy Italian cheese traditionally made from ewes' milk whey. It is soft and white, with a smooth texture and a slightly sweet flavor. It should be used within 2–3 days of purchase.

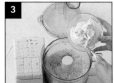

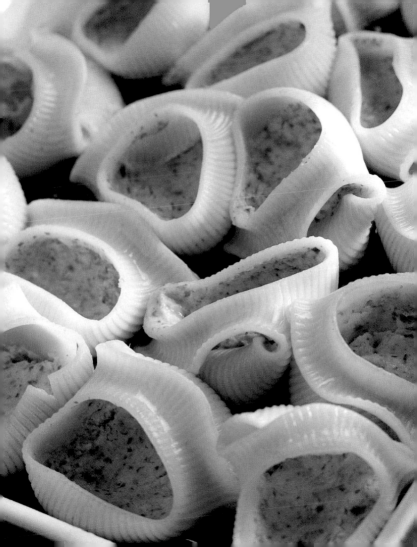

Rotelle with Spicy Italian Sauce

Serves 4

INGREDIENTS

2⅞ cup Italian red wine sauce
  (see Cook's Tip, bottom right)
5 tbsp olive oil

3 garlic cloves, crushed
2 fresh red chilies, chopped
1 green chili, chopped

3½ cups dried rotelle
salt and pepper
warm Italian bread, to serve

1 Make the Italian Red Wine Sauce (see Cook's Tip, right).

2 Heat 4 tbsp of the oil in a saucepan. Add the garlic and chilies and sauté for 3 minutes.

3 Stir in the Italian red wine sauce, season to taste, and simmer gently for about 20 minutes.

4 Bring a large pan of lightly salted water to a boil. Add the rotelle and the remaining oil and cook for 8 minutes, until just tender. Drain the pasta.

5 Toss the rotelle in the spicy sauce, transfer to a warm dish, and serve with warm Italian bread.

COOK'S TIP

Take care when using fresh chiles as they can burn your skin. Handle them as little as possible—wear rubber gloves if necessary. Wash your hands thoroughly afterward, and don't touch your face or eyes before you have washed your hands. Remove chili seeds before chopping the chiles, as they are the hottest part.

COOK'S TIP

To make Italian red wine sauce, first make a demi-glace sauce by combining ⅝ cup each brown stock and espagnole sauce, cook for 10 minutes, and strain. Mix ½ cup red wine, 2 tbsp red wine vinegar, 4 tbsp chopped shallots, 1 bay leaf and 1 thyme sprig in a small pan. Bring to a boil and reduce by about three-quarters. Add the demi-glace sauce to the pan and simmer for about 20 minutes. Season to taste and strain.

Tricolor Timballini

Serves 4

INGREDIENTS

1 tbsp butter, softened	1 egg yolk	⁵/₈ cup sieved tomatoes
1 cup dried white breadcrumbs	1 cup grated Swiss cheese	1 tbsp tomato paste
6 ounces dried tricolor spaghetti, broken into 2-inch lengths	1¼ cups Béchamel sauce	salt and pepper
	1 onion, finely chopped	fresh basil leaves, to garnish
3 tbsp olive oil	1 bay leaf	
	⁵/₈ cup dry white wine	

1 Grease four ¾ cup molds or ramekins with the butter. Evenly coat the insides with half the breadcrumbs.

2 Bring a saucepan of lightly salted water to a boil. Add the spaghetti and 1 tbsp of the oil and cook until just tender. Drain and transfer to a mixing bowl.

3 Add the egg yolk and cheese to the pasta and season. Mix in the béchamel sauce. Spoon the mixture into the ramekins and sprinkle with the remaining breadcrumbs.

4 Stand the ramekins on a cookie sheet and bake in a preheated oven at 425°F for 20 minutes. Set aside for 10 minutes.

5 Meanwhile, make the sauce. Heat the remaining oil in a pan and gently sauté the onion and bay leaf for 2-3 minutes.

6 Stir in the wine, sieved tomatoes, and tomato paste and season. Simmer for 20 minutes, until thickened. Remove and discard the bay leaf.

7 Turn the timballini out onto individual serving plates, garnish with the basil leaves, and serve with the tomato sauce.

Tagliarini with Gorgonzola

Serves 4

INGREDIENTS

2 tbsp butter

8 ounces Gorgonzola cheese,
roughly crumbled

5/8 cup heavy cream

2 tbsp dry white wine

1 tsp cornstarch

4 fresh sage sprigs, finely
chopped

14 ounces dried tagliarini

2 tbsp olive oil

salt and white pepper

1 Melt the butter in a saucepan, stir in 6 ounces of the Gorgonzola cheese and melt, over a low heat, for about 2 minutes.

2 Add the cream, wine, and cornstarch to the pan and beat with a whisk until fully incorporated.

3 Stir in the sage and season to taste with salt and white pepper. Bring to a boil over a low heat, whisking constantly, until the sauce thickens. Remove from the heat and set aside.

4 Bring a large pan of lightly salted water to a boil. Add the tagliarini and 1 tbsp of the olive oil. Cook the pasta for 12–14 minutes, or until just tender, drain and toss in the remaining oil. Transfer the pasta to a serving dish and keep warm.

5 Reheat the sauce over a low heat, whisking constantly. Spoon the Gorgonzola sauce over the tagliarini, generously sprinkle with the remaining crumbled cheese, and serve immediately.

COOK'S TIP

Gorgonzola is one of the world's oldest veined cheeses and, arguably, its finest. Always check that it is creamy yellow with delicate green veining. Avoid hard or discolored cheese. It should have a rich, piquant aroma, not a bitter smell. If you find Gorgonzola too strong or rich, substitute a milder blue cheese.

Gnocchi Piemontese

Serves 4

INGREDIENTS

1 pound warm mashed potato
⅝ cup self-rising flour
1 egg
2 egg yolks

1 tbsp olive oil
⅝ cup espagnole sauce

SAUCE:
4 tbsp butter

2 cups freshly grated Parmesan
    cheese
salt and pepper

1 Combine the mashed potato and flour in a bowl. Add the egg and egg yolks, season well, and mix together to form a dough.

2 Break off pieces of the dough and roll them between the palms of your hands to form small balls the size of a walnut. Flatten the balls with a fork into the shape of small circles.

3 Bring a large pan of lightly salted water to a boil. Add the gnocchi and olive oil and poach for 10 minutes.

4 Mix the espagnole sauce and the butter in a large saucepan over a gentle heat. Gradually blend in the grated Parmesan cheese.

5 Remove the gnocchi from the pan and toss in the sauce, transfer to 4 individual serving plates, and serve immediately.

COOK'S TIP

This dish also makes an excellent main meal with a crisp salad.

VARIATION

These gnocchi would also taste delicious with a tomato sauce, in Trentino-style. Mix together 1 cup finely chopped sun-dried tomatoes, 1 finely sliced celery stalk, 1 crushed garlic clove, and 6 tbsp red wine in a pan. Cook over a low heat for 15–20 minutes. Stir in 8 skinned, chopped, Italian plum tomatoes, season to taste with salt and pepper, and simmer over a low heat for a further 10 minutes.

Pasta Omelet

Serves 2

INGREDIENTS

4 tbsp olive oil
1 small onion, chopped
1 fennel bulb, thinly sliced
4¹/₂ ounces potato, diced
1 garlic clove, chopped

4 eggs
1 tbsp chopped fresh parsley
pinch of chili powder
3¹/₂ ounces cooked short pasta

2 tbsp stuffed green olives, halved
salt and pepper
fresh marjoram sprigs, to garnish
tomato salad, to serve

1 Heat half the oil in a skillet over a low heat and cook the onion, fennel, and potato, stirring, for 8-10 minutes, until the potato is just tender.

2 Add the garlic and fry for 1 minute. Remove the pan from the heat, transfer the vegetables to a plate, and set aside.

3 Beat the eggs until they are frothy. Stir in the parsley and season with salt, pepper, and a pinch of chili powder.

4 Heat 1 tablespoon of the remaining oil in a clean skillet. Add half of the egg mixture to the pan, then add the cooked vegetables, pasta, and half of the olives. Pour in the remaining egg mixture and cook until the sides begin to set.

5 Lift up the edges of the omelet with a spatula to allow the uncooked egg to spread underneath. Cook until the underside of the omelet is a light golden brown color.

6 Slide the omelet out of the pan onto a plate. Wipe the pan with paper towels and heat the remaining oil. Invert the omelet into the pan and cook until the other side is golden brown.

7 Slide the omelet onto a warmed serving dish and garnish with the remaining olives and the marjoram. Serve cut into wedges, with a tomato salad.

Spaghetti with Ricotta Cheese

Serves 4

INGREDIENTS

12 ounces dried spaghetti	$^1/_2$ cup ricotta cheese	1 tbsp pine nuts
3 tbsp olive oil	pinch of grated nutmeg	salt and pepper
3 tbsp butter	pinch of ground cinnamon	fresh parsley sprigs, to garnish
2 tbsp chopped fresh parsley	$^5/_8$ cup unsweetened yogurt	
1 cup freshly ground almonds	$^1/_2$ cup hot chicken stock	

1 Bring a large pan of lightly salted water to a boil. Add the spaghetti and 1 tbsp of the oil and cook until tender, but still firm to the bite.

2 Drain the pasta, return to the pan, and toss with the butter and chopped parsley. Set aside and keep warm.

3 To make the sauce, mix together the ground almonds, ricotta cheese, nutmeg, cinnamon, and unsweetened yogurt over a low heat to form a thick paste. Stir in the remaining oil, then gradually stir in the hot chicken stock, until smooth. Season the sauce with black pepper to taste.

4 Transfer the spaghetti to a warm serving dish, pour the sauce on top, and toss together well (see Cook's Tip). Sprinkle with the pine nuts, garnish with the fresh parsley, and serve the spaghetti warm.

COOK'S TIP

Use two large forks to toss spaghetti or other long pasta, so that it is thoroughly coated with the sauce. Special spaghetti forks are available from some cookware departments and kitchen stores. Holding one fork in each hand, gently ease the prongs under the pasta on each side and lift them toward the center. Continue until the pasta is completely coated.

Gnocchi Romana

Serves 4

INGREDIENTS

3 ⅛ cups milk

pinch of freshly grated nutmeg

6 tbsp butter, plus extra
    for greasing

1 ¼ cups cream of wheat

1 ½ cups grated Parmesan cheese

2 eggs, beaten

½ cup grated Swiss cheese

salt and pepper

fresh basil sprigs, to garnish

1 Pour the milk into a saucepan and bring to a boil. Remove from the heat and stir in the nutmeg, 2 tbsp of the butter, and salt and pepper to taste.

2 Gradually stir the semolina into the milk, whisking to prevent lumps forming, and return the pan to a low heat. Simmer, stirring constantly, for about 10 minutes, until the mixture is very thick.

3 Beat ⅔ cup of the Parmesan into the semolina mixture, then beat in the eggs. Continue beating until smooth. Set aside to cool slightly.

4 Spread out the semolina mixture in an even layer on a sheet of waxed paper or in a large, oiled baking pan. Smooth the surface with a damp spatula—it should be about ½-inch thick. Set aside to cool completely, then leave to chill for 1 hour.

5 Once chilled, cut out rounds of gnocchi, measuring about 1 ½ inches in diameter.

6 Grease a shallow ovenproof dish or 4 individual dishes. Lay the gnocchi trimmings in the base of the dish or dishes and cover with overlapping rounds of gnocchi.

7 Melt the remaining butter and drizzle over the gnocchi. Sprinkle with the remaining Parmesan and the Swiss cheese.

8 Bake in a preheated oven at 400°F for 25-30 minutes, until the top is crisp and golden brown. Garnish and serve.

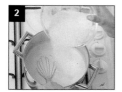

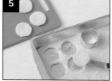

Three-Cheese Bake

Serves 4

INGREDIENTS

butter, for greasing	1 cup grated mozzarella or	fresh basil leaves (optional), to
14 ounces dried penne	halloumi cheese	garnish
1 tbsp olive oil	4 tbsp freshly grated	
2 eggs, beaten	Parmesan cheese	
1½ cups ricotta cheese	salt and black pepper	
4 fresh basil sprigs		

1 Lightly grease an ovenproof dish.

2 Bring a large pan of lightly salted water to a boil. Add the penne and olive oil and cook until just tender, but still firm to the bite. Drain the pasta, set aside, and keep warm.

3 Beat the eggs into the ricotta cheese and season to taste with salt and pepper.

4 Spoon half of the penne into the base of the dish and cover with half of the basil leaves.

5 Spoon over half of the ricotta cheese mixture. Sprinkle with the mozzarella or halloumi cheese and then top with the remaining basil leaves. Cover with the remaining penne and then spoon over the remaining ricotta cheese mixture. Lightly sprinkle with the grated Parmesan cheese.

6 Bake in a preheated oven at 375°F for 30–40 minutes, until golden brown and the cheese topping is bubbling.

7 Garnish with basil leaves, if desired, and serve hot.

VARIATION

Try substituting smoked Bavarian cheese for the mozzarella or halloumi and grated Cheddar cheese for the Parmesan, for a slightly different but just as delicious flavor.

Baked Rigatoni Filled with Tuna & Ricotta Cheese

Serves 4

INGREDIENTS

butter, for greasing	½ cup heavy cream	4 ounces sun-dried tomatoes,
1 pound dried rigatoni	2⅔ cups grated Parmesan	drained and sliced
1 tbsp olive oil	cheese	salt and black pepper
7 ounce can flaked tuna, drained		
1 cup ricotta cheese		

1 Lightly grease an ovenproof dish with butter.

2 Bring a large saucepan of lightly salted water to a boil. Add the rigatoni and olive oil and cook until just tender, but still firm to the bite. Drain the pasta and set aside until cool enough to handle.

3 In a bowl, mix together the tuna and ricotta cheese to form a soft paste. Spoon the mixture into a piping bag and use to fill the rigatoni. Arrange the filled pasta tubes side by side in the prepared ovenproof dish.

4 To make the sauce, mix the cream and Parmesan cheese, and season. Spoon the sauce over the rigatoni and top with the sun-dried tomatoes arranged in a criss-cross pattern. Bake in a preheated oven at 400°F for 20 minutes. Serve immediately.

VARIATION

For a vegetarian alternative of this recipe, simply substitute a mixture of pitted and chopped black olives and chopped walnuts for the tuna. Follow exactly the same cooking method.

Spaghetti with Anchovy & Pesto Sauce

Serves 4

INGREDIENTS

³/₈ cup olive oil

2 garlic cloves, crushed

2 ounce can anchovy fillets, drained

1 pound dried spaghetti

2 ounces pesto sauce

2 tbsp finely chopped fresh oregano

1 cup grated Parmesan cheese, plus extra for serving (optional)

salt and pepper

2 fresh oregano sprigs, to garnish

1 Reserve 1 tbsp of the oil and heat the remainder in a small saucepan. Add the garlic and fry for 3 minutes.

2 Lower the heat, stir in the anchovies, and cook, stirring occasionally, until the anchovies have disintegrated.

3 Bring a large saucepan of lightly salted water to a boil. Add the spaghetti and the remaining olive oil and cook until just tender.

4 Add the pesto sauce and chopped fresh oregano to the anchovy mixture and then season with black pepper to taste.

5 Drain the spaghetti and transfer to a warm serving dish. Pour over the pesto sauce and then sprinkle over the grated Parmesan cheese, if using.

6 Garnish with oregano sprigs and serve with extra cheese, if using.

VARIATION

For a vegetarian version of this recipe, simply substitute drained sun-dried tomatoes for the anchovy fillets.

COOK'S TIP

If you find canned anchovies much too salty, soak them in a saucer of milk for 5 minutes, drain, and pat dry with paper towels before using them.

Fettuccine with Anchovy & Spinach Sauce

Serves 4

INGREDIENTS

2 pounds fresh, young spinach leaves	6 tbsp olive oil	8 canned anchovy fillets, drained and chopped
14 ounces dried fettuccine	3 tbsp pine nuts	salt
	3 garlic cloves, crushed	

1 Trim off any tough spinach stalks. Rinse the spinach leaves and place them in a large saucepan with only the water that is clinging to them after washing. Cover and cook over a high heat, shaking the pan from time, until the spinach has wilted, but retains its color. Drain well, set aside and keep warm.

2 Bring a large saucepan of lightly salted water to a boil. Add the fettuccine and 1 tbsp of the oil and cook until it is just tender, but still firm to the bite.

3 Heat 4 tbsp of the remaining olive oil in a saucepan. Add the pine nuts and fry until golden. Remove from the pan and set aside.

4 Add the garlic to the pan and fry until golden. Add the anchovies and stir in the spinach. Cook, stirring, for 2-3 minutes, until heated through. Return the pine nuts to the pan, stirring until well combined.

5 Drain the fettuccine, toss in the remaining olive oil, and transfer to a warm serving dish. Spoon the anchovy and spinach sauce over the fettuccine, toss lightly, and serve immediately.

COOK'S TIP

If you are in a hurry, you can use frozen spinach. Thaw and drain it thoroughly, pressing out as much moisture as possible. Cut the leaves into strips and add to the dish with the anchovies in step 4.

Penne with Muscoli Fritti nell'Olio

Serves 4-6

INGREDIENTS

3½ cups dried penne
½ cup olive oil
1 pound mussels, cooked and shelled
1 tsp sea salt

⅔ cup all-purpose flour
3½ ounces sun-dried tomatoes, sliced
salt and pepper

TO GARNISH:
1 lemon, thinly sliced
basil leaves

1 Bring a large pan of lightly salted water to a boil. Add the penne and 1 tbsp of the olive oil and cook until the pasta is just tender, but still firm to the bite.

2 Drain the pasta and place in a serving dish. Set aside and keep warm.

3 Lightly sprinkle the mussels with the sea salt. Season the flour with salt and pepper, sprinkle into a bowl, and toss the mussels in the flour until well coated.

4 Heat the remaining oil in a skillet and fry the mussels, stirring frequently, until golden brown.

5 Toss the mussels with the penne and sprinkle with the sun-dried tomatoes. Garnish with lemon slices and basil leaves and serve.

VARIATION

You could substitute clams for the mussels. If using fresh clams, try smaller varieties, such as Venus.

COOK'S TIP

Sun-dried tomatoes have been used in Mediterranean countries for a long time, but have become popular elsewhere only quite recently. They are dried and then preserved in oil. They have a concentrated, almost roasted flavor and a dense texture. They should be drained and chopped or sliced before using.

Chili Polenta Chips

Serves 4

INGREDIENTS		
3 cups instant polenta	1 tbsp olive oil	1 tbsp chopped parsley
2 tsp chili powder	²/₃ cup sour cream	salt and pepper

1 Bring 6¼ cups water to a boil in a large saucepan. Add 2 teaspoons salt and then add the polenta in a steady stream, stirring constantly.

2 Reduce the heat slightly and continue stirring for about 5 minutes. It is essential to stir the polenta, otherwise it will stick to the bottom of the pan and burn. The polenta should have a thick consistency at this point and should be stiff enough to hold the spoon upright in the pan.

3 Add the chili powder to the polenta mixture and stir well. Season to taste with a little salt and pepper.

4 Spread the polenta out on to a board or cookie sheet to about 1½ inches thick. Let cool and set.

5 Cut the cooled polenta mixture into thin wedges.

6 Heat 1 tablespoon of oil in a pan. Add the polenta wedges and fry for 3–4 minutes on each side until golden and crispy. Alternatively, brush with melted butter and broil for 6–7 minutes, until golden. Drain the cooked polenta on paper towels.

7 Mix the sour cream with parsley and place in a small serving bowl.

8 Serve the polenta with the sour cream and parsley dip.

COOK'S TIP

Easy-cook instant polenta is widely available in supermarkets and is quick to make. It will keep for up to 1 week in the refrigerator. The polenta can also be baked in a preheated oven at 400°F for 20 minutes.

Polenta Kabobs

Serves 4

INGREDIENTS

3 cups water	8 slices prosciutto	salt and pepper
1½ cups instant polenta	(about 2¾ ounces)	salad greens, to serve
2 tbsp fresh thyme, stalks removed	1 tbsp olive oil	

1 Bring the water to a boil and add 1 teaspoon salt. Add the polenta in a steady stream, stirring constantly. Cook, stirring, for 5 minutes, or according to the instructions on the packet.

2 Add the fresh thyme to the polenta mixture and season to taste with salt and pepper.

3 Spread out the polenta, about 1 inch thick, on a board. Set aside to cool.

4 Using a sharp knife, cut the cooled polenta into 1-inch cubes.

5 Cut the prosciutto slices into 2 pieces lengthwise. Wrap the prosciutto around the polenta cubes.

6 Thread the prosciutto-wrapped polenta cubes onto skewers.

7 Brush the kabobs with a little oil and cook under a preheated broiler, turning frequently, for 7–8 minutes. Alternatively, barbecue the kabobs until golden. Transfer to serving plates and serve with salad greens.

VARIATION

Try flavoring the polenta with chopped oregano, basil, or marjoram instead of the thyme, if you prefer. You should use 3 tablespoons chopped herbs to every 3 cups instant polenta.

Risotto-Stuffed Bell Peppers

Serves 4

INGREDIENTS

4 red or orange bell peppers	3³/₄ cups hot vegetable	1³/₄ ounces Italian sausage, such as
1 tbsp olive oil	or chicken stock	Felino salami or other coarse
1 large onion, finely chopped	3 tbsp butter	Italian salami, chopped
1²/₃ cups risotto rice, washed	²/₃ cup grated pecorino cheese,	7 ounces mozzarella cheese, sliced
about 15 strands saffron		
²/₃ cup white wine		

1 Cut the bell peppers in half, leaving some of the stalk. Remove the seeds.

2 Place the bell peppers, cut side up, under a preheated broiler for 12–15 minutes, until softened and charred.

3 Meanwhile, heat the oil in a large skillet. Add the onion and sauté for 3–4 minutes, or until softened. Add the rice and saffron, stirring to coat in the oil, and cook for 1 minute.

4 Add the wine and stock slowly, a ladleful at a time, making sure that all the liquid is absorbed before adding the next ladleful of liquid. When all the liquid is absorbed, the rice should be cooked. Test by tasting a grain – if it is still crunchy, add a little more water and continue cooking. It should take at least 15 minutes to cook.

5 Stir in the butter, pecorino cheese, and the chopped Italian sausage.

6 Spoon the risotto into the bell peppers. Top with a slice of mozzarella and broil for 4–5 minutes, or until the cheese is bubbling. Serve hot.

VARIATION

Use tomatoes instead of the bell peppers, if you prefer. Halve 4 large tomatoes and scoop out the seeds. Follow steps 3–6, as there is no need to roast them.

Potato Gnocchi with Tomato Sauce

Serves 4

INGREDIENTS

12 ounces mealy potatoes, halved

$^2/_3$ cup self-rising flour, plus extra for rolling out

2 tsp dried oregano

2 tbsp oil

1 large onion, chopped

2 garlic cloves, chopped

14 ounce can chopped tomatoes

$^1/_2$ vegetable stock cube dissolved in $^1/_3$ cup boiling water

salt and pepper

2 tbsp basil, shredded, plus whole leaves to garnish

Parmesan cheese, grated, to serve

1 Bring a large pan of water to a boil. Add the potatoes and cook for 12–15 minutes, or until tender. Drain and cool.

2 Peel and then mash the potatoes with the salt and pepper, sifted flour, and oregano. Mix together with your hands to form a dough.

3 Heat the oil in a pan. Add the onions and garlic and sauté for 3–4 minutes. Add the tomatoes and stock and cook, uncovered, for

10 minutes. Season with salt and pepper to taste.

4 Roll the potato dough into a sausage about 1 inch in diameter. Cut the sausage into 1-inch lengths. Flour your hands, then press a fork into each piece to create a series of ridges on one side and the indent of your index finger on the other.

5 Bring a large pan of water to a boil and cook the gnocchi, in batches, for 2–3 minutes. They should rise to the

surface when cooked. Drain and keep warm.

6 Stir the basil into the tomato sauce and pour over the gnocchi. Garnish with basil leaves and freshly ground black pepper. Sprinkle with Parmesan and serve.

VARIATION

Try serving the gnocchi with Pesto Sauce for a change.

Baked Gnocchi

Serves 4

INGREDIENTS

1¾ cups vegetable stock

⅔ cup cream of wheat

1 tbsp thyme, stalks removed

1 egg, beaten

⅔ cup grated Parmesan cheese

3 tbsp butter

2 garlic cloves, crushed

salt and pepper

1 Place the stock in a large saucepan and bring to a boil. Add the cream of wheat in a steady trickle, stirring continuously. Keep stirring for 3–4 minutes, until the mixture is thick enough to hold a spoon upright. Set the mixture aside to cool slightly.

2 Add the thyme, egg, and half the cheese, and season to taste with salt and pepper.

3 Spread the mixture on a board in a layer about ½ inch thick. Set aside to cool and set.

4 When the mixture is cold, cut it into 1-inch squares, reserving any trimmings.

5 Grease an ovenproof dish, placing the reserved trimmings in the bottom. Arrange the cream of wheat squares on top and sprinkle with the remaining cheese.

6 Melt the butter in a pan and add the garlic and black pepper to taste. Pour the butter mixture over the gnocchi. Bake in a preheated oven at 425°F for 15–20 minutes, until puffed up and golden. Serve hot.

VARIATION

Try adding ½ tablespoon sun-dried tomato paste or ¼ cup finely chopped mushrooms, fried in butter, to the mixture in step 2. Follow the same cooking method.

Meat
& Poultry

*Pasta with meat or poultry is a classic combination.
Dishes range from easy, economic mid-week suppers
to sophisticated and elegant meals for special occasions.*

Most meat in Italy is sold ready boned and cut across the
grain. Veal is a great favorite and widely available. Pork
is also popular, cooked with lots of fragrant herbs, with
roast pig being the traditional dish of Umbria. Lamb is
often served for special occasions, cooked on a spit or
roasted in the oven with wine, garlic, and herbs.

Poultry dishes provide some of Italy's finest food. Every
part of the chicken is used, the leftovers generally being
used for making soups. Turkey, duck, goose, and guinea
fowl are also popular, as is game. Wild rabbit, hare, wild
boar, and deer are traditional fare, especially in Sardinia.

The recipes in this chapter include many
family favorites and some exciting variations
on traditional themes. Finally, there is a superb
collection of mouth-watering original recipes
featuring pasta, beef, lamb, pork, chicken, and
game. You will be astonished at how quickly and
easily you can prepare these gourmet dishes.

Spaghetti Bolognese

Serves 4

INGREDIENTS

3 tbsp olive oil
2 garlic cloves, crushed
1 large onion, finely chopped
1 carrot, diced
2 cups lean ground beef, veal,
   or chicken

3 ounces chicken livers,
   finely chopped
3½ ounces lean prosciutto, diced
⅝ cup Marsala
10 ounce can chopped
   plum tomatoes
1 tbsp chopped fresh basil leaves

2 tbsp tomato paste
salt and pepper
1 pound dried spaghetti

1 Heat 2 tbsp of the olive oil in a large saucepan. Add the garlic, onion, and carrot and sauté for 6 minutes.

2 Add the ground beef, veal, or chicken, the chicken livers, and prosciutto to the pan and cook over a medium heat, stirring occasionally, for 12 minutes, until well browned.

3 Stir in the Marsala, tomatoes, basil, and tomato paste and cook for 4 minutes. Season to taste with salt and pepper. Cover and simmer for about 30 minutes.

4 Remove the lid from the pan, stir, and simmer for a further 15 minutes.

5 Meanwhile, bring a large pan of lightly salted water to a boil. Add the spaghetti and the remaining oil and cook for about 12 minutes, until tender, but still firm to the bite. Drain and transfer to a serving dish. Pour the sauce over the pasta, toss, and serve hot.

VARIATION

Chicken livers are an essential ingredient in a classic Bolognese sauce to which they add richness. However, if you prefer not to use them, you can substitute the same quantity of ground beef.

Creamed Strips of Sirloin with Rigatoni

Serves 4

INGREDIENTS

6 tbsp butter
1 pound sirloin steak, trimmed
    and cut into thin strips
6 ounces button mushrooms,
    sliced
1 tsp mustard

pinch of freshly grated
    ginger root
2 tbsp dry sherry
$5/8$ cup heavy cream
salt and pepper
4 slices hot toast, cut into
    triangles, to serve

PASTA:
1 pound dried rigatoni
2 tbsp olive oil
2 fresh basil sprigs
8 tbsp butter

1 Preheat the oven to 375°F. Melt the butter in a large skillet and gently fry the steak, stirring frequently, for 6 minutes. Transfer to an ovenproof dish and keep warm.

2 Add the mushrooms to the remaining juices in the skillet and cook for 2–3 minutes. Add the mustard, ginger, and salt and pepper to taste. Cook for about 2 minutes, then add the sherry and cream. Cook for an additional 3 minutes, then pour the cream sauce over the steak.

3 Bake the steak and cream mixture in the preheated oven for 10 minutes.

4 Bring a large saucepan of lightly salted water to a boil. Add the rigatoni, olive oil, and 1 basil sprig and boil rapidly for 10 minutes, until tender but still firm to the bite. Drain the pasta and transfer to a warm serving plate. Toss the pasta with the butter and garnish with the remaining basil sprig.

5 Serve the steak with the pasta and triangles of warm toast. Serve the rigatoni separately.

Fresh Spaghetti with Italian Meatballs in Tomato Sauce

Serves 4

INGREDIENTS

2½ cups brown breadcrumbs
⅝ cup milk
2 tbsp butter
¼ cup whole-wheat flour
⅞ cup beef stock
14 ounce can chopped tomatoes

2 tbsp tomato paste
1 tsp sugar
1 tbsp finely chopped fresh
    tarragon
1 large onion, chopped
4 cups ground steak

1 tsp paprika
4 tbsp olive oil
1 pound fresh spaghetti
salt and pepper
fresh tarragon sprigs, to garnish

1 Soak the breadcrumbs in the milk for 30 minutes.

2 Melt half the butter in a pan. Stir in the flour and cook for 2 minutes. Gradually stir in the beef stock and cook, stirring constantly, for a further 5 minutes. Add the tomatoes, tomato paste, sugar, and tarragon. Season well and simmer for 25 minutes.

3 Mix the onion, steak, and paprika into the breadcrumbs and season. Shape into 14 meatballs.

4 Heat the oil and remaining butter in a skillet and fry the meatballs until brown all over. Place them in a deep casserole, pour the tomato sauce over the meatballs, cover, and bake in a preheated oven at 350°F for 25 minutes.

5 Cook the spaghetti in a pan of lightly salted boiling water for about 2–3 minutes, until tender, but still firm to the bite.

6 Meanwhile, remove the meatballs from the oven and allow them to cool for 3 minutes. Serve the meatballs and their sauce with the spaghetti, garnished with tarragon sprigs.

Layered Meat Loaf

Serves 6

INGREDIENTS

2 tbsp butter, plus extra
    for greasing
1 small onion, finely chopped
1 small red bell pepper, cored,
    seeded, and chopped
1 garlic clove, chopped
4 cups ground beef
¹/₂ cup white breadcrumbs
¹/₂ tsp cayenne pepper

1 tbsp lemon juice
¹/₂ tsp grated lemon rind
2 tbsp chopped fresh parsley
³/₄ cup dried short pasta, such
    as fusilli
1 tbsp olive oil
1 cup Italian cheese sauce
    4 bay leaves
6 ounces bacon

salt and pepper
salad greens, to garnish

1 Preheat the oven to 350°F. Melt the butter in a pan and sauté the onion and bell pepper for 3 minutes. Stir in the garlic and cook for 1 minute.

2 Put the meat into a bowl and mash with a wooden spoon until sticky. Add the onion mixture, breadcrumbs, cayenne pepper, lemon juice, lemon rind, and parsley. Season and set aside.

3 Bring a pan of salted water to a boil. Add the pasta and oil and cook for 8–10 minutes, until almost tender. Drain and stir into the Italian cheese sauce.

4 Grease a 2-pound loaf pan and arrange the bay leaves in the base. Stretch the bacon slices and line the base and sides of the pan with them. Spoon in half the meat mixture and smooth the surface.

Cover with the pasta mixed with Italian cheese sauce, then spoon in the remaining meat mixture. Level the top and cover with foil.

5 Bake the meat loaf for 1 hour, or until the juices run clear when a skewer is inserted in the center. Pour off any excess fat and turn out the loaf onto a warm serving dish. Garnish with salad greens.

Egg Noodles with Beef

Serves 4

INGREDIENTS

10 ounces egg noodles

3 tbsp walnut oil

1-inch piece fresh ginger root, cut into thin strips

5 scallions, finely shredded

2 garlic cloves, finely chopped

1 red bell pepper, cored, seeded, and thinly sliced

$3\frac{1}{2}$ ounces button mushrooms, thinly sliced

12 ounces fillet steak, cut into thin strips

1 tbsp cornstarch

5 tbsp dry sherry

3 tbsp soy sauce

1 tsp soft brown sugar

1 cup bean sprouts

1 tbsp sesame oil

salt and pepper

scallion strips, to garnish

1 Bring a large pan of water to a boil. Add the noodles and cook according to the instructions on the packet. Drain the noodles, set aside, and keep warm.

2 Heat the walnut oil in a preheated wok and stir-fry the ginger, scallions, and garlic for 45 seconds. Add the bell pepper, mushrooms, and steak and stir-fry for 4 minutes. Season to taste.

3 Mix together the cornstarch, sherry, and soy sauce in a small bowl to form a paste, and pour into the wok. Sprinkle in the brown sugar and stir-fry all of the ingredients for 2 minutes longer.

4 Add the bean sprouts, drained noodles, and sesame oil to the wok, stir and toss together for 1 minute. Transfer to serving plates, garnish with strips of scallion and serve.

COOK'S TIP

If you do not have a wok, you could prepare this dish in a skillet. However, a wok is preferable, as the round base ensures an even distribution of heat and it is easier to keep stirring and tossing the contents when stir-frying.

Tagliarini with Meatballs in Red Wine & Oyster Mushroom Sauce

Serves 4

INGREDIENTS

2 cups white breadcrumbs	4 tomatoes, skinned and	salt and pepper
⅝ cup milk	chopped	fresh basil sprigs, to garnish
2 tbsp butter	1 tbsp tomato paste	
9 tbsp olive oil	1 tsp brown sugar	
3 cups sliced	1 tbsp finely chopped fresh basil	
- oyster mushrooms	12 shallots, chopped	
¼ cup whole-wheat flour	4 cups ground steak	
⅞ cup beef stock	1 tsp paprika	
⅝ cup red wine	1 pound dried egg tagliarini	

1 Soak the breadcrumbs in the milk for 30 minutes.

2 Sauté the mushrooms in half the butter and 4 tbsp of the oil for 4 minutes. Stir in the flour. Add the stock and wine and simmer for 15 minutes. Add the tomatoes, tomato paste, sugar, and basil and simmer for 30 minutes.

3 Mix the shallots, steak, and paprika with the breadcrumbs and season. Shape into 14 meatballs.

4 Heat 4 tbsp of the remaining oil and the remaining butter in a skillet. Fry the meatballs until brown all over. Transfer to a deep casserole, pour in the red wine and the mushroom sauce, cover, and bake in a preheated oven at 350°F for 30 minutes.

5 Bring a pan of salted water to a boil. Add the pasta and the remaining oil and cook until tender. Drain and transfer to a serving dish. Pour the meatballs and sauce onto the pasta, garnish with the basil sprigs, and serve.

Sicilian Spaghetti

Serves 4

INGREDIENTS

⅝ cup olive oil, plus extra for
  brushing

2 eggplants

3 cups ground beef

1 onion, chopped

2 garlic cloves, crushed

2 tbsp tomato paste

14 ounce can chopped tomatoes

1 tsp Worcestershire sauce

1 tsp chopped fresh marjoram or
  oregano or ½ tsp dried
  marjoram or oregano

½ cup pitted black olives, sliced

1 green, red, or yellow bell
  pepper, cored, seeded, and

chopped

6 ounces dried spaghetti

1 cup freshly grated Parmesan
  cheese

salt and pepper

1 Brush an 8-inch loose-based round cake pan with oil, line the base with baking parchment, and brush with oil.

2 Slice the eggplant. Heat a little olive oil in a pan and fry the eggplant until browned on both sides. Drain on paper towels.

3 Put the beef, onion, and garlic in a saucepan and cook, stirring until browned. Add the tomato paste, tomatoes, Worcestershire sauce, marjoram or oregano, and salt and pepper. Simmer, stirring occasionally, for 10 minutes. Add the olives and bell pepper and cook for 10 minutes longer.

4 Bring a pan of salted water to a boil. Add the spaghetti and 1 tablespoon of olive oil and cook until tender, but still firm to the bite. Drain and turn the spaghetti into a bowl. Add the meat mixture and cheese and toss together.

5 Arrange eggplant slices over the base and up the sides of the cake pan. Add the spaghetti and then cover with the rest of the eggplant slices. Bake in a preheated oven at 400°F for 40 minutes. Let stand for 5 minutes, then invert onto a serving dish. Discard the baking parchment and serve immediately.

Beef & Pasta Bake

Serves 4

INGREDIENTS

2 pounds steak, cut into cubes
about ½ cup beef stock
1 pound dried macaroni
1¼ cups heavy cream
½ tsp garam masala
salt
fresh cilantro, to garnish
naan bread, to serve

KORMA PASTE:
½ cup blanched almonds
6 garlic cloves
1-inch piece fresh ginger root,
    coarsely chopped
6 tbsp beef stock
1 tsp ground cardamom
4 cloves, crushed
1 tsp cinnamon

2 large onions, chopped
1 tsp cilantro seeds
2 tsp ground cumin seeds
pinch of cayenne pepper
6 tbsp of sunflower oil

1 Grind the almonds finely using a pestle and mortar. Put the ground almonds and the rest of the korma paste ingredients into a food processor or blender and process well to make a very smooth paste.

2 Put the steak in a shallow dish and spoon over the korma paste, turning to coat the steak well. Marinate in the refrigerator for 6 hours.

3 Transfer the steak to a large saucepan, and simmer gently, adding a little beef stock if required, for 35 minutes.

4 Bring a large saucepan of salted water to a boil. Add the macaroni and cook for 10 minutes, until tender, but still firm to the touch. Drain the pasta and transfer to a deep casserole. Add the steak, heavy cream, and garam masala.

5 Bake in a preheated oven at 400°F for 30 minutes. Remove from the oven and allow to stand for 10 minutes. Garnish with fresh cilantro and serve with naan bread.

VARIATION

You could also make this dish using diced chicken and chicken stock, instead of steak and beef stock.

Lasagne Verde

Serves 4–6

INGREDIENTS

butter, for greasing
14 sheets precooked lasagne
$3^3/_4$ cups Béchamel sauce
$^3/_4$ cup grated mozzarella cheese
fresh basil (optional), to garnish

MEAT SAUCE:
$^1/_8$ cup olive oil
4 cups ground beef

1 large onion, chopped
1 celery stalk, diced
4 cloves garlic, crushed
$^1/_4$ cup all-purpose flour
$1^1/_4$ cups beef stock
$^5/_8$ cup red wine
1 tbsp chopped fresh parsley
1 tsp chopped fresh marjoram
1 tsp chopped fresh basil

2 tbsp tomato paste
salt and pepper

1 To make the meat sauce, heat the olive oil in a large skillet. Add the ground beef and cook, stirring frequently, until browned all over. Add the onion, celery, and garlic and cook for 3 minutes.

2 Sprinkle in the flour and cook, stirring constantly, for 1 minute. Gradually stir in the stock and red wine, season well with salt and pepper, and add the parsley, marjoram, and basil. Bring to a boil, lower the heat, and simmer for 35 minutes. Add the tomato paste and simmer for 10 minutes longer.

3 Lightly grease an ovenproof dish with a little butter. Arrange sheets of lasagne over the base of the dish, spoon a layer of meat sauce over the noodles, then béchamel sauce. Place another layer of lasagne on top and repeat the whole process twice, finishing with a layer of béchamel sauce. Lightly sprinkle with the grated mozzarella cheese.

4 Bake the lasagne in a preheated oven at 375°F for 35 minutes, until the top is golden brown and bubbling. Garnish with fresh basil, if desired, and serve immediately.

Pasticcio

Serves 6

INGREDIENTS

2 cups dried fusilli
1 tbsp olive oil, plus extra
    for brushing
4 tbsp heavy cream
salt
mixed salad, to serve

SAUCE:
2 tbsp olive oil
1 onion, thinly sliced

1 red bell pepper, cored, seeded,
    and chopped
2 garlic cloves, chopped
5¼ cups ground beef
14 ounce can chopped tomatoes
½ cup dry white wine
2 tbsp chopped fresh parsley
2 ounce can anchovies, drained
    and chopped
salt and pepper

TOPPING:
1¼ cups natural yogurt
3 eggs
pinch of freshly grated nutmeg
½ cup freshly grated Parmesan
    cheese

1 To make the sauce, heat the oil in a skillet and sauté the onion and red bell pepper for 3 minutes. Add the garlic and cook for 1 minute. Add the beef and cook until browned.

2 Add the tomatoes and wine and bring to a boil. Simmer for 20 minutes, until thickened.

Stir in the parsley, anchovies, and seasoning.

3 Bring a pan of salted water to a boil. Add the pasta and oil and cook for 10 minutes, until almost tender. Drain and transfer to a bowl. Stir in the cream.

4 For the topping, beat together the yogurt, eggs, and nutmeg.

5 Brush an ovenproof dish with oil. Spoon in half the pasta and cover with half the meat sauce. Repeat the process, then spread on the topping and sprinkle with cheese.

6 Bake in a preheated oven at 375°F for 25 minutes until golden. Serve with a mixed salad.

Fettuccine with Fillet of Veal & Pink Grapefruit in a Rose-Petal Butter Sauce

Serves 4

INGREDIENTS

1 pound dried fettuccine	⁵/₈ cup rose petal vinegar (see Cook's Tip)	TO GARNISH:
7 tbsp olive oil		12 pink grapefruit segments
1 tsp chopped fresh oregano	⁵/₈ cup fish stock	12 pink peppercorns
1 tsp chopped fresh marjoram	¹/₄ cup grapefruit juice	rose petals
³/₄ cup butter	¹/₄ cup heavy cream	fresh herb leaves
1 pound veal fillet, thinly sliced	salt	

1 Cook the fettuccine with 1 tbsp of the oil in a pan of salted boiling water for 12 minutes. Drain and transfer to a warm serving dish. Add 2 tbsp of the olive oil, the oregano, and marjoram.

2 Heat 4 tbsp of the butter with the remaining oil in a large skillet. Gently fry the veal for 6 minutes. Remove and place on top of the pasta.

3 Add the vinegar and fish stock to the pan and bring to a boil. Boil vigorously until reduced by two-thirds. Add the grapefruit juice and cream and simmer for 4 minutes. Dice the remaining butter, add to the pan, and whisk until fully incorporated.

4 Pour the sauce around the veal, garnish and serve.

COOK'S TIP

To make rose petal vinegar, infuse the petals of 8 pesticide-free roses in ⁵/₈ cup white wine vinegar for 48 hours.

Neapolitan Veal Cutlets with Mascarpone Cheese & Marille

Serves 4

INGREDIENTS

$^7/_8$ cup butter
4 9-ounce veal cutlets, trimmed
1 large onion, sliced
2 apples, peeled, cored, and
      sliced
6 ounces button mushrooms
1 tbsp chopped fresh tarragon

8 black peppercorns
1 tbsp sesame seeds
14 ounces dried marille
$^1/_2$ cup extra virgin olive oil
$^3/_4$ cup mascarpone cheese,
      broken into small pieces
salt and pepper

2 large beef tomatoes, cut in half
leaves of 1 fresh basil sprig
fresh basil leaves, to garnish

1 Melt 4 tbsp of the butter in a skillet and fry the veal for 5 minutes on each side. Transfer to a dish and keep warm.

2 Fry the onion and apples in the pan until lightly browned. Transfer to a dish, place the veal on top, and keep warm.

3 Fry the mushrooms, tarragon, and peppercorns in the remaining butter for 3 minutes. Sprinkle with the sesame seeds.

4 Bring a pan of salted water to a boil. Add the pasta and 1 tbsp of the oil and cook until tender. Drain and transfer to a serving plate.

5 Top the pasta with the mascarpone cheese and sprinkle with the remaining olive oil. Place the onions, apples and veal cutlets on top of the pasta. Spoon the mushrooms, peppercorns, and pan juices onto the cutlets, place the tomatoes and basil leaves around the edge, and place in a preheated oven at 300°F for 5 minutes. Season with salt and pepper to taste and serve immediately.

Stir-Fried Pork with Pasta & Vegetables

Serves 4

INGREDIENTS

3 tbsp sesame oil

12 ounces pork tenderloin, cut
   into thin strips

1 pound dried taglioni

1 tbsp olive oil

8 shallots, sliced

2 garlic cloves, finely chopped

1-inch piece fresh ginger
   root, grated

1 fresh green chili, finely
   chopped

1 red bell pepper, cored, seeded,
   and thinly sliced

1 green bell pepper, cored,
   seeded, and thinly sliced

3 zucchini, thinly sliced

2 tbsp ground almonds

1 tsp ground cinnamon

1 tbsp oyster sauce

2 ounces creamed coconut (see
   Cook's Tip), grated

salt and pepper

1 Heat the sesame oil in a preheated wok. Season the pork and stir-fry for 5 minutes.

2 Bring a pan of salted water to a boil. Add the taglioni and olive oil and cook for 12 minutes. Set aside and keep warm.

3 Add the shallots, garlic, ginger, and chili to the wok and stir-fry for 2 minutes. Add the bell peppers and zucchini and stir-fry for 1 minute.

4 Finally, add the ground almonds, cinnamon, oyster sauce, and creamed coconut to the wok and stir-fry for 1 minute.

5 Drain the taglioni and transfer to a serving dish. Top with the stir-fry and serve immediately.

COOK'S TIP

Creamed coconut is available from Chinese and Asian food stores and some large supermarkets. It is sold in compressed blocks and adds a concentrated coconut flavor to the dish.

Orecchiette with Pork in Cream Sauce, Garnished with Quail Eggs

Serves 4

INGREDIENTS

1 pound pork tenderloin,
  thinly sliced
4 tbsp olive oil
8 ounces button mushrooms,
  sliced

⁷/₈ cup Italian red wine sauce
1 tbsp lemon juice
pinch of saffron
3 cups dried orecchiette
4 tbsp heavy cream

12 quail eggs (see Cook's Tip)
salt

1 Pound the slices of pork until wafer thin, then cut into strips.

2 Heat the olive oil in a skillet and stir-fry the pork for 5 minutes, then stir-fry the mushrooms for a further 2 minutes.

3 Pour in the Italian red wine sauce, then simmer for 20 minutes.

4 Meanwhile, bring a large saucepan of lightly salted water to a boil. Add the lemon juice, saffron, and orecchiette and cook for 12 minutes, until tender but still firm to the bite. Drain the pasta and keep warm.

5 Stir the cream into the pan with the pork and heat gently for 3 minutes.

6 Boil the quail eggs for 3 minutes, cool them in cold water, and remove the shells.

7 Transfer the pasta to a warm serving plate, top with the pork and sauce, and garnish with the eggs. Serve immediately.

COOK'S TIP

In this recipe, the quail eggs are soft-cooked. As they are very difficult to shell when warm, they should be thoroughly cooled first. Otherwise, they will break up unattractively.

Stuffed Cannelloni

Serves 4

INGREDIENTS

8 dried cannelloni tubes
1 tbsp olive oil
$\frac{1}{4}$ cup freshly grated Parmesan
    cheese
fresh herb sprigs, to garnish

FILLING:
2 tbsp butter
$10\frac{1}{2}$ ounces frozen spinach,
    thawed and chopped

$\frac{1}{2}$ cup ricotta cheese
$\frac{1}{4}$ cup freshly grated
    Parmesan cheese
$\frac{1}{4}$ cup chopped ham
pinch of freshly grated nutmeg
2 tbsp heavy cream
2 eggs, lightly beaten
salt and pepper

SAUCE:
2 tbsp butter
$\frac{1}{4}$ cup all-purpose flour
$1\frac{1}{4}$ cups milk
2 bay leaves
pinch of freshly grated nutmeg

1 For the filling, melt the butter in a pan and stir-fry the spinach for 2–3 minutes. Remove from the heat and stir in the cheeses and the ham. Season with nutmeg, salt, and pepper. Beat in the cream and eggs to make a thick paste.

2 Cook the pasta with the oil for 10–12 minutes, until almost tender. Drain and set aside.

3 To make the sauce, melt the butter in a pan. Stir in the flour and cook, stirring, for 1 minute. Gradually stir in the milk and the bay leaves and simmer for 5 minutes. Add the nutmeg and seasoning. Remove from the heat and discard the bay leaves.

4 Spoon the filling into a piping bag and fill the cannelloni.

5 Spoon a little sauce into the base of an ovenproof dish. Arrange the cannelloni in the dish in a single layer and pour over the remaining sauce. Sprinkle with the Parmesan cheese and bake in a preheated oven at 375°F for 40–45 minutes. Garnish with fresh herb sprigs and serve.

Whole Wheat Spaghetti with Suprêmes of Chicken Nell Gwyn

Serves 4

INGREDIENTS

⅛ cup rapeseed oil	1 ounce zucchini, cut into	3 large oranges, peeled and cut
3 tbsp olive oil	matchstick strips	into segments
4 8-ounce chicken suprêmes	1 ounce red bell pepper, cut into	rind of 1 orange, cut into very
⅝ cup orange brandy	matchstick strips	fine strips
2 tbsp all-purpose flour	1 ounce leek, finely shredded	2 tbsp chopped fresh tarragon
⅝ cup freshly squeezed orange	14 ounces dried whole-	⅝ cup fromage frais or
juice	wheat spaghetti	ricotta cheese
		salt and pepper

1 Heat the rapeseed oil and 1 tbsp of the olive oil in a skillet. Add the chicken and cook quickly until golden brown. Add the orange brandy and cook for 3 minutes. Add the flour and cook for 2 minutes.

2 Lower the heat and add the orange juice, zucchini, bell pepper, and leek, and season. Simmer for 5 minutes until the sauce has thickened.

3 Meanwhile, bring a pan of salted water to a boil. Add the spaghetti and 1 tbsp of the olive oil and cook for 10 minutes, until just tender, but still firm to the bite. Drain, transfer to a serving dish, and drizzle the remaining oil on top.

4 Add half the orange segments, half the orange rind, the tarragon, and fromage frais or ricotta cheese to the sauce in the pan and cook for 3 minutes.

5 Place the chicken on top of the pasta, pour over a little sauce, garnish with orange segments and rind. Serve immediately.

Chicken & Mushroom Lasagne

Serves 4

INGREDIENTS

butter, for greasing	CHICKEN & MUSHROOM SAUCE:	3 ounces chicken livers,
14 sheets precooked lasagne	2 tbsp olive oil	finely chopped
3¾ cups béchamel sauce	2 garlic cloves, crushed	4 ounces prosciutto, diced
1 cup grated Parmesan cheese	1 large onion, finely	⅝ cup Marsala
	chopped	10 ounce can chopped tomatoes
	8 ounces exotic mushrooms,	1 tbsp chopped fresh basil leaves
	sliced	2 tbsp tomato paste
	2½ cups ground chicken	salt and pepper

1 To make the sauce, heat the olive oil in a large pan. Add the garlic, onion, and mushrooms and cook, stirring frequently, for 6 minutes.

2 Add the ground chicken, chicken livers, and prosciutto and cook over a low heat for 12 minutes, until the meat has browned.

3 Stir the Marsala, tomatoes, basil, and tomato paste into the pan and cook for 4 minutes. Season to taste, cover, and simmer for 30 minutes. Uncover the pan, stir, and simmer for an additional 15 minutes.

4 Arrange sheets of lasagne over the base of a greased ovenproof dish,

spoon a layer of chicken and mushroom sauce over the lasagne, then add a layer of béchamel sauce. Place another layer of lasagne on top and repeat the process twice, finishing with a layer of béchamel sauce. Sprinkle with the grated cheese and bake in a preheated oven at 375°F for 35 minutes until golden brown. Serve.

Tagliatelle with Chicken Sauce

Serves 4

INGREDIENTS

9 ounces fresh green tagliatelle
1 tbsp olive oil
salt
fresh basil leaves, to garnish

TOMATO SAUCE:
2 tbsp olive oil
1 small onion, chopped

1 garlic clove, chopped
14 ounce can chopped tomatoes
2 tbsp chopped fresh parsley
1 tsp dried oregano
2 bay leaves
2 tbsp tomato paste
1 tsp sugar
salt and pepper

CHICKEN SAUCE:
4 tbsp unsalted butter
14 ounces boned chicken breasts,
     skinned, and cut into thin
     strips
3/4 cup blanched almonds
1 1/4 cups heavy cream
salt and pepper

1 To make the tomato sauce, heat the oil in a pan and fry the onion until translucent. Add the garlic and cook for 1 minute. Stir in the tomatoes, parsley, oregano, bay leaves, tomato paste, and sugar. Season, bring to a boil, and simmer for 15–20 minutes, until reduced by half. Remove from the heat and discard the bay leaves.

2 To make the chicken sauce, melt the butter in a skillet and stir-fry the chicken and almonds for 5–6 minutes, until the chicken is cooked through.

3 Meanwhile, bring the cream to a boil in a pan and boil for about 10 minutes, until reduced by half. Pour the cream over the chicken and almonds,

stir, and season to taste. Set aside and keep warm.

4 Bring a large pan of salted water to a boil. Add the tagliatelle and olive oil and cook until tender. Drain and transfer to a warm serving dish. Spoon the tomato sauce over the pasta and arrange the chicken sauce on top. Garnish and serve.

Mustard-Baked Chicken with Pasta Shells

Serves 4

INGREDIENTS

8 chicken pieces
   (about 4 ounces each)
4 tbsp butter, melted
4 tbsp mild mustard (see
   Cook's Tip)

2 tbsp lemon juice
1 tbsp brown sugar
1 tsp paprika
3 tbsp poppy seeds
14 ounces fresh pasta shells

1 tbsp olive oil
salt and pepper

1 Arrange the chicken, smooth side down, in an ovenproof dish.

2 Mix together the butter, mustard, lemon juice, sugar, and paprika in a bowl and season to taste. Brush the mixture over the upper surfaces of the chicken pieces and bake in a preheated oven at 400°F for 15 minutes.

3 Remove the dish from the oven and carefully turn over the chicken

pieces. Coat the upper surfaces of the chicken with the remaining mustard mixture, sprinkle with poppy seeds, and return to the oven for 15 minutes longer.

4 Meanwhile, bring a large pan of lightly salted water to a boil. Add the pasta shells and olive oil and cook until tender, but still firm to the bite.

5 Drain the pasta and arrange on a warmed serving dish. Top with the

chicken, pour over the sauce, and serve immediately.

COOK'S TIP

Dijon is the type of mustard most often used in cooking, as it has a clean and only mildly spicy flavor. German mustard has a sweet-sour taste, with Bavarian mustard being slightly sweeter. American mustard is mild and sweet.

Tortellini

Serves 4

INGREDIENTS

4 ounces boned chicken
   breast, skinned
2 ounces prosciutto
1½ ounces cooked spinach,
   well drained
1 tbsp finely chopped onion
2 tbsp freshly grated
   Parmesan cheese

pinch of ground allspice
1 egg, beaten
1 pound Basic Pasta Dough
salt and pepper
2 tbsp chopped fresh parsley,
   to garnish

SAUCE:
1¼ cups light cream
2 garlic cloves, crushed
4 ounces button mushrooms,
   thinly sliced
4 tbsp freshly grated Parmesan
   cheese

1 Bring a pan of seasoned water to a boil. Add the chicken and poach for 10 minutes. Cool slightly, then put in a food processor with the prosciutto, spinach, and onion, and process until finely chopped. Stir in the Parmesan cheese, allspice, and egg and season to taste.

2 Thinly roll out the pasta dough and cut into 1½–2-inch rounds.

3 Place ½ tsp of the filling in the center of each round. Fold the pieces in half and press the edges to seal. Then wrap each piece around your index finger, cross over the ends, and curl the rest of the dough backward to make a navel shape.

4 Bring a pan of salted water to a boil. Add the tortellini, in batches, bring back to a boil, and cook for 5 minutes. Drain and transfer to a serving dish.

5 To make the sauce, bring the cream and garlic to a boil in a pan, then simmer for 3 minutes. Add the mushrooms and half the cheese, season, and simmer for 2–3 minutes. Pour the sauce over the pasta. Sprinkle with the remaining Parmesan, garnish and serve.

Chicken Suprêmes Filled with Tiger Shrimp on a Bed of Pasta

Serves 4

INGREDIENTS

4 7-ounce chicken
   suprêmes, trimmed
4 ounces large spinach leaves,
   trimmed and blanched in hot
   salted water
4 slices of prosciutto

12–16 raw tiger shrimp, shelled
   and deveined
4 tbsp butter, plus extra
   for greasing
1 pound dried tagliatelle
1 tbsp olive oil

3 leeks, shredded
1 large carrot, grated
5/8 cup thick mayonnaise
2 large cooked beets
salt

1 Place each suprême between 2 pieces of waxed paper and pound with a rolling pin to flatten.

2 Divide half of the spinach among the suprêmes, add a slice of prosciutto to each, and top with more spinach. Place 4 shrimp on top. Roll up each suprême to form a packet. Wrap each packet in greased foil, place on a cookie sheet and bake in a preheated oven at 400°F for 20 minutes.

3 Cook the pasta with the oil in salted boiling water, until tender. Drain and transfer to a warm dish.

4 Melt the butter and fry the leeks and carrot for 3 minutes. Transfer to the center of the pasta.

5 Work the mayonnaise and 1 beet in a food processor or blender until smooth. Rub through a strainer and pour around the pasta and vegetables.

6 Cut the remaining beet into diamond shapes and place them neatly around the mayonnaise. Remove the foil from the chicken and cut the suprêmes into thin slices. Arrange the slices on top of the vegetables and pasta, and serve.

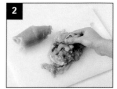

Chicken & Lobster on a Bed of Penne

Serves 6

INGREDIENTS

butter, for greasing

6 chicken breasts

1 pound dried penne rigate

6 tbsp extra virgin olive oil

1 cup freshly grated
   Parmesan cheese

salt

lemon wedges, to serve

FILLING:

4 ounces lobster meat, chopped

2 shallots, very finely chopped

2 figs, chopped

1 tbsp Marsala

2 tbsp breadcrumbs

1 large egg, beaten

salt and pepper

1 Grease 6 pieces of foil large enough to enclose each chicken breast and lightly grease a cookie sheet.

2 Place all of the filling ingredients into a mixing bowl and blend together thoroughly with a spoon.

3 Cut a pocket in each chicken breast with a sharp knife and fill with the lobster mixture. Wrap each chicken breast in foil, place the packets on the greased cookie sheet, and bake in a preheated oven at 400°F for 30 minutes.

4 Meanwhile, bring a large pan of lightly salted water to a boil. Add the pasta and 1 tablespoon of the olive oil and cook for about 10 minutes, or until tender but still firm to the bite. Drain the pasta thoroughly and transfer to a large serving plate. Sprinkle with the remaining olive oil and the grated Parmesan cheese, set aside, and keep warm until required.

5 Carefully remove the foil from around the chicken breasts. Slice the breasts very thinly and arrange over the pasta. Serve with lemon wedges.

COOK'S TIP

The cut of chicken known as suprême consists of the breast and wing. It is always skinned.

Chicken with Green Olives & Pasta

Serves 4

INGREDIENTS

3 tbsp olive oil

2 tbsp butter

4 chicken breasts, part boned

1 large onion, finely chopped

2 garlic cloves, crushed

2 red, yellow, or green bell
    peppers, cored, seeded, and
    cut into large pieces

9 ounces button mushrooms,
    sliced or quartered

6 ounces tomatoes, skinned
    and halved

$\frac{5}{8}$ cup dry white wine

$1\frac{1}{2}$ cups pitted green olives

4–6 tbsp heavy cream

14 ounces dried pasta

salt and pepper

chopped parsley, to garnish

1 Heat 2 tbsp of the oil and the butter in a skillet. Fry the chicken breasts until golden brown. Remove from the pan.

2 Add the onion and garlic to the pan and sauté over a medium heat until beginning to soften. Add the bell peppers and mushrooms and cook for 2–3 minutes. Add the tomatoes and season to taste with salt and pepper. Transfer the vegetables to a casserole and arrange the chicken on top.

3 Add the wine to the pan and bring to a boil. Pour the wine over the chicken. Cover and cook in a preheated oven at 350°F for 50 minutes.

4 Add the olives to the casserole and mix in until well combined. Pour in the cream, cover, and return to the oven for 10–20 minutes.

5 Bring a large pan of lightly salted water to a boil. Add the pasta and the remaining oil and cook until tender, but still firm to the bite. Drain well and transfer to a serving dish.

6 Arrange the chicken on top of the pasta, cover with the sauce, garnish with the parsley, and serve immediately. Alternatively, place the pasta in a large serving bowl and serve separately.

Sliced Breast of Duckling with Linguine

Serves 4

INGREDIENTS

4 10½-ounce boned breasts
of duckling
2 tbsp butter
⅜ cup finely chopped carrots
4 tbsp finely chopped shallots
1 tbsp lemon juice
⅝ cup meat stock
4 tbsp clear honey

¾ cup fresh or thawed
frozen raspberries
¼ cup all-purpose flour
1 tbsp Worcestershire sauce
14 ounces fresh linguine
1 tbsp olive oil
salt and pepper

TO GARNISH:
fresh raspberries
fresh sprigs of parsley

1 Trim and score the duck breasts and season well. Melt the butter in a skillet and fry the duck breasts until lightly colored.

2 Add the carrots, shallots, lemon juice, and half the meat stock and simmer for 1 minute. Stir in half the honey and half the raspberries. Sprinkle in half the flour and cook, stirring constantly, for 3 minutes. Add pepper and the Worcestershire sauce.

3 Stir in the remaining stock and cook for 1 minute. Stir in the remaining honey, raspberries, and flour. Cook for 3 minutes longer.

4 Remove the duck from the pan, but continue simmering the sauce.

5 Bring a large pan of salted water to a boil. Add the linguine and olive oil and cook until tender. Drain and divide between 4 individual plates.

6 Slice the duck breasts lengthwise into ¼-inch thick pieces. Pour a little sauce over the pasta and arrange the sliced duck in a fan shape on top of it. Garnish and serve.

Rigatoni & Pesto-Baked Partridge

Serves 4

INGREDIENTS

8 partridge pieces (about 4 ounces each)	1 tbsp brown sugar	cheese
4 tbsp butter, melted	6 tbsp pesto sauce	salt and pepper
4 tbsp Dijon mustard	1 pound dried rigatoni	
2 tbsp lime juice	1 tbsp olive oil	
	1⅓ cups freshly grated Parmesan	

1 Arrange the partridge pieces, smooth side down, in a single layer in a large, ovenproof dish.

2 Mix together the butter, Dijon mustard, lime juice, and brown sugar in a bowl. Season to taste with salt and pepper. Brush this mixture over the uppermost surfaces of the partridge pieces and bake in a preheated oven at 400°F for 15 minutes.

3 Remove the dish from the oven and coat the partridge pieces with 3 tbsp of the pesto sauce. Return to the oven and bake for a further 12 minutes.

4 Remove the dish from the oven and carefully turn over the partridge pieces. Coat the top of the partridges with the remaining mustard mixture and return to the oven for a further 10 minutes.

5 Meanwhile, bring a large pan of lightly salted water to a boil. Add the rigatoni and olive oil and cook for about 10 minutes, until tender, but still firm to the bite. Drain and transfer to a large serving dish. Toss the pasta with the remaining pesto sauce and the Parmesan.

6 Arrange the pieces of partridge on the serving dish with the rigatoni, pour the cooking juices on top, and serve immediately.

VARIATION

You could also prepare young pheasant in the same way.

Breast of Pheasant Lasagne with Baby Onions & Green Peas

Serves 4

INGREDIENTS

butter, for greasing
14 sheets precooked lasagne
3³/₄ cups Béchamel sauce
³/₄ cup grated mozzarella cheese

FILLING:
8 ounces pork fat, diced
2 tbsp butter
16 small onions
8 large pheasant breasts,
    thinly sliced

¹/₄ cup all-purpose flour
2¹/₂ cups chicken stock
bouquet garni
1 pound fresh peas, shelled
salt and pepper

1 Put the pork fat into a pan of boiling, salted water. Simmer for 3 minutes, drain and pat dry.

2 Fry the pork fat and onions in the butter until lightly browned. Remove from the pan.

3 Add the pheasant to the pan and cook over a low heat, until browned all over. Transfer to an ovenproof dish.

4 Stir the flour into the pan and cook until just brown, then blend in the stock. Pour over the pheasant, add the bouquet garni, and cook in a preheated oven at 400°F for 5 minutes.

5 Remove and discard the bouquet garni. Add the onions, pork fat, and peas and return to the oven for about 10 minutes.

6 Mince the pheasant breasts and pork in a food processor.

7 Lower the oven to 375°F. Make layers of lasagne, pheasant sauce, and béchamel sauce in a greased ovenproof dish, ending with béchamel sauce. Sprinkle with the cheese and bake in the oven for 30 minutes. Serve surrounded by the peas and onions.

Chicken Lasagne

Serves 4

INGREDIENTS
---

12 ounces fresh lasagne (about 9 sheets) or $5\frac{1}{2}$ ounces dried lasagne (about 9 sheets)
1 tbsp olive oil
1 red onion, finely chopped
1 garlic clove, crushed
$1\frac{1}{2}$ cups sliced mushrooms

12 ounces skinless chicken or turkey breast, cut into chunks
$\frac{2}{3}$ cup red wine, diluted with $\frac{1}{3}$ cup water
9 ounces tomato sauce
1 tsp sugar

BECHAMEL SAUCE:
5 tbsp butter
$\frac{1}{2}$ cup all-purpose flour
$2\frac{1}{2}$ cups milk
1 egg, beaten
1 cup grated Parmesan cheese
salt and pepper

1 Cook the lasagne in a pan of boiling water following the instructions on the packet. Lightly grease a deep ovenproof dish.

2 Heat the oil in a pan. Add the onion and garlic and sauté for 3–4 minutes. Add the mushrooms and chicken and stir-fry for 4 minutes, or until the meat browns.

3 Add the wine, bring to a boil, then lower the heat and simmer for 5 minutes. Stir in the tomato sauce and sugar and cook for 3–5 minutes, until the meat is tender and cooked through. The sauce should have thickened, but still be quite runny.

4 To make the béchamel sauce, melt the butter in a pan, stir in the flour, and cook for 2 minutes. Remove the pan from the heat and gradually add the milk, mixing to form a smooth sauce. Return the pan to the heat and bring to a boil, stirring until thickened. Cool slightly, then beat in the egg and half the cheese. Season to taste.

5 Place 3 sheets of lasagne in the base of the dish and cover with half the chicken mixture. Repeat the layers. Finish with the last 3 sheets of lasagne, pour the béchamel sauce on top, and sprinkle with the Parmesan. Bake in a preheated oven at 375°F for 30 minutes, until golden.

Cannelloni

Serves 4

INGREDIENTS

20 tubes dried cannelloni (about 7 oz) or 20 square sheets of fresh pasta (about 12 oz)

1¹/₈ cups ricotta cheese

5¹/₂ ounces frozen spinach, thawed

¹/₂ small red bell pepper, seeded and diced

2 scallions, chopped

²/₃ cup hot vegetable or chicken stock

1 portion of basil and tomato sauce

¹/₃ cup grated Parmesan or pecorino cheese

salt and pepper

1 If you are using dried cannelloni, check the packet instructions; many varieties do not need pre-cooking. If necessary, pre-cook your pasta. Bring a large saucepan of water to a boil, add 1 tablespoon oil, and cook the pasta for 3–4 minutes— it is easier to do this in batches. Drain thoroughly.

2 In a bowl, mix together the ricotta, spinach, bell pepper, and scallions and season to taste with salt and pepper.

3 Lightly butter an ovenproof dish, large enough to contain all the pasta tubes in a single layer. Spoon the ricotta and spinach mixture into the pasta tubes and place them into the prepared dish. If you are using fresh sheets of pasta, spread the ricotta mixture along one side of each fresh pasta square and roll up to form a tube.

4 Mix together the stock and basil and tomato sauce and pour over the pasta tubes.

5 Sprinkle the cheese over the cannelloni and bake in a preheated oven at 375°F for 20–25 minutes, or until the pasta is cooked through.

VARIATION

If you would prefer a creamier version, omit the stock and the basil and tomato sauce and replace with béchamel sauce.

Rich Beef Stew

Serves 4

INGREDIENTS

1 tbsp oil
1 tbsp butter
8 ounces baby onions, peeled
  and halved
1¼ pounds stewing steak, diced into
  1½-inch chunks

1¼ cups beef stock
⅔ cup red wine
4 tbsp chopped oregano
1 tbsp sugar
1 orange
1 ounce porcini or other dried

mushrooms
8 ounces fresh plum tomatoes
cooked rice or potatoes, to serve

1 Heat the oil and butter in a large skillet. Add the baby onions and sauté for 5 minutes, or until golden. Remove with a slotted spoon, set aside, and keep warm.

2 Add the beef to the skillet and cook, stirring, for 5 minutes, or until browned all over.

3 Return the onions to the skillet and add the stock, wine, oregano, and sugar, stirring to mix thoroughly. Transfer the mixture to an ovenproof casserole dish.

4 Pare the rind from the orange and cut it into strips. Slice the orange flesh into rings. Add the orange rings and the rind to the casserole. Cook in a preheated oven at 350°F for 1¼ hours.

5 Soak the porcini mushrooms for 30 minutes in a small bowl containing 4 tablespoons warm water.

6 Skin and halve the tomatoes. Add the tomatoes, porcini mushrooms, and their

soaking liquid to the casserole. Cook for a further 20 minutes, until the beef is tender and the juices thickened. Serve with cooked rice or potatoes.

VARIATION

Instead of fresh tomatoes, try using 8 sun-dried tomatoes, cut into wide strips.

Pork with Lemon & Garlic

Serves 4

INGREDIENTS

1 pound pork tenderloin

1/2 cup chopped almonds

2 tbsp olive oil

2/3 cup finely chopped prosciutto

2 garlic cloves, chopped

1 tbsp fresh oregano, chopped

finely grated rind of 2 lemons

4 shallots, finely chopped

3/4 cup ham or chicken stock

1 tsp sugar

1 Using a sharp knife, cut the pork tenderloin into 4 equal pieces. Place them between sheets of wax paper and pound each piece with a meat mallet or the end of a rolling pin to flatten it.

2 Cut a horizontal slit in each piece of pork to make a pocket.

3 Spread out the almonds on a cookie sheet. Lightly toast the almonds under a preheated broiler for 2–3 minutes, or until golden brown.

4 Mix the almonds with 1 tablespoon of the olive oil, the prosciutto, garlic, oregano, and the finely grated rind from 1 lemon. Carefully spoon the mixture into the pockets of the pork.

5 Heat the remaining olive oil in a large skillet. Add the chopped shallots and sauté for 2 minutes.

6 Add the pork to the skillet and cook for 2 minutes on each side or until browned all over.

7 Add the stock to the skillet, bring to a boil, cover, and simmer for 45 minutes, or until the pork is tender. Remove the meat from the skillet, set aside, and keep warm.

8 Using a grater, pare the remaining lemon. Add the rind and sugar to the pan and boil for 3–4 minutes, or until reduced and syrupy. Pour over the pork tenderloin and serve immediately.

Porkchops with Fennel & Juniper

Serves 4

INGREDIENTS

1/2 fennel bulb	finely grated rind and juice of	4 porkchops, each about 5 1/2 ounces
1 tbsp juniper berries, lightly crushed	1 orange	fresh bread and a crisp salad, to serve
about 2 tbsp olive oil		

1 Using a sharp knife, finely chop the fennel bulb, discarding all the green parts.

2 Grind the juniper berries in a mortar with a pestle. Mix the crushed juniper berries with the fennel flesh, olive oil, and orange rind.

3 Using a sharp knife, score a few cuts all over each chop.

4 Place the porkchops in a single layer in a roasting pan or an ovenproof dish. Spoon the fennel and juniper mixture over the porkchops.

5 Carefully pour the orange juice over the top of each porkchop, cover, and marinate in the refrigerator for about 2 hours.

6 Drain the porkchops and cook under a preheated broiler, for 10–15 minutes, depending on the thickness of the meat, until the pork is tender and cooked through, turning occasionally.

7 Transfer the porkchops to serving plates and serve with a crisp, fresh salad and plenty of fresh bread to mop up the cooking juices.

COOK'S TIP

Juniper berries are most commonly associated with gin, but they are often added to meat dishes in Italy for a delicate citrus flavor. They can be bought dried from most health-food shops and supermarkets.

Pork Cooked in Milk

Serves 4

INGREDIENTS

1 pound 12 ounces boneless leg of pork	1 onion, chopped	1 tbsp green peppercorns, crushed
1 tbsp oil	2 garlic cloves, chopped	2 fresh bay leaves
2 tbsp butter	¹/₂ cup diced pancetta	2 tbsp marjoram
	5 cups milk	2 tbsp thyme

1 Using a sharp knife, remove the fat from the pork. Shape the meat into a neat form, tying it in place with a length of string.

2 Heat the oil and butter in a large saucepan. Add the onion, garlic, and pancetta to the pan and cook for 2–3 minutes.

3 Add the pork to the pan and cook, turning occasionally, until it is browned all over.

4 Pour the milk in, add the peppercorns, bay leaves, marjoram, and thyme, and cook over a low heat for 1¼–1½ hours, or until tender. Watch the liquid carefully for the last 15 minutes of the cooking time because it tends to reduce very quickly and will then burn. If the liquid reduces and the pork is still not tender, add another ¹/₂ cup milk and continue cooking. Reserve the cooking liquid.

5 Remove the pork from the saucepan. Using a sharp knife, cut the meat into slices. Transfer the pork slices to serving plates and serve immediately with the sauce (see Cook's Tip).

COOK'S TIP

As the milk reduces naturally in this dish, it forms a thick and creamy sauce, which curdles slightly but tastes delicious.

Neapolitan Porkchops

Serves 4

INGREDIENTS

2 tbsp olive oil	2 tsp yeast extract	2 tbsp fresh basil, shredded
1 garlic clove, chopped	4 pork loin chops, each about	freshly grated Parmesan cheese,
1 large onion, sliced	4¹/₂ oz	to serve
14 ounce can tomatoes	³/₄ cup pitted black olives	

1 Heat the oil in a large skillet. Add the onions and garlic and sauté for 3–4 minutes, or until the onions are just beginning to soften.

2 Add the tomatoes and yeast extract to the skillet and simmer for about 5 minutes, or until the sauce just starts to thicken.

3 Cook the porkchops under a preheated broiler for 5 minutes on both sides, until the the meat is golden and cooked through. Set the porkchops aside and keep warm.

4 Add the olives and fresh shredded basil to the sauce in the skillet and stir quickly to combine.

5 Transfer the chops to warm serving plates. Top with the sauce, sprinkle with freshly grated Parmesan cheese, and serve immediately.

COOK'S TIP

Parmesan is a mature and exceptionally hard cheese produced in Italy. You need to add only a little, as it has a very strong flavor.

COOK'S TIP

There are many types of canned tomato available — for example plum tomatoes, or chopped tomatoes in water, or chopped sieved tomatoes (passata). The chopped variety are often canned with added flavors, such as garlic, basil, onion, chili, and mixed herbs, and are a good standby.

Roman Pan-Fried Lamb

Serves 4

INGREDIENTS

1 tbsp oil	3 sprigs thyme, stalks removed	1/2 cup pitted black olives, halved
1 tbsp butter	6 canned anchovy fillets	2 tbsp chopped parsley, to garnish
1 1/4 pounds lamb (shoulder or leg), cut in 1-inch cubes	2/3 cup red wine	mashed potato, to serve
4 garlic cloves, peeled	2/3 cup lamb or vegetable stock	
	1 tsp sugar	

1 Heat the oil and butter in a large skillet. Add the cubes of lamb and cook for 4–5 minutes, stirring, until the meat is browned all over.

2 Using a pestle and mortar, grind together the garlic, thyme, and anchovies to make a smooth paste.

3 Add the wine and lamb or vegetable stock to the skillet, stirring to mix. Stir in the garlic and anchovy paste, together with the sugar.

4 Bring the mixture to a boil, reduce the heat, cover and simmer for 30–40 minutes, or until the lamb is tender. For the last 10 minutes of the cooking time, remove the lid in order to allow the sauce to reduce slightly.

5 Stir the olives into the sauce and mix.

6 Transfer the lamb and the sauce to a serving dish and garnish with freshly chopped parsley. Serve with creamy mashed potatoes.

COOK'S TIP

Rome is the capital of both the region of Lazio and Italy and thus has become a focal point for specialities from all over Italy. Food from this region tends to be fairly simple and quick to prepare, all with plenty of herbs and seasonings giving really robust flavors.

Lamb Noisettes with Bay & Lemon

Serves 4

INGREDIENTS

4 lamb chops	²/₃ cup white wine	pared rind of 1 lemon
1 tbsp oil	²/₃ cup lamb or vegetable stock	salt and pepper
1 tbsp butter	2 bay leaves	

1 Using a sharp knife, carefully remove the bone from each lamb chop, keeping the meat intact. Alternatively, ask your butcher to prepare the lamb noisettes for you.

2 Shape the meat into rounds and secure with a length of string.

3 In a large skillet, heat together the oil and butter until the mixture is just beginning to froth. Add the lamb noisettes to the skillet and cook for 2–3 minutes on each side, or until browned all over.

4 Remove the skillet from the heat, drain off all of the fat, and discard.

5 Return the skillet to the heat. Add the wine, stock, bay leaves, and lemon rind to the skillet and cook over a medium heat for 20–25 minutes, or until the lamb is tender.

6 Season the lamb and sauce to taste with a little salt and pepper.

7 Transfer to serving plates. Remove the string and serve the noisettes with the sauce.

COOK'S TIP

Your local butcher will offer you good advice on how to prepare the lamb noisettes, if you are wary of preparing them yourself.

Chicken Marengo

Serves 4

INGREDIENTS

1 tbsp olive oil	8 slices white bread	¹/₂ cup pitted black olives, chopped
8 chicken pieces	3 tbsp butter, melted	1 tsp sugar
10¹/₂ ounces tomato sauce	2 garlic cloves, crushed	fresh basil, to garnish
³/₄ cup white wine	3¹/₂ ounces mixed mushrooms (such	
2 tsp dried mixed herbs	as button, oyster, and ceps)	

1 Using a sharp knife, remove the bone from each of the chicken pieces.

2 Heat the oil in a large skillet. Add the chicken pieces and cook, turning occasionally, for 4–5 minutes, or until browned all over.

3 Add the tomato sauce, wine, and mixed herbs to the skillet. Bring to a boil and then simmer for 30 minutes, or until the chicken is tender and the juices run clear when a toothpick is inserted into the thickest part of the meat.

4 Mix the melted butter and crushed garlic together. Lightly toast the slices of bread and brush with the garlic butter.

5 Add the remaining oil to a separate skillet and cook the mushrooms for 2–3 minutes, or until just brown.

6 Add the olives and sugar to the chicken mixture and warm through.

7 Transfer the chicken and sauce to serving plates. Serve with the bruschetta (fried bread) and fried mushrooms.

COOK'S TIP

If you have time, marinate the chicken pieces in the wine and herbs in the refrigerator for 2 hours. This will make the chicken more tender and accentuate the wine flavor of the sauce.

Prosciutto-Wrapped Chicken

Serves 4

INGREDIENTS

4 skinless chicken breasts	8 slices prosciutto	$^2/_3$ cup chicken stock
$^1/_2$ cup cream cheese, flavored with herbs and garlic	$^2/_3$ cup red wine	1 tbsp brown sugar

1 Using a sharp knife, make a horizontal slit along the length of each chicken breast to form a pocket.

2 Beat the cheese with a wooden spoon to soften it. Spoon the cheese into the pocket of the chicken breasts.

3 Wrap 2 slices of prosciutto around each chicken breast and secure in place with a length of string.

4 Pour the wine and chicken stock into a large skillet and bring to a boil over a medium heat.

When the mixture is just starting to boil, add the sugar and stir to dissolve.

5 Add the chicken breasts to the skillet. Lower the heat and simmer for about 12–15 minutes, or until the chicken is tender and the juices run clear when a toothpick is inserted into the thickest part of the meat.

6 Remove the chicken from the pan, set aside, and keep warm.

7 Reheat the sauce and boil until reduced and thickened. Remove the string and cut the chicken

into slices. Pour the sauce over the chicken to serve.

VARIATION

Try adding 2 finely chopped sun-dried tomatoes to the soft cheese in step 2, if desired.

Chicken with Balsamic Vinegar

Serves 4

INGREDIENTS

4 boneless chicken thighs	1 tbsp oil	2 tbsp fresh thyme
2 garlic cloves, crushed	1 tbsp butter	salt and pepper
¾ cup red wine	4 shallots	cooked polenta or rice, to serve
3 tbsp white wine vinegar	3 tbsp balsamic vinegar	

1 Using a sharp knife, make a few slashes in the skin of the chicken. Brush the chicken with the crushed garlic and place in a non-metallic dish.

2 Pour the wine and white wine vinegar over the chicken and season to taste with a little salt and pepper. Cover and marinate in the refrigerator for as long as possible, preferably overnight.

3 Carefully remove the chicken pieces with a slotted spoon, draining well, and reserve the marinade.

4 Heat the oil and butter in a skillet. Add the shallots and sauté for 2–3 minutes, or until they begin to soften.

5 Add the chicken pieces to the skillet and cook for about 3-4 minutes, turning, until browned all over. Reduce the heat and add half the reserved marinade. Cover and cook for 15-20 minutes, adding more marinade when necessary.

6 Add the balsamic vinegar and thyme and cook for a further 4 minutes.

7 Transfer to serving plates and serve with polenta or rice.

COOK'S TIP

To make the chicken pieces look a little neater, use toothpicks to hold them together or secure them with a length of string.

Saltimbocca

Serves 4

INGREDIENTS

4 turkey fillets or 4 veal escalopes, about 1 pound in total	8 sage leaves	$^3/_4$ cup white wine
$3^3/_4$ ounces prosciutto	1 tbsp olive oil	$^3/_4$ cup chicken stock
	1 onion, finely chopped	

1 Place the turkey or veal between sheets of wax paper. Pound the meat with a meat mallet or the end of a rolling pin to flatten it slightly. Cut each escalope in half.

2 Trim the prosciutto to fit each piece of turkey or veal and place over the meat. Lay a sage leaf on top. Roll up the escalopes and secure with a toothpick.

3 Heat the oil in a skillet and sauté the onion for 3–4 minutes. Add the turkey or veal rolls to the skillet and cook for 5 minutes, until golden brown all over.

4 Pour the wine and stock into the skillet and simmer for 15 minutes if using turkey, and 20 minutes for veal, or until tender. Serve immediately.

VARIATION

Try a similar recipe called Bocconcini, *meaning "little mouthfuls." Follow the same method as here, but replace the sage leaf with a piece of Swiss cheese.*

COOK'S TIP

If using turkey rather than veal, watch it carefully, as turkey tends to turn dry very quickly if overcooked.

Escalopes with Italian Sausage & Capers

Serves 4

INGREDIENTS

1 tbsp olive oil	finely grated rind and juice of	4 turkey or veal escalopes, each
6 canned anchovy fillets, drained	1 orange	about 4¹/₂ ounces
1 tbsp capers, drained	³/₄ cup diced Italian sausage	salt and pepper
1 tbsp fresh rosemary, stalks removed	3 tomatoes, skinned and chopped	crusty bread or cooked polenta,
		to serve

1 Heat the oil in a large skillet. Add the anchovies, capers, fresh rosemary, orange rind and juice, Italian sausage, and tomatoes and cook for about 5–6 minutes, stirring occasionally.

2 Meanwhile, place the turkey or veal escalopes between sheets of wax paper. Pound the meat with a meat mallet or the end of a rolling pin to flatten it.

3 Add the meat to the mixture in the skillet. Season to taste with salt and pepper, cover, and cook for 3–5 minutes on each side, or slightly longer if the meat is thicker.

4 Transfer to serving plates and serve with fresh crusty bread or cooked polenta.

VARIATION

Try using 4-minute steaks, slightly flattened, instead of the turkey or veal. Cook them for 4–5 minutes on top of the sauce in the skillet.

COOK'S TIP

Polenta is typical of northern Italian cuisine. It is often fried or toasted and used to mop up the juices of the main course.

Italian Sausage & Bean Casserole

Serves 4

INGREDIENTS

8 Italian sausages	1 green bell pepper	2 tbsp sun-dried tomato paste
1 tbsp olive oil	8 ounces fresh tomatoes, skinned and	14 ounce can cannellini beans
1 large onion, chopped	chopped or 14 ounce can	mashed potato or rice, to serve
2 garlic cloves, chopped	tomatoes, chopped	

1 Seed the bell pepper and cut it into thin strips.

2 Prick the Italian sausages all over with a fork. Cook them, under a preheated broiler for 10–12 minutes, turning occasionally, until brown all over. Set aside and keep warm.

3 Heat the oil in a large skillet. Add the onion, garlic, and bell pepper strips to the skillet and cook for 5 minutes, stirring occasionally, or until the onion has softened.

4 Add the tomatoes to the skillet and simmer the mixture over a medium heat, stirring occasionally, for about 5 minutes, or until slightly reduced and thickened.

5 Stir the sun-dried tomato paste, cannellini beans, and Italian sausages into the mixture in the skillet. Cook for about 4–5 minutes, or until the mixture is piping hot. Add 4–5 tablespoons of water, stirring well, if the mixture becomes too dry during cooking.

6 Transfer the Italian sausage and bean casserole to serving plates and serve with mashed potato or cooked rice.

COOK'S TIP

Italian sausages are coarse in texture and have quite a strong flavor. They can be found in speciality sausage shops, Italian delicatessens, and some supermarkets. Game sausages are the only substitutes in this recipe.

Broiled Chicken with Pesto Toasts

Serves 4

INGREDIENTS

8 part-boned chicken thighs

olive oil, for brushing

1²/₃ cups sieved tomatoes

¹/₂ cup green or red
    pesto sauce

12 slices French bread

1 cup freshly grated
    Parmesan cheese

¹/₂ cup pine nuts
    or slivered almonds

basil sprig, to garnish

1 Put the chicken in a single layer in a wide flameproof dish and brush with oil. Place under a preheated broiler for about 15 minutes, turning occasionally, until golden brown.

2 Pierce the thighs with the point of a sharp knife to ensure that the there is no trace of pink in the juices.

3 Pour off any excess fat. Warm the sieved tomatoes and half the pesto sauce in a small saucepan and pour over the chicken. Broil for a few more minutes, turning until coated.

4 Meanwhile, spread the remaining pesto onto the slices of bread. Arrange the bread over the chicken and sprinkle with the Parmesan cheese. Scatter the pine nuts over the cheese. Broil for 2–3 minutes, until browned and bubbling. Serve hot, garnished with a basil sprig.

COOK'S TIP

Leaving the skin on means the chicken will have a higher fat content, but many people like the rich taste and crispy skin, especially when it is blackened by the barbecue. The skin also keeps in the cooking juices.

Boned Chicken with Parmesan

Serves 6

INGREDIENTS

1 chicken, weighing about 5 pounds	1 cup freshly grated	2 garlic cloves, crushed
8 slices mortadella or salami	Parmesan cheese	1 egg, beaten
2 cups fresh white	6 tablespoons chopped fresh basil	pepper
or brown bread crumbs	or parsley	fresh spring vegetables, to serve

1 Bone the chicken, keeping the skin intact. Dislocate each leg by breaking it at the thigh joint. Cut down each side of the backbone, taking care not to pierce the breast skin.

2 Pull the backbone clear of the flesh and discard. Remove the ribs, severing any attached flesh with a sharp knife.

3 Scrape the flesh from each leg and cut away the bone at the joint with a knife or shears.

4 Use the bones for stock. Lay out the boned chicken on a board, skin side down. Arrange the mortadella slices over the chicken, overlapping slightly.

5 Put the bread crumbs, Parmesan cheese, garlic, and basil or parsley in a bowl. Season well with pepper and mix. Stir in the beaten egg to bind the mixture together. Pile the mixture down the middle of the boned chicken, roll the meat around it, and tie securely with fine cotton string.

6 Place in a roasting pan and brush lightly with olive oil. Roast in a preheated oven at 400°F for 1½ hours, or until the juices run clear when the chicken is pierced with a sharp knife.

7 Serve hot or cold, in slices, with fresh spring vegetables.

VARIATION

Replace the mortadella with slices of bacon, if desired.

Italian Chicken Spirals

Serves 4

INGREDIENTS

4 skinless, boneless, chicken breasts	2 cups whole wheat pasta spirals	1 tablespoon lemon juice
1 cup fresh basil leaves		1 tablespoon olive oil
2 tablespoons hazelnuts	2 sun-dried tomatoes or fresh tomatoes	1 tablespoon capers
1 garlic clove, crushed		1/2 cup black olives
		salt and pepper

1 Beat the chicken breasts with a rolling pin to flatten evenly.

2 Place the basil and hazelnuts in a food processor and process until finely chopped. Mix with the garlic, salt, and pepper.

3 Spread the basil mixture over the chicken breasts and roll up from one short end to enclose the filling. Wrap the chicken rolls tightly in foil so that they hold their shape, then seal the ends well.

4 Bring a large pan of lightly salted water to boil and cook the pasta until tender, but still firm to the bite.

5 Place the chicken parcels in a steamer basket or colander set over the pan, cover tightly, and steam for 10 minutes. Meanwhile, dice the tomatoes.

6 Drain the pasta and return to the pan with the lemon juice, olive oil, tomatoes, capers, and olives. Heat through.

7 Pierce the chicken with a a sharp knife to make sure that the juices run clear and not pink, then slice the chicken, arrange it over the pasta, and serve.

VARIATION

Sun-dried tomatoes have a wonderful, rich flavor, but if you can't find them, use fresh tomatoes.

Prosciutto-Wrapped Chicken Cushions

Serves 4

INGREDIENTS

1/2 cup frozen spinach, thawed	2 tablespoons butter	2/3 cup dry white or red wine
1/2 cup ricotta cheese	1 tablespoon olive oil	1 1/4 cups chicken stock
pinch grated nutmeg	12 small onions or shallots	salt and pepper
4 skinless, boneless chicken breasts, each weighing 6 ounces	1 1/2 cups button mushrooms, sliced	carrot purée and green beans, to serve
4 slices prosciutto	1 tablespoon all-purpose flour	

1 Put the spinach into a strainer and press out the water with a spoon. Mix with the ricotta and nutmeg and season with salt and pepper to taste.

2 Using a sharp knife, slit each chicken breast through the side and enlarge each cut to form a pocket. Fill with the spinach mixture, reshape the chicken breasts, wrap each breast tightly in a slice of ham, and secure with toothpicks. Cover and chill in the refrigerator.

3 Heat the butter and oil in a skillet and brown the chicken breasts for 2 minutes on each side. Transfer the chicken to a large, shallow ovenproof dish and keep warm until required.

4 Fry the onions and mushrooms for 2–3 minutes, until lightly browned. Stir in the all-purpose flour, then gradually add the wine and stock. Bring to a boil, stirring constantly. Season to taste and spoon the mixture around the chicken.

5 Cook the chicken, uncovered, in a preheated oven at 400°F for 20 minutes. Turn the breasts over and cook for a further 10 minutes. Remove the toothpicks and serve with the sauce, together with carrot purée and green beans, if desired.

Chicken Pepperonata

Serves 4

INGREDIENTS

8 skinless chicken thighs	1 large red bell pepper, thinly sliced	1 tablespoon chopped oregano
2 tablespoons whole wheat flour	1 large yellow bell pepper, thinly sliced	salt and pepper
2 tablespoons olive oil	1 large green bell pepper, thinly sliced	fresh oregano, to garnish
1 small onion, thinly sliced		crusty whole-wheat bread, to serve
1 garlic clove, crushed	14 ounce can chopped tomatoes	

1 Remove and discard the skin from the chicken thighs and toss them in the flour.

2 Heat the oil in a wide skillet and fry the chicken quickly until sealed and lightly browned, then remove from the pan. Add the onion to the pan and gently fry until soft. Add the garlic, bell peppers, tomatoes, and oregano, then bring to a boil, stirring.

3 Arrange the chicken over the vegetables, season well with salt and pepper, then cover tightly, and simmer for 20–25 minutes, or until the chicken is cooked completely and tender.

4 Season to taste, garnish with oregano, and serve with crusty whole-wheat bread.

COOK'S TIP

If you do not have fresh oregano, use canned tomatoes with herbs already added.

COOK'S TIP

For extra flavor, halve the bell peppers and broil under a preheated broiler until the skins are charred. Let cool, then remove the skins and seeds. Slice the bell peppers thinly and use in the recipe.

Fish & Seafood

Fish markets in Italy are fascinating, with a
huge variety on display, but as most of the catch
comes from the Mediterranean, it is not
always easy to find an equivalent elsewhere.
Pasta is a natural partner for fish and seafood. Both
are cooked quickly to preserve their flavor and
texture, they are packed full of nutritional goodness,
and the varieties available are almost infinite.
The superb recipes in this chapter demonstrate the
full range of these qualities. Try a quick,
easy, and satisfying supper, or one of the more
unusual and sophisticated dishes. There are dishes
to suit all tastes—freshwater and sea fish, shellfish
and other seafood—and to suit all pockets.
All are easy to make; the only problem
is choosing which one to cook next.

Cannelloni Filetti di Sogliola

Serves 6

INGREDIENTS

12 small fillets of sole
(about 4 ounces each)
⁵⁄₈ cup red wine
6 tbsp butter
3⁷⁄₈ cups sliced
button mushrooms
4 shallots, finely chopped

4 ounces tomatoes, chopped
2 tbsp tomato paste
¹⁄₂ cup all-purpose
flour, sifted
⁵⁄₈ cup warm milk
2 tbsp heavy cream
6 dried cannelloni tubes

6 ounces cooked, peeled shrimp,
preferably freshwater
salt and pepper
1 fresh fennel sprig, to garnish

1 Brush the fillets with a little wine, season, then roll them up, skin side inward. Secure with a skewer or toothpick.

2 Arrange the fish rolls in a single layer in a large skillet, add the remaining red wine, and poach for about 4 minutes. Remove the fish, reserving the cooking liquid.

3 Melt the butter in another pan. Sauté the mushrooms and shallots for 2 minutes, then add the tomatoes and tomato paste. Season the flour and stir it into the pan. Stir in the reserved cooking liquid and half the milk. Cook over a low heat, stirring, for 4 minutes. Remove from the heat and stir in the cream.

4 Bring a pan of salted water to a boil. Add the cannelloni and cook for 8 minutes, until tender but still firm to the bite. Drain and set aside to cool.

5 Remove the skewers or toothpicks from the fish rolls. Put 2 sole fillets into each cannelloni tube with 2–3 shrimp and a little red wine sauce. Arrange the cannelloni in an ovenproof dish, pour over the sauce and bake in a preheated oven at 400°F for 20 minutes.

6 Transfer the cannelloni to individual serving plates, garnish, and serve with the red wine sauce.

Sea Bass with Olive Sauce on a Bed of Macaroni

Serves 4

INGREDIENTS

1 pound dried macaroni
1 tbsp olive oil
8 4-ounce sea bass medallions

TO GARNISH:
lemon slices
shredded leek
shredded carrot

SAUCE:
2 tbsp butter
4 shallots, chopped
2 tbsp capers
1½ cups pitted green olives, chopped
4 tbsp balsamic vinegar
1¼ cups fish stock

1¼ cups heavy cream
juice of 1 lemon
salt and pepper

1 To make the sauce, melt the butter in a skillet and fry the shallots for 4 minutes. Add the capers and olives and cook for 3 minutes longer.

2 Stir in the balsamic vinegar and fish stock, bring to a boil, and reduce by half. Add the cream, stirring, and reduce again by half. Season to taste and stir in the lemon juice. Remove from the heat, set aside, and keep warm.

3 Bring a pan of salted water to a boil. Add the pasta and olive oil and cook for 12 minutes, until tender but still firm to the bite.

4 Meanwhile, lightly broil the sea bass medallions for 3–4 minutes on each side, until cooked through, but still moist and delicate.

5 Drain the pasta and transfer to a large serving dish. Top the pasta with the fish medallions and then pour on the olive sauce. Garnish with a few lemon slices, shredded leek, and shredded carrot and serve immediately.

Spaghetti alla Bucaniera

Serves 4

INGREDIENTS

³/₄ cup all-purpose flour	1 carrot, diced	salt and pepper
1 pound brill or sole fillets, skinned and chopped	1 leek, finely chopped	chopped fresh parsley, to garnish
1 pound hake fillets, skinned and chopped	1¹/₄ cups hard cider	crusty brown bread, to serve
6 tbsp butter	1¹/₄ cups medium sweet cider	
4 shallots, finely chopped	2 tsp anchovy extract	
2 garlic cloves, crushed	1 tbsp tarragon vinegar	
	1 pound dried spaghetti	
	1 tbsp olive oil	

1 Season the flour with salt and pepper to taste. Sprinkle ¹/₄ cup of the seasoned flour onto a shallow plate. Press the fish pieces into the seasoned flour so that they are thoroughly coated.

2 Melt the butter in a flameproof casserole. Add the fish fillets, shallots, garlic, carrot, and leek and cook over a low heat, stirring frequently, for about 10 minutes.

3 Sprinkle over the remaining seasoned flour and cook, stirring constantly, for 2 minutes. Gradually stir in the cider, anchovy extract, and tarragon vinegar. Bring to a boil and simmer over a low heat for 35 minutes. Alternatively, bake in a preheated oven at 350°F for 30 minutes.

4 About 15 minutes before the end of the cooking time, bring a large

pan of lightly salted water to a boil. Add the spaghetti and olive oil and cook for about 12 minutes, until tender but still firm to the bite. Drain the spaghetti thoroughly and transfer to a large serving dish.

5 Arrange the fish on top of the spaghetti and cover with the sauce. Garnish with chopped parsley and serve immediately with warm, crusty brown bread.

Steamed Pasta Pudding

Serves 4

INGREDIENTS

1 cup dried short-cut macaroni or other short pasta	6 black peppercorns	salt and pepper
1 tbsp olive oil	$^1/_2$ cup heavy cream	fresh dill or parsley sprigs, to garnish
1 tbsp butter, plus extra for greasing	2 eggs, separated	tomato sauce, to serve
1 pound white fish fillets, such as cod or haddock	2 tbsp chopped fresh dill or parsley	
2–3 fresh parsley sprigs	pinch of freshly grated nutmeg	
	$^2/_3$ cup freshly grated Parmesan cheese	

1 Bring a pan of salted water to a boil. Add the pasta and olive oil and cook until tender, but still firm to the bite. Drain the pasta, add the butter, cover, and keep warm.

2 Place the fish in a skillet. Add the parsley sprigs, peppercorns, and enough water to cover. Bring to a boil, cover, and simmer for 10 minutes. Remove the fish, reserving the cooking liquid.

3 Skin the fish and cut into bite-size pieces. Combine the cream, egg yolks, chopped dill or parsley, nutmeg, and cheese, and mix with the pasta in a bowl. Spoon in the fish and enough of the reserved cooking liquid to make a moist, but firm mixture. Whisk the egg whites until stiff, then fold them into the mixture.

4 Grease a heatproof bowl and spoon in the fish mixture to within $1^1/_2$ inches of the rim. Cover the top with greased baking paper and foil and tie securely with a piece of string.

5 Stand the bowl on a trivet in a saucepan. Add boiling water to reach halfway up the sides. Cover and steam for $1^1/_2$ hours. Invert the pudding onto a serving plate. Garnish and serve with the tomato sauce.

Red Mullet Fillets with Orecchiette, Amaretto, & Orange Sauce

Serves 4

INGREDIENTS

³/₄ cup all-purpose flour

8 red mullet fillets

2 tbsp butter

⁵/₈ cup fish stock

1 tbsp crushed almonds

1 tsp pink peppercorns

1 orange, peeled and cut into segments

1 tbsp orange liqueur

grated rind of 1 orange

1 pound dried orecchiette

1 tbsp olive oil

⁵/₈ cup heavy cream

4 tbsp amaretto

salt and pepper

TO GARNISH:

2 tbsp snipped fresh chives

1 tbsp toasted almonds

1 Season the flour and sprinkle into a shallow bowl. Press the fish fillets into the flour to coat. Melt the butter in a skillet and fry the fish over a low heat for 3 minutes, until browned.

2 Add the fish stock to the pan and cook for 4 minutes. Carefully remove the fish, cover with foil, and keep warm.

3 Add the almonds, pink peppercorns, half the orange, the orange liqueur, and orange rind to the pan. Simmer until the liquid has reduced by half.

4 Meanwhile, bring a large saucepan of lightly salted water to a boil. Add the orecchiette and olive oil and cook for 15 minutes, until tender but still firm to the bite.

5 Meanwhile, season the sauce and stir in the cream and amaretto. Cook for 2 minutes. Return the fish to the pan to coat with the sauce.

6 Drain the pasta and transfer to a serving dish. Top with the fish fillets and their sauce. Garnish with orange segments, chives, and toasted almonds. Serve.

Vermicelli with Fillets of Red Mullet

Serves 4

INGREDIENTS

2¼ pounds red mullet fillets
1¼ cups dry white wine
4 shallots, finely chopped
1 garlic clove, crushed
3 tbsp mixed fresh herbs
finely grated rind and juice of
   1 lemon

pinch of freshly grated nutmeg
3 anchovy fillets, roughly
   chopped
2 tbsp heavy cream
1 tsp cornstarch
1 pound dried vermicelli
1 tbsp olive oil
salt and pepper

TO GARNISH:
1 fresh mint sprig
lemon slices
lemon rind

1 Put the fish fillets in a large casserole. Pour the wine over and add the shallots, garlic, chopped herbs, lemon rind and juice, nutmeg, and anchovies. Season to taste. Cover and bake in a preheated oven at 350°F for 35 minutes.

2 Carefully transfer the mullet to a warm dish. Set aside and keep warm while you prepare the sauce and pasta.

3 Pour the cooking liquid into a pan and bring to a boil. Simmer for 25 minutes, until reduced by half. Mix together the cream and cornstarch and stir into the sauce to thicken.

4 Bring a pan of salted water to a boil. Add the vermicelli and olive oil and cook until tender, but still firm to the bite. Drain the pasta and transfer to a warm serving dish.

5 Arrange the red mullet fillets on top of the vermicelli and pour the sauce over it. Garnish with a fresh mint sprig, slices of lemon, and strips of lemon rind and serve immediately.

COOK'S TIP

The best red mullet is sometimes called golden mullet, although it is bright red in color.

Spaghetti al Tonno

Serves 4

INGREDIENTS

7 ounce can tuna, drained
2 ounce can anchovies, drained
$1\frac{1}{8}$ cups olive oil

1 cup roughly chopped parsley
$\frac{5}{8}$ cup crème fraîche
1 pound dried spaghetti

2 tbsp butter
salt and pepper
black olives, to garnish
crusty bread, to serve

1 Remove any bones from the tuna. Put the tuna into a food processor or blender, together with the anchovies, 1 cup of the olive oil, and the parsley. Process until smooth.

2 Spoon the crème fraîche into the food processor or blender and process again for a few seconds to blend well. Season to taste.

3 Bring a large pan of lightly salted water to a boil. Add the spaghetti and the remaining olive oil and cook until tender, but still firm to the bite.

4 Drain the spaghetti, return to the saucepan and place over a medium heat. Add the butter and toss well to coat. Spoon in the sauce and quickly toss into the spaghetti, using 2 forks, until well combined.

5 Remove the pan from the heat and divide the spaghetti between 4 warm individual plates. Garnish with the olives and serve immediately with warm, crusty bread.

VARIATION

If desired, you could add 1–2 garlic cloves to the sauce, substitute $\frac{1}{2}$ cup chopped fresh basil for half the parsley, and garnish with capers instead of black olives.

Casserole of Fusilli & Smoked Haddock with Egg Sauce

Serves 4

INGREDIENTS

2 tbsp butter, plus extra
    for greasing
1 pound smoked haddock fillets,
    cut into 4 slices
2½ cups milk
¼ cup all-purpose flour

pinch of freshly grated nutmeg
3 tbsp heavy cream
1 tbsp chopped fresh parsley,
    plus extra to garnish
2 eggs, hard cooked and mashed
    to a pulp

4 cups dried fusilli
1 tbsp lemon juice
salt and pepper
boiled new potatoes and beets,
    to serve

1 Grease a casserole with butter. Put the haddock in the casserole and pour in the milk. Bake in a preheated oven at 400°F for 15 minutes. Carefully pour the cooking liquid into a pitcher without breaking up the fish.

2 Melt the butter in a saucepan and stir in the flour. Gradually whisk in the reserved cooking liquid. Season with salt, pepper, and nutmeg. Stir in the cream, parsley, and mashed egg and cook for 2 minutes.

3 Bring a large saucepan of lightly salted water to a boil. Add the fusilli and lemon juice and cook until tender, but still firm to the bite.

4 Drain the pasta and tip it over the fish. Top with the sauce and return to the oven for 10 minutes.

5 Garnish and serve the casserole with boiled new potatoes and beets.

VARIATION

You can use any type of dried pasta for this casserole. Try penne, conchiglie, or rigatoni.

Ravioli of Lemon Sole & Haddock

Serves 4

INGREDIENTS

1 pound lemon sole fillets, skinned

1 pound haddock fillets, skinned

3 eggs beaten

1 pound cooked potato gnocchi

3 cups fresh breadcrumbs

1/4 cup heavy cream

1 pound Basic Pasta Dough

1 1/4 cups Italian red wine sauce

2/3 cup freshly grated Parmesan cheese

salt and pepper

1 Flake the fish fillets in a large mixing bowl.

2 Mix the eggs, cooked potato gnocchi, breadcrumbs, and cream in a bowl until combined. Add the fish to the bowl and season to taste.

3 Roll out the pasta dough on a lightly floured counter and cut out 3-inch rounds.

4 Place a spoonful of the fish stuffing on each round. Dampen the edges slightly and fold the pasta rounds over, pressing together to seal.

5 Bring a large saucepan of lightly salted water to a boil. Add the ravioli and cook for 15 minutes.

6 Transfer the ravioli, using a slotted spoon, to a large serving dish. Pour the Italian red wine sauce over the ravioli, sprinkle with the Parmesan cheese, and serve immediately.

COOK'S TIP

For square ravioli, divide the dough into two. Wrap half in plastic wrap and thinly roll out the other half. Cover with a clean, damp dish cloth while you roll the remaining dough. Spoon the filling at regular intervals brushing the gaps with water or beaten egg. Cover with the second sheet of dough and press firmly between the filling to seal and expel any air. Cut into squares.

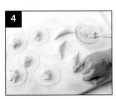

Poached Salmon Steaks with Penne

Serves 4

INGREDIENTS

4 10-ounce fresh salmon steaks
4 tbsp butter
$^3/_4$ cup dry white wine
sea salt
8 peppercorns
fresh dill sprig
fresh tarragon sprig
1 lemon, sliced

1 pound dried penne
2 tbsp olive oil
lemon slices and fresh
    watercress, to garnish

LEMON & WATERCRESS SAUCE:
2 tbsp butter
$^1/_4$ cup all-purpose flour

$^5/_8$ cup warm milk
juice and finely grated rind of
    2 lemons
2 ounces watercress, chopped
salt and pepper

1 Put the salmon in a large, nonstick pan. Add the butter, wine, a pinch of sea salt, the peppercorns, dill, tarragon, and lemon. Cover, bring to a boil, and simmer for 10 minutes.

2 Using a fish slice, remove the salmon. Strain and reserve the cooking liquid. Remove and discard the salmon skin and center bones.

Place the fish on a warm dish, cover, and keep warm.

3 Bring a saucepan of salted water to a boil. Add the penne and 1 tbsp of the oil and cook for 12 minutes. Drain and toss in the remaining olive oil. Place on a warm serving dish, top with the salmon steaks, and keep warm.

4 To make the sauce, melt the butter and stir

in the flour for 2 minutes. Stir in the milk and about 7 tbsp of the reserved cooking liquid. Add the lemon juice and rind and cook, stirring, for 10 minutes.

5 Add the watercress to the sauce, stir gently, and season to taste.

6 Pour the sauce over the salmon and penne, garnish, and serve.

Spaghetti with Smoked Salmon

Serves 4

INGREDIENTS

1 pound dried buckwheat
  spaghetti
2 tbsp olive oil
1/2 cup crumbled feta cheese
salt
fresh cilantro or parsley leaves,
  to garnish

SAUCE:
1 1/4 cups heavy cream
5/8 cup whiskey or brandy
4 1/2 ounces smoked salmon
pinch of cayenne pepper
black pepper

2 tbsp chopped fresh cilantro
  or parsley

1 Bring a large pan of lightly salted water to a boil. Add the spaghetti and 1 tbsp of the olive oil and cook until tender, but still firm to the bite. Drain and toss in the remaining olive oil. Cover, shake the pan, set aside, and keep warm.

2 Pour the cream into a small saucepan and bring to simmering point, but do not let it boil. Pour the whiskey or brandy into another small saucepan and

bring to simmering point, but do not allow it to boil. Remove both pans from the heat and mix together the cream and whiskey or brandy.

3 Cut the smoked salmon into thin strips and add to the cream mixture. Season to taste with cayenne and black pepper. Just before serving, add the chopped fresh cilantro or parsley and stir until well combined.

4 Transfer the spaghetti to a warm serving dish, pour the sauce on, and toss thoroughly with 2 large forks. Scatter the crumbled feta cheese over the top, garnish with the cilantro or parsley leaves, and serve immediately.

COOK'S TIP

Serve this rich and luxurious dish with a green salad tossed in a lemony dressing.

Trout with Pasta colle Acciughe & Smoked Bacon

Serves 4

INGREDIENTS

butter, for greasing
4 9½-ounce trout, gutted
    and cleaned
12 anchovies in oil, drained
    and chopped
2 apples, peeled, cored, and
    sliced

4 fresh mint sprigs
juice of 1 lemon
12 slices bacon
1 pound dried tagliatelle
1 tbsp olive oil
salt and pepper

TO GARNISH:
2 apples, cored and sliced
4 fresh mint sprigs

1 Open up the cavities of each trout and wash with warm salt water.

2 Season each cavity with salt and black pepper. Divide the anchovies, sliced apples, and mint sprigs between each of the cavities. Sprinkle the lemon juice into each cavity.

3 Carefully wrap each trout with three slices of bacon in a spiral, covering all of the fish except for the head and tail.

4 Arrange the trout on a deep, greased cookie sheet with the loose ends of bacon tucked neatly underneath. Season with black pepper to taste and bake in a preheated oven at 400°F for 20 minutes, turning the trout over after 10 minutes.

5 Meanwhile, bring a large pan of lightly salted water to a boil. Add the tagliatelle and olive oil and cook for 12 minutes, until tender, but still firm to the bite. Drain and transfer to a serving dish.

6 Remove the trout from the oven and arrange on the tagliatelle. Garnish with sliced apples and fresh mint sprigs and serve immediately.

Farfalle with a Medley of Seafood

Serves 4

INGREDIENTS

12 raw tiger shrimp
12 raw shrimp
4¹/₂ ounces freshwater shrimp
1 pound fillet of sea bream
4 tbsp butter
12 scallops, shelled
juice and finely grated rind of
    1 lemon

pinch of saffron powder or
    threads
4 cups vegetable stock
⁵/₈ cup rose petal vinegar
1 pound dried farfalle
1 tbsp olive oil
⁵/₈ cup white wine
1 tbsp pink peppercorns

4 ounces baby carrots
⁵/₈ cup heavy cream or fromage
    frais
salt and pepper

1 Peel and devein all of the shrimp. Thinly slice the sea bream. Melt the butter in a pan, add the sea bream, scallops, and shrimp, and cook for about 1–2 minutes.

2 Season with black pepper. Add the lemon juice and grated rind. Very carefully add the saffron powder or a few strands of saffron to the cooking juices (not to the seafood).

3 Remove the seafood from the pan, set aside and keep warm. Retain the juices.

4 Return the pan to the heat and add the vegetable stock. Bring to a boil and reduce by one-third. Add the vinegar and cook for 4 minutes, until reduced.

5 Bring a pan of salted water to a boil. Add the farfalle and olive oil and cook until tender, but still firm to the bite. Drain and transfer to a warm plate and top with the seafood.

6 Add the wine, peppercorns, and carrots to the pan and reduce the sauce for 6 minutes. Add the cream or fromage frais and simmer for 2 minutes. Pour the sauce over the seafood and pasta and serve.

Seafood Lasagne

Serves 4

INGREDIENTS

1 pound finnan haddock, filleted,
  skin removed and flesh flaked
4 ounces shrimp
4 ounces sole fillet, skin removed
  and flesh sliced
juice of 1 lemon
4 tbsp butter

3 leeks, very thinly sliced
$\frac{1}{2}$ cup all-purpose flour
$2\frac{1}{3}$ cups milk
2 tbsp clear honey
$1\frac{3}{4}$ cups grated mozzarella
  cheese
1 pound precooked lasagne

$\frac{2}{3}$ cup freshly grated
  Parmesan cheese
black pepper

1 Put the haddock fillet, shrimp, and sole fillet into a large bowl and season with black pepper to taste and a little lemon juice. Set aside while you start to make the sauce.

2 Melt the butter in a large saucepan. Add the leeks and cook, stirring occasionally, for 8 minutes. Add the flour and cook, stirring constantly, for 1 minute. Gradually stir in enough milk to make a thick, creamy sauce.

3 Blend in the honey and mozzarella cheese and cook for 3 minutes longer. Remove the pan from the heat and mix in the fish and shrimp.

4 Make alternate layers of fish sauce and lasagne in an ovenproof dish, finishing with a layer of fish sauce on top. Generously sprinkle the grated Parmesan cheese and bake in a preheated oven at 350°F for 30 minutes. Serve the lasagne immediately.

VARIATION

For a cider sauce, substitute 1 finely chopped shallot for the leeks, $1\frac{1}{4}$ cups cider, and $1\frac{1}{4}$ cups heavy cream for the milk and 1 tsp mustard for the honey.

For a Tuscan sauce, substitute 1 finely chopped fennel bulb for the leeks and omit the honey.

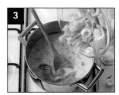

Spaghetti with Seafood Sauce

Serves 4

INGREDIENTS

8 ounces dried spaghetti, broken
    into 6-inch lengths
2 tbsp olive oil
1¼ cups chicken stock
1 tsp lemon juice
1 small cauliflower, cut into
    florets
2 carrots, thinly sliced
14 ounces snow peas

4 tbsp butter
1 onion, sliced
8 ounces zucchini, sliced
1 garlic clove, chopped
12 ounces frozen, cooked, peeled
    shrimp, defrosted
2 tbsp chopped fresh parsley
⅓ cup freshly grated
    Parmesan cheese

½ tsp paprika
salt and pepper
4 unpeeled, cooked shrimp,
    to garnish

1 Bring a pan of salted water to a boil. Add the spaghetti and 1 tbsp of the olive oil and cook until tender, but still firm to the bite. Drain and toss with the remaining olive oil, cover, and keep warm.

2 Bring the chicken stock and lemon juice to a boil. Add the cauliflower and carrots and cook for 3–4 minutes.

Remove from the pan and set aside. Add the snow peas to the pan and cook for 1–2 minutes. Set aside with the other vegetables.

3 Melt half of the butter in a skillet and sauté the onion and zucchini for about 3 minutes. Add the garlic and shrimp to the skillet and cook for a further 2–3 minutes, until thoroughly heated through.

Stir in the reserved vegetables and heat through. Season with salt and pepper to taste and stir in the remaining butter.

4 Transfer the pasta to a warm serving dish. Pour over the sauce and add the parsley. Toss well and sprinkle with the Parmesan and paprika, garnish with the unpeeled shrimp, and serve.

Macaroni & Shrimp Bake

Serves 4

INGREDIENTS

3 cups dried short-cut macaroni

1 tbsp olive oil, plus extra
for brushing

6 tbsp butter, plus extra for
greasing

2 small fennel bulbs, thinly sliced
and fronds reserved

6 ounces mushrooms, thinly
sliced

6 ounces peeled, cooked shrimp

pinch of cayenne pepper

1¼ cups Béchamel sauce (see
Cook's Tip)

²/₃ cup freshly grated
Parmesan cheese

2 large tomatoes, sliced

1 tsp dried oregano

salt and pepper

1 Bring a saucepan of salted water to a boil. Add the pasta and oil and cook until tender, but still firm to the bite. Drain and return to the pan. Add 2 tbsp of butter, cover, shake the pan, and keep warm.

2 Melt the remaining butter in a pan. Sauté the fennel for 3–4 minutes. Stir in the mushrooms and cook for 2 minutes. Stir in the shrimp, then remove the pan from the heat.

3 Stir the pasta, cayenne pepper and shrimp mixture into the béchamel sauce. Pour into a greased ovenproof dish. Sprinkle with the Parmesan cheese and arrange the tomato slices around the edge. Brush the tomatoes with olive oil and sprinkle the oregano on top.

4 Bake in a preheated oven at 350°F for 25 minutes, until golden brown. Serve immediately.

COOK'S TIP

For béchamel sauce, melt 2 tbsp butter. Stir in ¼ cup flour. Cook, stirring, for 2 minutes. Gradually, stir in 1¼ cups warm milk. Add 2 tbsp finely chopped onion, 5 white peppercorns, and 2 parsley sprigs, and season with salt, dried thyme, and grated nutmeg. Simmer, stirring, for 15 minutes. Strain before using.

Pasta Packets

Serves 4

INGREDIENTS

1 pound dried fettuccine	1 pound 10 ounces large raw	$\frac{1}{2}$ cup dry white wine
$\frac{5}{8}$ cup pesto sauce	shrimp, peeled and deveined	salt and pepper
4 tsp extra virgin olive oil	2 garlic cloves, crushed	lemon wedges, to serve

1 Cut out 4 × 12-inch squares of baking paper.

2 Bring a large saucepan of lightly salted water to a boil. Add the fettuccine and cook for 2–3 minutes, until just softened. Drain thoroughly, keep warm, and set aside.

3 Mix together the fettuccine and half of the pesto sauce. Spread out the paper squares and put 1 tsp olive oil in the middle of each. Divide the fettuccine between the squares, then divide the shrimp, and place on top of the fettuccine.

4 Mix together the remaining pesto sauce and the garlic and spoon it over the shrimp. Season each packet with salt and black pepper and sprinkle with the white wine.

5 Dampen the edges of the baking paper and wrap the packets loosely, twisting the edges to seal.

6 Place the packets on a cookie sheet and bake in a preheated oven at 400°F for about 10–15 minutes. Transfer the packets to 4 warm individual plates and serve with lemon wedges.

COOK'S TIP

Traditionally, these packets are designed to look like old-fashioned money bags. The resemblance is more effective with baking paper than with foil.

Farfallini Buttered Lobster

Serves 4

INGREDIENTS
---

2 1-pound, 9-ounce lobsters,
    split into halves
juice and grated rind of
    1 lemon
1/2 cup butter
4 tbsp fresh white breadcrumbs
2 tbsp brandy

5 tbsp heavy cream
    or crème fraîche
1 pound dried farfallini
1 tbsp olive oil
2/3 cup freshly grated
    Parmesan cheese
salt and pepper

TO GARNISH:
1 kiwi fruit, sliced
4 large, unpeeled, cooked shrimp
fresh dill sprigs

---

1 Carefully discard the stomach sac, vein, and gills from each lobster. Remove all the meat from the tail and chop. Crack the claws and legs, remove the meat, and chop. Transfer the meat to a bowl and add the lemon juice and rind.

2 Clean the shells and place in a warm oven at 325°F to dry out.

3 Melt 2 tbsp of the butter in a skillet. Add the breadcrumbs and fry for about 3 minutes, until crisp and golden brown.

4 Melt the remaining butter in a saucepan. Add the lobster meat and heat through gently. Add the brandy and cook for a further 3 minutes, then add the cream or crème fraîche, and season to taste.

5 Meanwhile, bring a large pan of lightly salted water to a boil. Add the farfallini and olive oil and cook for 12 minutes, until tender, but still firm to the bite. Drain and spoon the pasta into the lobster shells. Top with the buttered lobster and sprinkle with a little grated Parmesan cheese and the breadcrumbs. Broil for 2–3 minutes, until a light golden brown color.

6 Transfer the lobster shells to a warm serving dish, garnish with the, kiwi fruit, unpeeled shrimp, and dill sprigs, and serve.

Pasta Shells with Mussels

Serves 4–6

INGREDIENTS

2¾ pounds mussels
1 cup dry white wine
2 large onions, chopped
½ cup unsalted butter

6 large garlic cloves, finely
  chopped
5 tbsp chopped fresh parsley
1¼ cups heavy cream
14 ounces dried pasta shells

1 tbsp olive oil
salt and pepper
crusty bread, to serve

1 Scrub and debeard the mussels under cold running water. Discard any that do not close when sharply tapped. Put the mussels into a large saucepan with the wine and half of the onions. Cover and cook over a medium heat until the shells open.

2 Remove the pan from the heat. Drain the mussels and reserve the cooking liquid. Discard any mussels that have not opened. Strain the cooking liquid and reserve.

3 Melt the butter in a pan and sauté the remaining onion until translucent. Stir in the garlic and cook for 1 minute. Gradually stir in the reserved cooking liquid, then the parsley and cream. Season and simmer.

4 Cook the pasta with the oil until just tender, but still firm to the bite. Drain, return to the pan, cover and keep warm.

5 Reserve a few mussels for the garnish and remove the remainder from their shells. Stir the shelled mussels into the cream sauce and warm briefly. Transfer the pasta to a serving dish. Pour the sauce over the pasta and toss to coat. Garnish with the reserved mussels and serve with bread.

COOK'S TIP

Pasta shells are ideal because the sauce collects in the cavities and impregnates the pasta with flavor.

Saffron Mussel Tagliatelle

Serves 4

INGREDIENTS

2¹/₄ pounds mussels	1¹/₄ cups heavy cream	1 tbsp olive oil
⁵/₈ cup white wine	pinch of saffron threads or	salt and pepper
1 medium onion, finely chopped	saffron powder	3 tbsp chopped fresh parsley,
2 tbsp butter	1 egg yolk	to garnish
2 garlic cloves, crushed	juice of ¹/₂ lemon	
2 tsp cornstarch	1 pound dried tagliatelle	

1 Scrub and debeard the mussels under cold running water. Discard any that do not close when sharply tapped. Put the mussels in a pan with the wine and onion. Cover and cook over a high heat until the shells open.

2 Drain and reserve the cooking liquid. Discard any mussels that are still closed. Reserve a few mussels for the garnish and remove the remainder from their shells.

3 Strain the cooking liquid into a saucepan. Bring to a boil and reduce by about half. Remove the pan from the heat.

4 Melt the butter in a saucepan and fry the garlic for 2 minutes, until golden brown. Stir in the cornstarch and cook, stirring, for 1 minute. Gradually stir in the cooking liquid and the cream. Crush the saffron threads and add to the pan. Season to taste and simmer for 2–3 minutes, until the sauce has thickened.

5 Stir in the egg yolk, lemon juice, and shelled mussels. Do not allow the mixture to boil.

6 Bring a pan of salted water to a boil. Add the pasta and oil and cook until tender. Drain and transfer to a serving dish. Add the mussel sauce and toss. Garnish with the parsley and reserved mussels and serve.

Baked Scallops with Pasta in Shells

Serves 4

INGREDIENTS

12 scallops
3 tbsp olive oil
3 cups small, dried whole-wheat
    pasta shells
⅝ cup fish stock

1 onion, chopped
juice of 2 lemons
⅝ cup heavy cream
2 cups freshly grated
    cheddar cheese

salt and pepper
crusty brown bread, to serve

1 Remove the scallops from their shells. Scrape off the skirt and the black intestinal thread. Reserve the white part (the flesh) and the orange part (the coral or roe). Carefully ease the flesh and coral from the shell with a short, but very strong knife.

2 Wash the shells thoroughly and dry them well. Put the shells on a cookie sheet, sprinkle lightly with about two-thirds of the olive oil, and set aside.

3 Meanwhile, bring a large saucepan of lightly salted water to a boil. Add the pasta shells and remaining olive oil and cook for about 12 minutes, until tender, but still firm to the bite. Drain and spoon about 1 ounce of pasta into each scallop shell.

4 Put the scallops, fish stock, and onion in an ovenproof dish and season to taste with pepper. Cover with foil and bake in a preheated oven at 350°F for 8 minutes.

5 Remove the dish from the oven. Remove the foil and, using a slotted spoon, transfer the scallops to the shells. Add 1 tbsp of the cooking liquid to each shell, together with a drizzle of lemon juice and a little cream, and top with the grated cheese.

6 Increase the oven temperature to 450°F and return the scallops to the oven for 4 minutes. Serve the scallops in their shells with crusty brown bread and butter.

Vermicelli with Clams

Serves 4

INGREDIENTS

14 ounces dried vermicelli,
spaghetti, or other long pasta
2 tbsp olive oil
2 tbsp butter
2 onions, chopped

2 garlic cloves, chopped
2 7-ounce jars clams in water
1/2 cup white wine
4 tbsp chopped fresh parsley
1/2 tsp dried oregano

pinch of freshly grated nutmeg
salt and pepper

TO GARNISH:
2 tbsp Parmesan cheese shavings
fresh basil sprigs

1 Bring a large pan of lightly salted water to a boil. Add the pasta and half the olive oil and cook until tender, but still firm to the bite. Drain, return to the pan, and add the butter. Cover the pan, shake well, and keep warm.

2 Heat the remaining oil in a pan over a medium heat. Add the onions and sauté until they are translucent. Stir in the garlic and cook for 1 minute.

3 Strain the liquid from 1 jar of clams and add the liquid to the pan, with the wine. Stir, bring to simmering point, and simmer for 3 minutes. Drain the second jar of clams and discard the liquid.

4 Add the clams, parsley, and oregano to the pan and season with pepper and nutmeg. Lower the heat and cook until the sauce is completely heated through.

5 Transfer the pasta to a serving dish and pour over the sauce. Garnish and serve immediately.

COOK'S TIP

There are many different types of clams found along almost every coast in the world. Those traditionally used in this dish are the very tiny ones—only 1–2 inches across—known in Italy as vongole.

Squid & Macaroni Stew

Serves 4–6

INGREDIENTS

2 cups dried short-cut macaroni or other small pasta shapes	⅝ cup red wine	salt and pepper
7 tbsp olive oil	12 ounces tomatoes, skinned and thinly sliced	crusty bread, to serve
2 onions, sliced	2 tbsp tomato paste	
12 ounces prepared squid, cut into 1½-inch strips	1 tsp dried oregano	
1 cup fish stock	2 bay leaves	
	2 tbsp chopped fresh parsley	

1 Bring a large pan of lightly salted water to a boil. Add the pasta and 1 tbsp of the olive oil and cook for 3 minutes. Drain and keep warm.

2 Heat the remaining oil in a pan and sauté the onions until translucent. Add the squid and stock and simmer for 5 minutes. Pour in the wine, tomatoes, tomato paste, oregano, and bay leaves. Bring the sauce to a boil, season to taste, and cook for 5 minutes.

3 Stir the pasta into the pan, cover, and simmer for about 10 minutes, or until the squid and macaroni are tender and the sauce has thickened. If the sauce remains too liquid, uncover the pan and continue cooking for a few minutes.

4 Discard the bay leaves. Reserve a little parsley and stir the remainder into the pan. Transfer to a warm serving dish and sprinkle with the remaining parsley. Serve with crusty bread.

COOK'S TIP

To prepare squid, peel off the outer skin, then cut off the head and tentacles. Extract the transparent flat oval bone from the body and discard. Remove the sac of black ink, then turn the body sac inside out. Wash in cold water. Cut off the tentacles and discard the rest; wash thoroughly.

Pasta Vongole

Serves 4

INGREDIENTS

1½ pounds fresh clams or 10 ounce can clams, drained	2 tbsp olive oil	salt and pepper
14 ounces mixed seafood, such as shrimps, squid, and mussels, thawed if frozen	2 cloves garlic, finely chopped	1½ pounds fresh pasta or 12 ounces dried pasta
	⅔ cup white wine	
	⅔ cup fish stock	
	2 tbsp chopped tarragon	

1 If you are using fresh clams, scrub them clean and discard any that are already open.

2 Heat the oil in a large skillet. Add the garlic and the clams to the pan and cook for 2 minutes, shaking the pan to ensure that all the clams are coated in the oil.

3 Add the remaining seafood mixture to the skillet and cook for a further 2 minutes.

4 Pour the wine and stock over the mixed seafood, and bring to a boil. Cover the skillet, reduce the heat, and simmer for 8–10 minutes, or until the shells open. Discard any clams or mussels that do not open.

5 Meanwhile, cook the pasta in a saucepan of boiling water according to the instructions on the packet, or until it is cooked through, but still has "bite." Drain.

6 Stir the tarragon into the sauce and season to taste.

7 Transfer the pasta to a serving dish, pour the sauce over it, and serve.

VARIATION

Red clam sauce can be made by adding 8 tablespoons of tomato sauce along with the stock in step 4. Follow the same cooking method.

Smoked Cod Polenta

Serves 4

INGREDIENTS

6¼ cups water

3 cups instant polenta

7 ounces chopped frozen spinach, thawed

3 tbsp butter

⅔ cup grated pecorino cheese

¾ cup milk

1 pound skinless smoked cod fillet

4 eggs, beaten

salt and pepper

1 Bring the water to a boil and add 2 teaspoons salt. Add the polenta in a steady stream, stirring constantly. Cook, stirring, for 5 minutes, or according to the instructions on the packet.

2 Stir the spinach, butter, and half the pecorino cheese into the polenta. Season to taste with salt and pepper.

3 Divide the polenta between 4 individual ovenproof dishes, spreading the polenta evenly across the bases and up the sides of the dishes.

4 In a large skillet, bring the milk to a boil. Add the smoked cod and cook, turning once, for 8–10 minutes, or until tender. Remove the fish with a slotted spoon.

5 Remove the pan from the heat. Mix the milk and eggs together.

6 Using a fork, flake the fish into small pieces and place it in the center of the dishes.

7 Pour the milk and egg mixture over the fish.

8 Sprinkle the remaining cheese on top and bake in a preheated oven at 375°F for 25–30 minutes, or until set and golden. Serve hot.

VARIATION

Try using 12 ounces cooked chicken breast with 2 tablespoons chopped tarragon, instead of the fish.

Celery & Salt Cod Casserole

Serves 4

INGREDIENTS

9 ounces salt cod, soaked overnight	3 celery stalks, chopped	1/2 cup pine nuts
1 tbsp oil	14 ounce can tomatoes, chopped	2 tbsp roughly chopped tarragon
4 shallots, finely chopped	2/3 cup fish stock	2 tbsp capers
2 garlic cloves, chopped		crusty bread or mashed potatoes, to serve

1 Drain the salt cod, rinse it under plenty of running water, and drain again thoroughly. Remove and discard any skin and bones. Pat the fish dry with paper towels and cut it into chunks.

2 Heat the oil in a large skillet. Add the shallots and garlic and cook for 2–3 minutes. Add the celery and cook for a further 2 minutes, then add the tomatoes and stock.

3 Bring the mixture to a boil, reduce the heat, and simmer for 5 minutes.

4 Add the fish and cook for 10 minutes, or until tender.

5 Meanwhile, spread the pine nuts out on a cookie sheet. Place under a preheated broiler and toast for 2–3 minutes, or until golden.

6 Stir the tarragon, capers, and pine nuts into the fish casserole and heat gently to warm through.

7 Transfer to serving plates and serve with fresh crusty bread or mashed potatoes.

COOK'S TIP

Salt cod is a useful ingredient to have on hand, and once soaked, can be used in the same way as any other fish. It does, however, have a stronger flavor than normal, and it is, of course, slightly salty. It can be found in fish markets, larger supermarkets, and delicatessens.

Salt Cod Fritters

Makes 28 cakes

INGREDIENTS

3/4 cup self-rising flour
1 egg, beaten
2/3 cup milk
9 ounces salt cod, soaked overnight

1 small red onion, finely chopped
1 small fennel bulb, finely chopped
1 fresh red chili, finely chopped
2 tbsp oil

TO SERVE:
crisp salad, chili relish, cooked rice,
    and fresh vegetables

1 Sift the flour into a large bowl. Make a well in the center of the flour and add the egg.

2 Using a wooden spoon, gradually draw in the flour, slowly adding the milk, and mix to form a smooth batter. Let stand for 10 minutes.

3 Drain the salt cod and rinse it in under running water. Drain again thoroughly.

4 Remove and discard the skin and any bones from the fish, then mash the flesh with a fork.

5 Place the fish in a large bowl and combine with the onion, fennel, and chili. Add the mixture to the batter and blend together.

6 Heat the oil in a large skillet and, taking about 1 tablespoon of the mixture at a time, spoon it into the hot oil. Cook the fritters, in batches, for 3–4 minutes on each side, until golden and slightly puffed. Keep warm while cooking the remaining mixture.

7 Serve with salad and a chili relish for a light meal or with vegetables and rice.

COOK'S TIP

If you prefer larger fritters, use 2 tablespoons per fritter and cook for slightly longer.

Sardinian Red Mullet

Serves 4

INGREDIENTS

1/3 cup golden raisins	1 zucchini, cut into	4 red mullet, filleted
2/3 cup red wine	2-inch sticks	1 3/4 ounce can anchovy fillets,
2 tbsp olive oil	2 oranges	drained
2 medium onions, sliced	2 tsp cilantro seeds, lightly crushed	2 tbsp chopped, fresh oregano

1 Place the golden raisins in a bowl. Add the red wine and set aside to soak for 10 minutes.

2 Heat the oil in a large skillet. Add the onions and sauté for 2 minutes.

3 Add the zucchini to the skillet and sauté for a further 3 minutes, or until tender.

4 Using a grater, pare long, thin strips from one of the oranges. Using a sharp knife, remove the skin from both of the oranges, then segment them by slicing between the lines of pith.

5 Add the orange zest to the skillet. Add the red wine, golden raisins, cilantro seeds, red mullet, and anchovies to the pan and simmer for 10–15 minutes, or until the fish is cooked through.

6 Stir in the oregano and set aside to cool. Place the mixture in a large bowl, cover, and chill in the refrigerator for at least 2 hours to allow the flavors to mingle. Transfer to serving plates and serve.

COOK'S TIP

Red mullet is usually available all year round — frozen, if not fresh — from your fish store or supermarket. If you cannot get ahold of it, try using tilapia. This dish can also be served warm, if you prefer.

Herrings with Hot Pesto Sauce

Serves 4

INGREDIENTS

4 herrings or small mackerel,
    cleaned and gutted
2 tbsp olive oil

8 ounces tomatoes, peeled, seeded,
    and chopped
8 canned anchovy fillets, chopped

about 30 fresh basil leaves
$^1/_2$ cup pine nuts
2 garlic cloves, crushed

1 Cook the herrings under a preheated broiler for about 8-10 minutes on each side, or until the skin is slightly charred on both sides.

2 Meanwhile, heat 1 tablespoon of the olive oil in a large saucepan.

3 Add the tomatoes and anchovies to the saucepan and cook over a medium heat for 5 minutes.

4 Meanwhile, place the basil, pine nuts, garlic, and remaining oil into a food processor and blend

to form a smooth paste. Alternatively, pound the ingredients by hand in a mortar with a pestle.

5 Add the pesto mixture to the saucepan containing the tomato and anchovy mixture, and stir to heat through.

6 Spoon some of the pesto sauce onto warm individual serving plates. Place the fish on top and pour the rest of the pesto sauce over the fish. Serve immediately.

COOK'S TIP

Try barbecuing the fish for an extra charbroiled flavor, if desired.

Broiled Stuffed Sole

Serves 4

INGREDIENTS

1 tbsp olive oil

2 tbsp butter

1 small onion, finely chopped

1 garlic clove, chopped

3 sun-dried tomatoes, chopped

2 tbsp lemon thyme

1 cup bread crumbs

1 tbsp lemon juice

4 small sole, gutted and cleaned

salt and pepper

lemon wedges, to garnish

fresh salad greens, to serve

1 Heat the oil and butter in a skillet until it is just beginning to froth.

2 Add the onion and garlic to the skillet and cook, stirring, for 5 minutes, until just softened.

3 To make the stuffing, mix the tomatoes, thyme, bread crumbs, and lemon juice in a bowl, and season to taste.

4 Add the stuffing mixture to the skillet and stir well to mix

5 Using a sharp knife, pare the skin from the bone inside the slit of the fish to make a pocket. Spoon the tomato and herb stuffing into the pocket.

6 Cook the fish under a preheated broiler for 6 minutes on each side, or until golden brown.

7 Transfer the stuffed fish to warm serving plates and garnish with lemon wedges. Serve immediately with fresh salad greens.

COOK'S TIP

Lemon thyme has a delicate lemon scent and flavor. Ordinary thyme can be used instead, but mix it with 1 teaspoon lemon rind to add extra flavor.

Sole Fillets in Marsala & Cream

Serves 4

INGREDIENTS

STOCK:
2¹/₂ cups water
bones and skin from the sole fillets
1 onion, peeled and halved
1 carrot, peeled and halved
3 fresh bay leaves

SAUCE:
1 tbsp olive oil
1 tbsp butter
4 shallots, finely chopped
3¹/₂ ounces baby button
    mushrooms, wiped and halved

1 tbsp peppercorns, lightly crushed
8 sole fillets
¹/₃ cup Marsala
²/₃ pint heavy cream

1 To make the stock, place the water, fish bones and skin, onion, carrot, and bay leaves in a saucepan and bring to a boil.

2 Reduce the heat and simmer the mixture for 1 hour, or until the stock has reduced to about ²/₃ cup. Drain the stock through a fine strainer, discarding the bones and vegetables, and set aside.

3 To make the sauce, heat the oil and butter in a skillet. Add the shallots and cook, stirring, for 2–3 minutes, or until just softened.

4 Add the mushrooms to the skillet and cook, stirring occasionally, for a further 2–3 minutes, or until they are just beginning to brown.

5 Add the peppercorns and sole fillets to the skillet. Fry the sole fillets for 3–4 minutes on each side, or until a golden brown color.

6 Pour the wine and stock over the fish and simmer for 3 minutes. Remove the fish with a fish slice or a slotted spoon, set aside, and keep warm.

7 Increase the heat and boil the mixture in the skillet for about 5 minutes, or until the sauce has reduced and thickened.

8 Pour in the cream, return the fish to the skillet, and heat through. Serve with cooked vegetables of your choice.

Fresh Baked Sardines

Serves 4

INGREDIENTS

2 tbsp olive oil	3 tbsp fresh thyme, stalks removed	4 eggs, beaten
2 large onions, sliced into rings	8 sardine fillets or about 2¼ pounds	⅔ pint milk
3 garlic cloves, chopped	sardines, filleted	salt and pepper
2 large zucchini, cut into sticks	1 cup grated Parmesan cheese	

1 Heat 1 tablespoon of the olive oil in a skillet. Add the onion rings and chopped garlic and sauté for about 2–3 minutes.

2 Add the zucchini to the skillet and cook, stirring occasionally, for about 5 minutes, or until golden.

3 Stir 2 tablespoons of thyme into the mixture.

4 Place half the onions and zucchini in the base of a large ovenproof dish. Top with the sardine fillets and half the grated Parmesan cheese.

5 Place the remaining onions and zucchini on top and sprinkle with the remaining thyme.

6 Mix the eggs and milk together in a bowl and season to taste with salt and pepper. Pour the mixture over the vegetables and sardines in the dish. Sprinkle the remaining Parmesan cheese over the top.

7 Bake in a preheated oven at 350°F for 20–25 minutes, or until golden and set. Serve the fresh baked sardines hot, straight from the oven.

VARIATION

If you cannot find sardines that are large enough to fillet, use small mackerel instead.

Marinated Fish

Serves 4

INGREDIENTS

4 mackerel	2 tbsp extra-virgin olive oil	2 garlic cloves, crushed
4 tbsp chopped marjoram	finely grated rind and juice of 1 lime	salt and pepper

1 Under gently running water, scrape the mackerel with the blunt side of a knife to remove any scales.

2 Using a sharp knife, make a slit in the stomach of the fish and cut horizontally along until the knife will go no farther very easily. Gut the fish and rinse under water. You may prefer to remove the heads before cooking, but it is not necessary.

3 Using a sharp knife, cut 4–5 diagonal slashes on each side of the fish. Place the fish in a shallow, nonmetallic dish.

4 To make the marinade, mix together the marjoram, olive oil, lime rind and juice, garlic, and salt and pepper in a bowl.

5 Pour the mixture over the fish. Marinate in the refrigerator for 30 minutes.

6 Cook the mackerel, under a preheated broiler, for 5–6 minutes on each side, brushing occasionally with the reserved marinade, until golden.

7 Transfer the fish to serving plates. Pour over any remaining marinade before serving.

COOK'S TIP

If the lime is too hard to squeeze, microwave on high for 30 seconds to release the juice. This dish is also excellent cooked on the grill.

Orange Mackerel

Serves 4

INGREDIENTS

2 tbsp oil	1 tbsp oats	salt and pepper
4 scallions, chopped	½ cup pitted mixed green and black	crisp salad greens, to serve
2 oranges	olives, chopped	
½ cup ground almonds	8 mackerel fillets	

1 Heat the oil in a skillet. Add the scallions, stirring occasionally, and cook for about 2 minutes.

2 Finely grate the rind of the oranges, then, using a sharp knife, cut away the remaining skin and white pith.

3 Using a sharp knife, segment the oranges by cutting down either side of the lines of pith to loosen each segment. Do this over a plate so that you can reserve any juice left over from the oranges. Cut each orange segment in half.

4 Lightly toast the almonds, under a preheated broiler, for 2–3 minutes, or until golden; watch them carefully as they brown very quickly.

5 Mix the scallions, oranges, any juice, the ground almonds, oats, and olives together in a bowl and season to taste with salt and pepper.

6 Spoon the orange mixture along the center of each mackerel fillet. Roll up each mackerel fillet, securing it in place with a toothpick.

7 Bake in a preheated oven at 375°F for 25 minutes, until the fish is tender.

8 Transfer to serving plates and serve warm with salad greens.

Italian Cod

Serves 4

INGREDIENTS

2 tbsp butter	2 sprigs rosemary, stalks removed	3 tbsp walnut oil
2 cups whole-wheat bread crumbs	2 tbsp chopped parsley	1 small fresh red chili, diced
$^1/_4$ cup chopped walnuts	4 cod fillets, each about $5^1/_2$ oz	salad greens, to serve
grated rind and juice of 2 lemons	1 garlic clove, crushed	

1 Melt the butter in a large skillet.

2 Remove the skillet from the heat and add the bread crumbs, walnuts, the rind and the juice of 1 lemon, half the rosemary, and half the parsley.

3 Arrange the cod fillets in a single layer in a shallow, foil-lined roasting pan. Press the bread crumb mixture over the top of the cod fillets.

4 Bake in a preheated oven at 400°F for 25–30 minutes, or until tender.

5 Mix the garlic, the remaining lemon rind and juice, rosemary, parsley, and chili in a bowl. Beat in the walnut oil and mix to combine. Drizzle the dressing over the cod fillets as soon as they are cooked.

6 Transfer to serving plates and serve immediately.

VARIATION

If desired, the walnuts may be omitted from the crust. In addition, extra-virgin olive oil can be used instead of walnut oil, if you prefer.

COOK'S TIP

The "hotness" of chiles varies, so use them with caution. As a general guide, the smaller the chili the hotter it will be.

Mussel Casserole

Serves 4

INGREDIENTS

2¼ pounds mussels	1 onion, finely chopped	3½ ounces tomato sauce
⅔ cup white wine	3 garlic cloves, chopped	1 tbsp chopped marjoram
1 tbsp oil	1 red chili, finely chopped	toast or crusty bread, to serve

1 Scrub the mussels to remove any mud or sand.

2 Remove the beards from the mussels by pulling away the hairy protrusion between the two shells. Rinse the mussels in a bowl of clean water. Discard any mussels that do not close when they are tapped – they are dead and should not be eaten.

3 Place the mussels in a large saucepan. Pour in the wine and cook for 5 minutes, shaking the pan occasionally until the shells open. Remove and discard any mussels that do not open.

4 Remove the mussels from the saucepan with a slotted spoon. Strain the cooking liquid through a fine strainer set over a bowl, reserving the cooking liquid.

5 Heat the oil in a large skillet. Add the onion, garlic, and chili and cook for 4–5 minutes, or until softened.

6 Add the reserved cooking liquid to the pan and cook for 5 minutes, or until reduced.

7 Stir in the tomato sauce, marjoram, and mussels and cook until hot.

8 Transfer to serving bowls and serve with toast or plenty of crusty bread to mop up the juices.

COOK'S TIP

Finger bowls are individual bowls of warm water with a slice of lemon floating in them. They are used to clean your fingers at the end of a meal.

Stuffed Squid

Serves 4

INGREDIENTS

8 prepared whole squid	2 sun-dried tomatoes, chopped	$^3/_4$ cup fish stock
6 canned anchovies, chopped	3 cups bread crumbs	cooked rice, to serve
2 garlic cloves, chopped	1 tbsp olive oil	
2 tbsp rosemary, stalks removed and leaves chopped	1 onion, finely chopped	
	$^3/_4$ cup white wine	

1 Remove the tentacles from the body of the squid and chop the flesh finely.

2 Grind the anchovies, garlic, rosemary, and tomatoes to a paste in a mortar with a pestle.

3 Add the bread crumbs and the chopped squid tentacles and mix. If the mixture is too dry to form a thick paste at this point, add 1 teaspoon water.

4 Spoon the paste into the body sacs of the squid, then tie a length of cotton around the end of each sac to fasten them. Do not overfill the sacs, because they will expand during cooking.

5 Heat the oil in a skillet. Add the onion and sauté, stirring, for 3–4 minutes, or until golden.

6 Add the stuffed squid to the skillet and cook for 3–4 minutes, or until golden brown all over.

7 Add the wine and stock and bring to a boil. Reduce the heat, cover, and then simmer for 15 minutes.

8 Remove the lid and cook for a further 5 minutes, until the squid is tender and the juices have reduced. Serve with cooked rice.

COOK'S TIP

If you cannot buy whole squid, use squid pieces and stir the paste into the sauce with the wine and stock.

Genoese Seafood Risotto

Serves 4

INGREDIENTS

5 cups hot fish or chicken stock
1²/₃ cups risotto rice, washed
3 tbsp butter
2 garlic cloves, chopped

9 ounces mixed, preferably raw,
seafood, such as jumbo shrimp,
squid, mussels, clams, and small
shrimp

2 tbsp chopped oregano, plus extra
for garnishing
²/₃ cup grated pecorino or
Parmesan cheese

1 In a large saucepan, bring the stock to a boil. Add the rice and cook, stirring, for about 12 minutes, until the rice is tender or according to the instructions on the packet. Drain thoroughly, reserving any excess liquid.

2 Heat the butter in a large skillet and add the garlic, stirring.

3 Add the raw mixed seafood to the skillet and cook for 5 minutes. If the seafood is already cooked through, sauté for 2–3 minutes.

4 Stir the oregano into the seafood mixture in the skillet.

5 Add the cooked rice to the skillet and cook, stirring constantly, for 2–3 minutes, or until heated through. Add the reserved stock if the mixture gets too sticky.

6 Add the pecorino or Parmesan cheese and mix well.

7 Transfer the risotto to warm serving dishes and serve immediately.

COOK'S TIP

The Genoese are excellent cooks, and they make particularly delicious fish dishes flavored with the local olive oil.

Vegetables, & Salads, Bakes

The recipes in this chapter offer something special for every occasion: filling vegetarian suppers, unusual vegetable side dishes, main courses, and side salads. You could even take many of the salads on a picnic and, of course, they are perfect as accompaniments for summer barbecues.

Many of the recipes are classic dishes, others are imaginative and sometimes surprising new combinations of vegetables and pasta. Try making a sophisticated family meal using an unusual vegetable such as fennel. Whatever you choose, in this section you will find a range of superb side dishes to get the tastebuds tingling.

Tagliatelle with Pumpkin

Serves 4

INGREDIENTS

1 pound 2 ounces pumpkin or butternut squash, peeled and seeded	about 1¼ cups chicken or vegetable stock
3 tbsp olive oil	4 ounces prosciutto
1 onion, finely chopped	9 ounces dried tagliatelle
2 garlic cloves, crushed	⅝ cup heavy cream
4–6 tbsp chopped fresh parsley	salt and pepper
pinch of freshly grated nutmeg	freshly grated Parmesan cheese, to serve

1 Cut the pumpkin or butternut squash in half and scoop out the seeds. Cut the pumpkin or squash into ½-inch cubes.

2 Heat 2 tbsp of the oil in a large saucepan. Add the onion and garlic and fry over a low heat for about 3 minutes, until soft. Add half of the parsley and cook for 1 minute.

3 Add the pumpkin or squash pieces and cook for 2–3 minutes. Season to taste with salt, pepper, and nutmeg.

4 Add half of the stock to the pan, bring to a boil, cover, and simmer for 10 minutes, or until the pumpkin or squash is tender, adding more stock, if necessary.

5 Add the prosciutto to the pan and cook, stirring frequently for 2 minutes longer.

6 Bring a large pan of lightly salted water to a boil. Add the tagliatelle and the remaining oil and cook for 12 minutes, until tender, but still firm to the bite. Drain and transfer to a warm serving dish.

7 Stir the cream into the pumpkin and ham mixture and heat through. Spoon over the pasta, sprinkle with the remaining parsley, and serve with the Parmesan.

Eggplant Cake

Serves 4

INGREDIENTS

1 eggplant, thinly sliced
5 tbsp olive oil
2 cups dried fusilli
2½ cups Béchamel sauce
¾ cup grated cheddar cheese
butter, for greasing
⅓ cup freshly grated Parmesan
   cheese
salt and pepper

LAMB SAUCE:
2 tbsp olive oil
1 large onion, sliced
2 celery stalks, thinly sliced
1 pound ground lamb
3 tbsp tomato paste
5½ ounces bottled sun-dried
   tomatoes, drained and
   chopped

1 tsp dried oregano
1 tbsp red wine vinegar
⅝ cup chicken stock
salt and pepper

1 Spinkle the eggplant slices with salt and set aside for 45 minutes.

2 To make the sauce, fry the onion and celery in the oil for 3–4 minutes. Add the lamb and cook until browned. Stir in the remaining sauce ingredients and cook for 20 minutes.

3 Rinse the eggplant slices, drain, and pat dry. Heat 4 tbsp of the oil in a skillet. Fry the eggplant slices for about 4 minutes on each side. Remove from the skillet and drain well.

4 Cook the fusilli with the oil in a pan of salted boiling water, until tender, but still firm to the bite. Drain and keep warm.

5 Gently heat the béchamel sauce. Stir in the cheddar cheese and then stir half of the cheese sauce into the fusilli.

6 Make layers of fusilli, lamb sauce, and eggplant slices in a greased dish. Spread the remaining cheese sauce over the top. Sprinkle with the Parmesan and bake in a preheated oven at 375°F for 25 minutes. Serve hot or cold.

Fettuccine all'Alfredo

Serves 4

INGREDIENTS

2 tbsp butter	1 tbsp olive oil	pinch of freshly grated nutmeg
⁷/₈ cup heavy cream	1 cup freshly grated Parmesan	salt and pepper
1 pound fresh fettuccine	cheese, plus extra	fresh parsley sprigs, to garnish
	to serve	

1 Put the butter and ⁵/₈ cup of the cream in a large saucepan and bring the mixture to a boil over a medium heat. Reduce the heat and then simmer gently for about 1½ minutes, or until slightly thickened.

2 Meanwhile, bring a large saucepan of lightly salted water to a boil. Add the fettuccine and olive oil and cook for 2–3 minutes, until tender, but still firm to the bite. Drain the fettuccine and then pour the cream and butter sauce over the top.

3 Toss the fettuccine in the sauce over a low heat until thoroughly coated.

4 Add the remaining cream, the Parmesan cheese, and nutmeg to the fettuccine mixture and season to taste with salt and pepper. Toss thoroughly to coat while heating through.

5 Transfer the fettuccine mixture to a warm serving plate and garnish with the fresh sprig of parsley. Serve immediately, with extra grated Parmesan cheese on the side.

VARIATION

This classic Roman dish is often served with the addition of strips of ham and fresh peas. Add 2 cups shelled cooked peas and 6 ounces ham strips with the Parmesan cheese in step 4.

Macaroni Bake

Serves 4

INGREDIENTS

4 cups dried short-cut macaroni
1 tbsp olive oil
4 tbsp beef drippings
1 pound potatoes, thinly sliced

1 pound onions, sliced
2 cups grated mozzarella
cheese
⅝ cup heavy cream

salt and pepper
crusty brown bread and butter,
to serve

1 Bring a large saucepan of lightly salted water to a boil. Add the macaroni and olive oil and cook for about 12 minutes, until tender, but still firm to the bite. Drain the macaroni thoroughly, set aside, and keep warm.

2 Melt the drippings in a large flameproof casserole, then remove from the heat.

3 Make alternate layers of potatoes, onions, macaroni, and grated cheese in the dish,

seasoning well with salt and pepper between each layer and finishing with a layer of cheese on top. Finally, pour the cream over the top layer of cheese.

4 Bake in a preheated oven at 400°F for 25 minutes. Remove the dish from the oven and carefully brown the top under a broiler.

5 Serve the bake straight from the dish with lots of crusty brown bread and butter, as a main course. Alternatively, you could

serve the dish as a vegetable accompaniment with your favorite main course.

VARIATION

For a stronger flavor, use mozzarella affumicata, *a smoked version of this cheese, or Swiss cheese instead of the mozzarella.*

Creamy Pasta & Broccoli

Serves 4

INGREDIENTS

4 tbsp butter

1 large onion, finely chopped

1 pound dried ribbon pasta

1 pound broccoli, broken into
  florets

⅝ cup boiling vegetable stock

1 tbsp all-purpose flour

⅝ cup light cream

½ cup grated mozzarella cheese

freshly grated nutmeg

salt and white pepper

fresh apple slices, to garnish

1 Melt half of the butter in a large saucepan over a medium heat. Add the onion and sauté for 4 minutes.

2 Add the broccoli and pasta to the pan and cook, stirring constantly, for 2 minutes. Add the vegetable stock, bring back to a boil, and simmer for a further 12 minutes. Season with salt and white pepper.

3 Meanwhile, melt the remaining butter in a saucepan over a medium heat. Sprinkle in the flour and cook, stirring constantly, for 2 minutes. Gradually stir in the cream and bring to simmering point, but do not boil. Add the grated cheese and season with salt and a little freshly grated nutmeg.

4 Drain the pasta and broccoli mixture and pour in the cheese sauce. Cook, stirring occasionally, for 2 minutes. Transfer the pasta and broccoli mixture to a warm serving dish, and serve garnished with slices of fresh apple.

VARIATION

This dish would also be delicious and look just as colorful made with Cape broccoli, which is actually a purple variety of cauliflower and not broccoli at all.

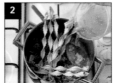

Paglia e Fieno

Serves 4

INGREDIENTS

4 tbsp butter
1 pound fresh peas, shelled
$^{7}/_{8}$ cup heavy cream

1 pound mixed fresh green and
    white spaghetti or tagliatelle
1 tbsp olive oil

$^{2}/_{3}$ cup freshly grated Parmesan
    cheese, plus extra to serve
pinch of freshly grated nutmeg
salt and pepper

1 Melt the butter in a large saucepan. Add the peas and cook, over a low heat, for 2–3 minutes.

2 Using a measuring pitcher, pour $^{5}/_{8}$ cup of the cream into the pan, bring to a boil, and simmer for 1–1$^{1}/_{2}$ minutes, Remove the pan from the heat.

3 Meanwhile, bring a large pan of lightly salted water to a boil. Add the spaghetti or tagliatelle

and olive oil and cook for 2–3 minutes, until just tender, but still firm to the bite. Remove the pan from the heat, drain the pasta thoroughly, and return to the pan.

4 Add the peas and cream sauce to the pasta. Return the pan to the heat and add the remaining cream and the grated Parmesan cheese. Season to taste with salt, black pepper, and a pinch of grated nutmeg.

5 Using 2 forks, gently toss the pasta to coat with the peas and cream sauce, while it is heating through.

6 Transfer the pasta to a serving dish and serve immediately, with extra Parmesan cheese.

Green Tagliatelle with Garlic

Serves 4

INGREDIENTS

2 tbsp walnut oil
1 bunch scallions, sliced
2 garlic cloves, thinly sliced
3¼ cups sliced mushrooms
1 pound fresh green and white
    tagliatelle
1 tbsp olive oil

8 ounces frozen spinach, thawed
    and drained
½ cup full-fat soft cheese with
    garlic and herbs
4 tbsp light cream
½ cup chopped, unsalted
    pistachio nuts
salt and pepper

TO GARNISH:
2 tbsp shredded fresh basil
fresh basil sprigs
Italian bread, to serve

1 Heat the walnut oil in a large skillet. Add the scallions and garlic and sauté for 1 minute, until just softened.

2 Add the mushrooms to the pan, stir well, cover, and cook over a low heat for about 5 minutes, until softened.

3 Meanwhile, bring a large saucepan of lightly salted water to a boil. Add the tagliatelle and olive oil and cook for 3–5 minutes, until tender, but still firm to the bite. Drain the tagliatelle thoroughly and return to the saucepan.

4 Add the spinach to the skillet and heat through for about 1–2 minutes. Add the cheese to the pan and allow to melt slightly. Stir in the cream and cook, stirring occasionally and without allowing the mixture to come to a boil, until it is heated through.

5 Pour the sauce over the pasta, season to taste, and mix well. Heat through gently, stirring constantly, for 2–3 minutes.

6 Transfer the pasta to a serving dish and sprinkle with the pistachio nuts and shredded basil. Garnish with the basil sprigs and serve.

Spaghetti Olio e Aglio

Serves 4

½ cup olive oil	3 tbsp roughly chopped fresh
3 garlic cloves, crushed	parsley
1 pound fresh spaghetti	salt and pepper

1 Reserve 1 tbsp of the olive oil and heat the remainder in a medium saucepan. Add the garlic and a pinch of salt and cook over a low heat, stirring constantly, until golden brown, then remove the pan from the heat. Do not allow the garlic to burn as it will taint its flavor. (If it does burn, you will have to start all over again!)

2 Meanwhile, bring a large saucepan of lightly salted water to a boil. Add the spaghetti and remaining olive oil and cook for 2–3 minutes, until tender, but still firm to the bite. Drain the spaghetti thoroughly and return to the pan.

3 Add the oil and garlic mixture to the spaghetti and toss to coat thoroughly. Season with pepper, add the chopped fresh parsley, and toss to coat again.

4 Transfer the spaghetti to a warm serving dish and serve immediately.

COOK'S TIP

It is worth buying the best-quality olive oil for dishes such as this one which makes a feature of its flavor. Extra virgin oil is produced from the first pressing and has the lowest acidity. It is more expensive than other types of olive oil, but has the finest flavor. Virgin olive oil is slightly more acidic, but is also well flavored. Oil simply labeled pure has usually been heat-treated and refined by mechanical means and, consequently, lacks character and flavor.

Patriotic Pasta

Serves 4

INGREDIENTS

4 cups dried farfalle	1 pound cherry tomatoes	salt and pepper
4 tbsp olive oil	3 ounces arugula	Pecorino cheese, to garnish

1 Bring a large saucepan of lightly salted water to a boil. Add the farfalle and 1 tbsp of the olive oil and cook until tender, but still firm to the bite. Drain the farfalle thoroughly and return to the pan.

2 Cut the cherry tomatoes in half and trim the arugula, using a sharp knife.

3 Heat the remaining olive oil in a large saucepan. Add the tomatoes and cook for 1 minute. Add the farfalle and the arugula and gently mix. Heat through and season to taste.

4 Meanwhile, using a vegetable peeler, shave thin slices of Pecorino cheese.

5 Transfer the farfalle and vegetables to a warm serving dish. Garnish with the Pecorino cheese shavings and serve immediately.

COOK'S TIP

Pecorino cheese is a hard ewe's milk cheese which resembles Parmesan and is often used for grating over a variety of dishes. It has a sharp flavor and is used only in small quantities.

COOK'S TIP

Arugula is a small plant with irregular-shaped leaves rather like those of turnip greens. The flavor is distinctively peppery and slightly reminiscent of radish. It has always been popular in Italy, both in salads and for serving with pasta, and has recently enjoyed a revival in the United States and Britain.

Mediterranean Spaghetti

Serves 4

INGREDIENTS

2 tbsp olive oil

1 large, red onion, chopped

2 garlic cloves, crushed

1 tbsp lemon juice

4 baby eggplants, quartered

2½ cups sieved tomatoes

2 tsp superfine sugar

2 tbsp tomato paste

14 ounce can artichoke hearts,
  drained and halved

1 cup pitted black olives

12 ounces dried spaghetti

2 tbsp butter

salt and pepper

fresh basil sprigs, to garnish

olive bread, to serve

1 Heat 1 tbsp of the olive oil in a large skillet. Add the onion, garlic, lemon juice, and eggplant and cook over a low heat for 4–5 minutes, until the onion and eggplant are lightly golden brown.

2 Pour in the sieved tomatoes, season to taste with salt and black pepper, and stir in the sugar and tomato paste. Bring to a boil, lower the heat slightly, and then simmer, stirring occasionally, for about 20 minutes.

3 Carefully stir in the artichoke hearts and black olives and cook for 5 minutes.

4 Meanwhile, bring a large saucepan of lightly salted water to a boil. Add the spaghetti and the remaining olive oil and cook for 7–8 minutes, until the pasta is tender, but still firm to the bite.

5 Drain the spaghetti thoroughly and toss with the butter. Transfer to a serving dish.

6 Pour the vegetable sauce over the spaghetti, garnish with the sprigs of fresh basil, and serve immediately with olive bread.

Spinach & Mushroom Lasagne

Serves 4

INGREDIENTS

8 tbsp butter, plus extra for
    greasing
2 garlic cloves, finely chopped
4 ounces shallots
8 ounces exotic mushrooms,
    such as chanterelles

1 pound spinach, cooked,
    drained and finely chopped
2 cups grated cheddar cheese
$^1/_4$ tsp freshly grated nutmeg
1 tsp chopped fresh basil
2 ounces all-purpose flour

$2^1/_2$ cups hot milk
$^2/_3$ cup grated Cheshire cheese
salt and pepper
8 sheets precooked lasagne

1 Lightly grease an ovenproof dish.

2 Melt 4 tbsp of the butter in a saucepan. Add the garlic, shallots, and mushrooms and sauté over a low heat for 3 minutes. Stir in the spinach, cheddar cheese, nutmeg, and basil. Season well and set aside.

3 Melt the remaining butter in another saucepan. Add the flour and cook, stirring constantly, for 1 minute. Gradually stir in the hot milk, whisking constantly until smooth. Stir in $^1/_4$ cup of the Cheshire cheese and season to taste.

4 Spread half of the mushroom and spinach mixture over the base of the prepared dish. Cover with a layer of lasagne and then with half of the cheese sauce. Repeat the process and sprinkle with the remaining Cheshire cheese. Bake in a preheated oven at 400°F for 30 minutes, until golden brown.

VARIATION

Substitute 4 bell peppers for the spinach. Roast in a preheated oven at 400°F for 20 minutes. Rub off the skins under cold water, seed, and chop before using.

Ravioli with Vegetable Stuffing

Serves 4

INGREDIENTS

1 pound Basic Pasta Dough 1 tbsp olive oil	STUFFING:	3 garlic cloves
6 tbsp butter	2 large eggplant	1 large onion
⅝ cup light cream	3 large zucchini	½ cup olive oil
1 cup freshly grated Parmesan cheese	6 large tomatoes	2 ounces tomato paste
	1 large green bell pepper	½ tsp chopped fresh basil
	1 large red bell pepper	salt and pepper

1 To make the stuffing, cut the eggplant and zucchini into 1-inch chunks. Sprinkle the eggplant with salt and set aside for 20 minutes. Rinse the eggplant and drain thoroughly.

2 Blanch the tomatoes in boiling water for 2 minutes. Drain, skin, and chop the flesh. Core and seed the bell peppers and cut into 1-inch pieces. Chop the garlic and onion.

3 Heat the oil in a saucepan. Add the garlic and onion and sauté for 3 minutes. Stir in the eggplant, zucchini, tomatoes, bell peppers, tomato paste, and basil. Season with salt and pepper to taste, cover, and leave to simmer for about 20 minutes, stirring frequently.

4 Roll out the pasta dough and cut out 3-inch rounds. Put a spoonful of the vegetable stuffing onto each round. Dampen the edges and fold the pasta rounds over, pressing together to seal.

5 Bring a pan of salted water to a boil.and cook the ravioli with the for 3–4 minutes. Drain and transfer to a greased ovenproof dish, dotting with butter. Pour in the cream and sprinkle with the Parmesan cheese. Bake in a preheated oven at 400°F for 20 minutes.

Zucchini & Eggplant Lasagne

Serves 6

INGREDIENTS

2¼ pounds eggplant
8 tbsp olive oil
2 tbsp garlic and herb butter
1 pound zucchini, sliced
2 cups grated
   mozzarella cheese
2½ cups sieved tomatoes

6 sheets precooked green
   lasagne
2½ cups Béchamel sauce
⅔ cup freshly grated
   Parmesan cheese
1 tsp dried oregano
salt and pepper

1 Thinly slice the eggplant and place in a colander. Sprinkle with salt and set aside for 20 minutes. Rinse and pat dry with paper towels.

2 Heat 4 tbsp of the olive oil in a large skillet. Fry half the eggplant slices over a low heat for 6–7 minutes, until golden. Drain on paper towels. Repeat with the remaining oil and eggplant slices.

3 Melt the garlic and herb butter in the skillet. Add the zucchini and fry for 5–6 minutes, until golden brown all over. Drain on paper towels.

4 Place half the eggplant and zucchini slices in a large ovenproof dish. Season with pepper and sprinkle with half the mozzarella cheese. Spoon half the sieved tomatoes over the cheese and top

with 3 sheets of lasagne. Repeat the process, ending with a layer of lasagne.

5 Top with the béchamel sauce and sprinkle the Parmesan cheese and oregano. Put the dish on a cookie sheet and bake in a preheated oven at 425°F for 30–35 minutes, until golden brown. Serve immediately.

Pasta & Bean Casserole

Serves 6

INGREDIENTS

1¼ cups dried navy beans,
  soaked overnight and drained

8 ounces dried penne

6 tbsp olive oil

3½ cups vegetable stock

2 large onions, sliced

2 garlic cloves, chopped

2 bay leaves

1 tsp dried oregano

1 tsp dried thyme

5 tbsp red wine

2 tbsp tomato paste

2 celery stalks, sliced

1 fennel bulb, sliced

1⅝ cups sliced mushrooms

8 ounces tomatoes, sliced

1 tsp dark brown sugar

4 tbsp dry white breadcrumbs

salt and pepper

salad greens and crusty bread,
  to serve

1 Put the navy beans in a large saucepan and add sufficient cold water to cover. Bring to a boil and continue to boil vigorously for 20 minutes. Drain, set aside, and keep warm.

2 Bring a large saucepan of lightly salted water to a boil. Add the penne and 1 tbsp of the olive oil and cook for about 3 minutes. Drain the pasta, set aside, and keep warm.

3 Put the beans in a large, flameproof casserole. Add the vegetable stock and stir in the remaining olive oil, the onions, garlic, bay leaves, oregano, thyme, wine, and tomato paste. Bring to a boil, then cover, and cook in a preheated oven at 350°F for 2 hours.

4 Add the penne, celery, fennel, mushrooms, and tomatoes to the casserole and season to taste with salt and pepper. Stir in the sugar and top with the breadcrumbs. Cover the dish and cook in the oven for 1 hour.

5 Serve hot with salad greens and crusty bread.

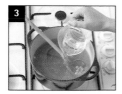

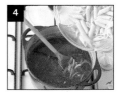

Creamed Spaghetti & Mushrooms

Serves 4

INGREDIENTS

4 tbsp butter

2 tbsp olive oil

6 shallots, sliced

6 cups sliced
    button mushrooms

1 tsp all-purpose flour

$^{5}/_{8}$ cup heavy cream

2 tbsp port

4 ounces sun-dried
    tomatoes, chopped

freshly grated nutmeg

1 pound dried spaghetti

1 tbsp freshly chopped parsley

salt and pepper

6 triangles of fried white bread,
    to serve

1 Heat the butter and 1 tbsp of the oil in a large saucepan. Add the shallots and cook for 3 minutes. Add the mushrooms and cook over a low heat for 2 minutes. Season with salt and black pepper, sprinkle in the flour, and cook, stirring constantly, for 1 minute.

2 Gradually stir in the cream and port, add the sun-dried tomatoes and a pinch of grated nutmeg, and cook over a low heat for 8 minutes.

3 Bring a large saucepan of lightly salted water to a boil. Add the spaghetti and remaining olive oil and cook for 12–14 minutes, until tender but still firm to the bite.

4 Drain the spaghetti and return to the pan. Add the mushroom sauce and cook for 3 minutes. Transfer the spaghetti and mushroom sauce to a large serving plate and sprinkle with chopped parsley. Serve with crispy triangles of fried bread.

VARIATION

Non-vegetarians could add 4 ounces prosciutto, cut into thin strips and heated gently in 2 tbsp butter, to the pasta along with the mushroom sauce.

Vegetable Pasta Stir-Fry

Serves 4

INGREDIENTS

14 ounces dried whole-wheat
    pasta shells or other short
    pasta shapes
1 tbsp olive oil
2 carrots, thinly sliced
4 ounces baby corncobs
3 tbsp corn oil
1-inch piece fresh ginger root,
    thinly sliced
1 large onion, thinly sliced

1 garlic clove, thinly sliced
3 celery stalks, thinly sliced
1 small red bell pepper, cored,
    seeded, and cut into
    matchstick strips
1 small green bell pepper, cored,
    seeded, and cut into
    matchstick strips
1 tsp cornstarch
2 tbsp water

3 tbsp soy sauce
3 tbsp dry sherry
1 tsp clear honey
a dash of hot pepper sauce
    (optional)
salt

1 Bring a large saucepan of lightly salted water to a boil. Add the pasta and olive oil and cook until tender, but still firm to the bite. Drain, return to the pan, and keep warm.

2 Bring a saucepan of lightly salted water to a boil. Add the carrots and corncobs and cook for 2 minutes. Drain, rinse in cold water, and drain again.

3 Heat the corn oil in a preheated wok or large skillet. Add the ginger root and stir-fry over a medium heat for 1 minute to flavor the oil. Remove the ginger from the oil with a slotted spoon and discard.

4 Add the onion, garlic, celery, and bell peppers to the wok or skillet and stir-fry for 2 minutes. Add the carrots and baby corncobs and stir-fry for 2 minutes. Stir in the pasta.

5 Mix together the cornstarch and water to make a smooth paste. Stir in the soy sauce, sherry, and honey. Pour the cornstarch mixture into the pasta and cook, stirring occasionally, for 2 minutes. Stir in a dash of pepper sauce, if liked. Transfer to a serving dish and serve.

Macaroni & Corn Pancakes

Serves 4

INGREDIENTS

2 corncobs

4 tbsp butter

4 ounces red bell peppers, cored, seeded, and finely diced

2¹/₂ cups dried short-cut macaroni

⁵/₈ cup heavy cream

¹/₄ cup all-purpose flour

4 egg yolks

4 tbsp olive oil

salt and pepper

TO SERVE:

oyster mushrooms

fried leeks

1 Bring a saucepan of water to a boil, add the corncobs and cook for about 8 minutes. Drain and rinse under cold running water for 3 minutes. Carefully cut away the kernels onto paper towels and set aside to dry.

2 Melt 2 tbsp of the butter in a skillet. Add the bell peppers and cook over a low heat, stirring occasionally, for 4 minutes. Drain thoroughly and pat dry with paper towels.

3 Bring a large pan of lightly salted water to a boil. Add the macaroni and cook for 12 minutes, until tender, but still firm to the bite. Drain the macaroni and leave to cool in cold water.

4 Beat together the cream, flour, a pinch of salt, and the egg yolks in a bowl until smooth. Add the corn and bell peppers to the cream and egg mixture. Drain the macaroni and toss into the corn and

cream mixture. Season well with black pepper to taste.

5 Heat the remaining butter with the oil in a large skillet. Drop spoonfuls of the mixture into the pan and press down until the mixture forms a flat pancake. Fry until golden on both sides, and all the mixture is used up. Serve immediately with oyster mushrooms and fried leeks.

384

Vermicelli Flan

Serves 4

INGREDIENTS

6 tbsp butter, plus extra,
   for greasing
8 ounces dried vermicelli or
   spaghetti
1 tbsp olive oil
1 onion, chopped
5 ounces button mushrooms

1 green bell pepper, cored,
   seeded, and sliced into thin
   rings
$\frac{5}{8}$ cup milk
3 eggs, lightly beaten
2 tbsp heavy cream
1 tsp dried oregano

freshly grated nutmeg
1 tbsp freshly grated
   Parmesan cheese
salt and pepper
tomato and basil salad,
   to serve

1 Grease the base and sides of an 8-inch loose-based flan pan with butter.

2 Bring a large pan of lightly salted water to a boil. Add the vermicelli and olive oil and cook until tender, but still firm to the bite. Drain and toss in 2 tbsp of the butter.

3 Press the pasta onto the base and around the sides of the flan pan to make a flan case.

4 Melt the remaining butter in a skillet. Add the onion and sauté until it is translucent.

5 Add the mushrooms and bell pepper rings to the skillet and cook, stirring and turning constantly, for 2–3 minutes. Spoon the onion, mushroom and bell peppers into the flan case and press down evenly over the base.

6 Beat together the milk, eggs, and cream, stir in

the oregano, and season to taste with nutmeg and black pepper. Carefully pour the mixture over the vegetables and sprinkle with the cheese.

7 Bake the flan in a preheated oven at 350°F for 40–45 minutes, until the filling has set.

8 Slide the flan out of the pan and serve warm with a tomato and basil salad.

Fettuccine with Olive, Garlic, & Walnut Sauce

Serves 4–6

INGREDIENTS

2 thick slices whole-wheat bread, crusts removed

1¼ cups milk

2½ cups shelled walnuts

2 garlic cloves, crushed

1 cup pitted black olives

²⁄₃ cup freshly grated Parmesan cheese

8 tbsp extra virgin olive oil

⁵⁄₈ cup heavy cream

1 pound fresh fettuccine

salt and pepper

2–3 tbsp chopped fresh parsley

1 Put the bread in a shallow dish, pour the milk over it, and set aside to soak until the liquid has been absorbed.

2 Spread the walnuts out on a cookie sheet and toast in a preheated oven at 375°F for about 5 minutes, until golden. Set aside to cool.

3 Put the soaked bread, walnuts, garlic, olives, Parmesan cheese, and 6 tbsp of the olive oil in a food processor and purée. Season to taste with a little salt and black pepper and stir in the cream.

4 Bring a large pan of lightly salted water to a boil. Add the fettuccine and 1 tablespoon of the remaining oil and cook for 2–3 minutes, until tender but still firm to the bite. Drain the pasta and toss with the remaining olive oil, until well combined.

5 Divide the fettuccine between individual plates and spoon the olive, garlic, and walnut sauce on top. Sprinkle with the fresh parsley and serve.

Linguine with Braised Fennel

Serves 4

INGREDIENTS

6 fennel bulbs	1/4 cup all-purpose flour	1 pound dried linguine
5/8 cup vegetable stock	7 tbsp heavy cream	1 tbsp olive oil
2 tbsp butter	1 tbsp Madeira	salt and pepper
6 slices bacon, diced		
6 shallots, quartered		

1 Trim the fennel bulbs, then gently peel off and reserve the first layer of the bulbs. Cut the bulbs into quarters and put them in a large saucepan, together with the vegetable stock and the reserved outer layers. Bring to a boil, lower the heat, and simmer for 5 minutes.

2 Using a slotted spoon, transfer the fennel to a large dish. Discard the outer layers of the fennel bulb. Bring the vegetable stock to a boil and allow to reduce by half. Set aside.

3 Melt the butter in a skillet. Add the bacon and shallots and fry for 4 minutes. Add the flour, reduced stock, cream, and Madeira and cook, stirring constantly, for 3 minutes, until the sauce is smooth. Season to taste and pour over the fennel.

4 Bring a large saucepan of lightly salted water to a boil. Add the linguine and olive oil and cook for 10 minutes, until tender, but still firm to the bite. Drain and transfer to a deep ovenproof dish.

5 Add the fennel and sauce and braise in a preheated oven at 350°F for 20 minutes. Serve immediately from the dish.

COOK'S TIP

Fennel will keep in the salad drawer of the refrigerator for 2–3 days, but it is best eaten as fresh as possible. Cut surfaces turn brown quickly, so do not prepare it too much in advance of cooking.

Baked Eggplant with Pasta

Serves 4

INGREDIENTS

8 ounces dried penne or other
short pasta shapes
4 tbsp olive oil, plus extra for
brushing
2 eggplant
1 large onion, chopped

2 garlic cloves, crushed
14 ounce can chopped tomatoes
2 tsp dried oregano
2 ounces mozzarella cheese,
thinly sliced
⅓ cup freshly grated

Parmesan cheese
2 tbsp dry breadcrumbs
salt and pepper
salad greens, to serve

1 Bring a pan of salted water to a boil. Add the pasta and 1 tbsp of the olive oil and cook until tender, but still firm to the bite. Drain and keep warm.

2 Cut the eggplant in half lengthwise and score around the inside, being careful not to pierce the shells. Scoop out the flesh with a spoon. Brush the insides of the shells with olive oil. Chop the flesh and set aside.

3 Sauté the onion in the remaining oil until translucent. Add the garlic and cook for 1 minute. Add the chopped eggplant and cook for 5 minutes. Add the tomatoes and oregano and season to taste. Bring to a boil and simmer until thickened. Remove from the heat and stir in the pasta.

4 Brush a cookie sheet with oil and arrange the eggplant shells in a

single layer. Divide half the tomato and pasta mixture between them. Sprinkle the mozzarella on, then pile the remaining tomato and pasta mixture on top. Mix the Parmesan cheese and breadcrumbs together and sprinkle over the top.

5 Bake in a preheated oven at 400°F for 25 minutes, until the topping is golden brown. Serve hot with salad greens.

Pasta with Green Vegetable Sauce

Serves 4

INGREDIENTS

2 cups dried gemelli or other
    pasta shapes
1 tbsp olive oil
1 head green broccoli, cut
    into florets
2 zucchini, sliced
8 ounces asparagus spears

4 ounces snow peas
4 ounces frozen peas
2 tbsp butter
3 tbsp vegetable stock
4 tbsp heavy cream
freshly grated nutmeg
2 tbsp chopped fresh parsley

2 tbsp freshly grated
    Parmesan cheese
salt and pepper

1 Bring a large saucepan of lightly salted water to a boil. Add the pasta and olive oil and cook until tender, but still firm to the bite. Drain, return to the pan, cover, and keep warm.

2 Steam the broccoli, zucchini, asparagus spears, and snow peas over a pan of boiling salted water until they are just beginning to soften. Remove from the heat and rinse in cold water. Drain thoroughly, and set aside.

3 Bring a small pan of lightly salted water to a boil. Add the frozen peas and cook for 3 minutes. Drain the peas, rinse in cold water, and then drain again. Set aside with the other vegetables.

4 Put the butter and vegetable stock in a pan over a medium heat. Add all of the vegetables, reserving a few of the asparagus spears, and toss carefully with a wooden spoon until they have

heated through, taking care not to break them up.

5 Stir in the cream and heat through without bringing to a boil. Add the seasoning and nutmeg.

6 Transfer the pasta to a warmed serving dish and stir in the chopped parsley. Spoon the vegetable sauce on top and sprinkle with Parmesan. Arrange the reserved asparagus spears in a pattern on top and serve.

Tagliatelle with Garlic Butter

Serves 4

INGREDIENTS

1 pound strong white flour, plus extra for dredging	4 eggs, beaten	3 garlic cloves, finely chopped
2 tsp salt	3 tbsp olive oil	2 tbsp chopped, fresh parsley
	5 tbsp butter, melted	pepper

1 Sift the flour into a large bowl and stir in the salt.

2 Make a well in the middle of the dry ingredients and add the eggs and 2 tablespoons of oil. Using a wooden spoon, stir in the eggs, gradually drawing in the flour. After a few minutes the dough will be too stiff to use a spoon and you will need to use your fingers.

3 Once all of the flour has been incorporated, turn the dough out onto a floured surface and knead for about 5 minutes, until smooth and elastic. If you find the dough is too wet, add a little more flour and continue kneading. Cover the dough with plastic wrap and set aside to rest for at least 15 minutes.

4 The basic dough is now ready. Roll the dough out thinly and create the pasta shapes required. This can be done by hand or with the aid of a pasta machine. The results from a machine are usually neater and thinner, but not necessarily better.

5 To make the tagliatelle by hand, fold the thinly rolled pasta sheets into 3 and, with a sharp knife, cut out long, thin strips, about ½ inch wide.

6 To cook, bring a large pan of water to a boil, add 1 tablespoon of oil and the pasta. It will take 2–3 minutes to cook, and the texture should have a slight bite to it. Drain thoroughly.

7 Mix together the butter, garlic, and parsley. Stir into the pasta and serve immediately with plenty of black pepper.

COOK'S TIP

Generally allow about 5½ ounces fresh pasta or about 3½ ounces dried pasta per person.

Spicy Tomato Tagliatelle

Serves 4

INGREDIENTS

3 tbsp butter

1 onion, finely chopped

1 garlic clove, crushed

2 small fresh red chiles, seeded
    and diced

1 pound fresh tomatoes, skinned,
    seeded, and diced

³/₄ cup vegetable stock

2 tbsp tomato paste

1 tsp sugar

salt and pepper

1¹/₂ pounds fresh green and white
    tagliatelle, or 12 ounces dried

1 Melt the butter in a large saucepan. Add the onion and garlic and sauté for 3–4 minutes, or until softened.

2 Add the chiles to the pan and continue cooking for about 2 minutes.

3 Add the tomatoes and stock, reduce the heat, and simmer for 10 minutes, stirring.

4 Pour the sauce into a food processor and blend for 1 minute, until smooth. Alternatively, push the sauce through a strainer.

5 Return the sauce to the pan and add the tomato paste, sugar, and salt and pepper to taste. Gently reheat over a low heat, until piping hot.

6 Cook the tagliatelle in a pan of boiling water according to the instructions on the packet or until it is cooked, but still has "bite." Drain the tagliatelle, transfer to serving plates, and serve with the tomato sauce.

VARIATION

Try topping your pasta dish with ¹/₃ cup diced pancetta or unsmoked bacon, dry-fried for 5 minutes, until crispy.

Basil & Tomato Pasta

Serves 4

INGREDIENTS

1 tbsp olive oil	1 tbsp sun-dried tomato paste	1 1/2 pounds fresh farfalle or
2 sprigs rosemary	12 fresh basil leaves, plus extra to	12 ounces dried farfalle
2 cloves garlic, unpeeled	garnish	
1 pound tomatoes, halved	salt and pepper	

1 Place the rosemary, garlic, and tomatoes, skin side up, in a roasting pan, with half of the oil.

2 Drizzle with the remaining oil and cook under a preheated broiler for 20 minutes, or until the tomato skins are slightly charred.

3 Peel the skin from the tomatoes. Roughly chop the tomato flesh and place in a pan.

4 Squeeze the pulp from the garlic cloves and mix with the tomato flesh and sun-dried tomato paste.

5 Roughly tear the fresh basil leaves into smaller pieces and then stir them into the sauce. Season with a little salt and pepper to taste.

6 Cook the farfalle in a saucepan of boiling water according to the instructions on the packet, or until it is cooked through, but still has "bite." Drain.

7 Gently heat the tomato and basil sauce.

8 Transfer the farfalle to serving plates and serve with the basil and tomato sauce.

COOK'S TIP

This sauce tastes just as good when served cold in a pasta salad.

Basil & Pine Nut Pesto

Serves 4

INGREDIENTS

about 40 fresh basil leaves

3 garlic cloves, crushed

$^1/_4$ cup pine nuts

$^2/_3$ cup finely grated Parmesan cheese

2-3 tbsp extra-virgin olive oil

salt and pepper

$1^1/_2$ pounds fresh pasta or 12 ounces dried pasta

1 Rinse the basil leaves and pat them dry with paper towels.

2 Put the basil leaves, garlic, pine nuts, and grated Parmesan into a food processor and blend for about 30 seconds, or until smooth. Alternatively, pound the ingredients by hand, using a mortar and pestle.

3 If you are using a food processor, keep the motor running and slowly add the olive oil. Alternatively, add the oil drop by drop while stirring briskly. Season with salt and pepper.

4 Meanwhile, cook the pasta in a saucepan of boiling water according to the instructions on the packet, or until it is cooked through, but still has "bite." Drain.

5 Transfer the pasta to a serving dish and add the pesto. Toss to mix well and serve hot.

VARIATION

Try making a walnut version of this pesto. Substitute $^1/_4$ cup walnuts for the pine nuts and add 1 tablespoon walnut oil in step 2.

COOK'S TIP

You can store pesto in the refrigerator for about 4 weeks. Cover the surface of the pesto with olive oil before sealing the container or bottle, to prevent the basil from oxidizing and turning black.

Pasta & Sicilian Sauce

Serves 4

INGREDIENTS

1 pound tomatoes, halved
$^1/_4$ cup pine nuts

$^1/_3$ cup golden raisins
1$^3/_4$ ounce can anchovies, drained
and halved lengthwise

2 tbsp concentrated tomato paste
1$^1/_2$ pounds fresh or
12 ounces dried penne

1 Cook the tomatoes under a preheated broiler for about 10 minutes. Cool slightly, then once cool enough to handle, carefully peel off the skin and dice the flesh, using a sharp knife.

2 Place the pine nuts on a cookie sheet and lightly toast under the broiler for 2–3 minutes or until golden.

3 Soak the golden raisins in a bowl of warm water for about 20 minutes. Drain the raisins thoroughly.

4 Place the tomatoes, pine nuts, and golden raisins in a small pan and gently heat.

5 Add the anchovies and tomato paste, heating the sauce for a further 2–3 minutes, or until hot.

6 Cook the pasta in a saucepan of boiling water according to the instructions on the packet, or until it is cooked through, but still has "bite." Drain thoroughly.

7 Transfer the pasta to a serving plate and serve with the hot Sicilian sauce.

VARIATION

Add 3$^1/_2$ ounces bacon, broiled for 5 minutes, until crispy, then chopped, instead of the anchovies, if you prefer.

COOK'S TIP

If you are making fresh pasta, remember that pasta dough prefers warm conditions and responds well to handling. Do not chill and do not use a marble surface for kneading.

Tortelloni

Makes 36 pieces

INGREDIENTS

about 10½ ounces fresh pasta, rolled out to thin sheets	3 garlic cloves, crushed	⅓ cup finely grated pecorino cheese, plus extra to garnish
5 tbsp butter	¾ cup finely chopped mushrooms	1 tbsp oil
4 tbsp finely chopped shallots	½ celery stalk, finely chopped	salt and pepper

1 Using a serrated pasta cutter, cut 2-inch squares from the sheets of fresh pasta. To make 36 tortellini you will need 72 squares. Once the pasta is cut, cover the squares with plastic wrap to keep them from drying out.

2 Heat 3 tbsp of the butter in a skillet. Add the shallots, 1 crushed garlic clove, the mushrooms, and celery, and cook for 4–5 minutes.

3 Remove the pan from the heat, stir in the cheese, and season with salt and pepper.

4 Spoon ½ teaspoon of the mixture onto the middle of 36 pasta squares. Brush the edges of the squares with water and top with the remaining 36 squares. Press the edges together to seal. Set aside to rest for 5 minutes.

5 Bring a large pan of water to a boil, add the oil, and cook the tortellini, in batches, for 2–3 minutes. The tortellini will rise to the surface when cooked and the pasta should be tender with a slight "bite." Remove from the pan with a slotted spoon and drain thoroughly.

6 Meanwhile, melt the remaining butter in a pan. Add the remaining garlic and plenty of pepper and cook for 1–2 minutes.

7 Transfer the tortellini to serving plates and pour the garlic butter over them. Garnish with grated pecorino cheese and serve immediately.

Milanese Sun-Dried Tomato Risotto

Serves 4

INGREDIENTS

1 tbsp olive oil	about 15 strands saffron	8 sun-dried tomatoes, cut into strips
2 tbsp butter	2/3 cup white wine	1 cup frozen peas, thawed
1 large onion, finely chopped	3 3/4 cups hot vegetable or chicken	1/3 cup shredded prosciutto
1 2/3 cups risotto rice, washed	stock	1 cup grated Parmesan cheese

1 Heat the oil and butter in a large skillet. Add the onion and sauté for 4–5 minutes, or until softened.

2 Add the rice and saffron to the skillet, stirring well to coat the rice in the oil, and cook for 1 minute.

3 Add the wine and stock slowly to the rice mixture in the pan, a ladleful at a time, stirring and making sure that all the liquid is absorbed before adding the next ladleful of liquid.

4 About halfway through adding the stock, stir in the tomatoes.

5 When all the wine and stock is incorporated, the rice should be cooked. Test by tasting a grain — if it is still crunchy, add a little more water and continue cooking. It should take at least 15 minutes to cook.

6 Stir in the peas, prosciutto, and cheese. Cook for 2–3 minutes, stirring, until hot. Serve with extra Parmesan.

COOK'S TIP

Italian rice is a round, short-grained variety with a nutty flavor, which is essential for a good risotto. Arborio is the very best kind to use. The finished dish should have moist, but separate grains. This is achieved by adding the hot stock a little at a time, adding more only when the last addition is fully absorbed. Do not leave the risotto to cook by itself: it needs constant watching to see when more liquid is required.

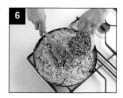

Mushroom Risotto

Serves 4

INGREDIENTS

2 tbsp olive oil

1 large onion, finely chopped

1 garlic clove, crushed

7 ounces mixed mushrooms, such as ceps, oyster, porcini, and button, wiped and sliced if large

1¹/₃ cups risotto rice, washed

pinch saffron threads

3 cups hot vegetable stock

²/₃ cup white wine

1 cup grated Parmesan cheese, plus extra for serving

2 tbsp chopped thyme

salt and pepper

1 Heat the oil in a large skillet. Add the onions and garlic and sauté for 3–4 minutes, or until softened.

2 Add the mushrooms to the skillet and cook for a further 3 minutes, or until they are just beginning to brown.

3 Add the rice and saffron to the skillet and stir to coat the rice in the oil.

4 Mix together the stock and wine and add to the skillet, a ladleful at a time. Stir the rice mixture and allow the liquid to be fully absorbed before adding more liquid, a ladleful at a time.

5 When all the wine and stock is incorporated, the rice should be cooked. Test by tasting a grain — if it is still crunchy, add a little more water and continue cooking. It should take at least 15 minutes to cook.

6 Stir in the cheese and thyme, and season with freshly ground black pepper.

7 Transfer the risotto to serving dishes and serve sprinkled with extra Parmesan cheese.

COOK'S TIP

Exotic mushrooms each have their own distinctive flavors and make a change from button mushrooms. However, they can be quite expensive, so you can always use a mixture with crimini or button mushrooms instead.

Chicken Risotto alla Milanese

Serves 4

INGREDIENTS

¹/₂ cup butter	2¹/₂ cups chicken stock	¹/₂ cup grated Parmesan cheese,
2 pounds chicken meat, thinly sliced	²/₃ cup white wine	to serve
1 large onion, chopped	1 teaspoon crumbled saffron	
2¹/₂ cups risotto rice	salt and pepper	

1 Heat 4 tablespoons of the butter in a deep skillet, and fry the chicken and onion until golden brown.

2 Add the rice, stir well, and cook for 15 minutes.

3 Heat the stock until boiling and gradually add to the rice. Add the white wine, saffron, and salt and pepper to taste and mix well. Simmer over low heat for 20 minutes, stirring occasionally, and adding more stock if the risotto becomes too dry.

4 Let stand for a few minutes and just before serving, add a little more stock and simmer for a further 10 minutes. Serve the risotto, sprinkled with the grated Parmesan cheese and the remaining butter.

COOK'S TIP

A risotto should have moist, but separate grains. Stock should be added a little at a time and only when the last addition has been completely absorbed.

VARIATION

The possibilities for risotto are almost endless—try adding any of the following just at the end of cooking time: cashews and corn, lightly sautéed zucchini and basil, or artichokes and oyster mushrooms.

Golden Chicken Risotto

Serves 4

INGREDIENTS

2 tablespoons sunflower oil	3 skinless, boneless chicken	6 1/4 cups chicken stock
1 tablespoon butter or margarine	breasts, diced	7 ounce can corn
1 medium leek, thinly sliced	12 ounces risotto rice	1/2 cup toasted unsalted peanuts
1 large yellow bell pepper, diced	few strands saffron	1/2 cup grated Parmesan cheese
		salt and pepper

1 Heat the oil and butter or margarine in a large saucepan. Fry the leek and bell pepper for 1 minute, then stir in the chicken, and cook, stirring until golden brown.

2 Stir in the rice and cook for 2–3 minutes.

3 Stir in the saffron strands and salt and pepper to taste. Add the stock, a little at a time, cover, and cook over low heat, stirring occasionally, for about 20 minutes, until the rice is tender and most of the liquid has been absorbed. Do not let the risotto dry out — add more stock if necessary.

4 Stir in the corn, peanuts, and Parmesan cheese, then adjust the seasoning to taste. Serve the risotto hot.

COOK'S TIP

Risottos can be frozen, before adding the Parmesan cheese, for up to 1 month, but remember to reheat this risotto thoroughly as it contains chicken.

Niçoise with Pasta Shells

Serves 4

INGREDIENTS

12 ounces dried small pasta
  shells
1 tbsp olive oil
4 ounces green beans
1³/₄ ounce can anchovies,
  drained
¹/₈ cup milk

2 small crisp lettuce heads
1 pound or 3 large beef
  tomatoes
4 hard-cooked eggs
8 ounce can tuna, drained
1 cup pitted black olives
salt and pepper

VINAIGRETTE DRESSING:
¹/₄ cup extra virgin olive oil
¹/₈ cup white wine vinegar
1 tsp wholegrain mustard
salt and pepper

1 Bring a large saucepan of lightly salted water to a boil. Add the pasta and the olive oil and cook until tender, but still firm to the bite. Drain and rinse in cold water.

2 Bring a small saucepan of lightly salted water to a boil. Add the beans and cook for 10–12 minutes, until tender, but still firm to the bite. Drain, rinse in cold water,

drain thoroughly once more, and then set aside.

3 Put the anchovies in a shallow bowl, cover with the milk, and set aside for 10 minutes. Meanwhile, tear the lettuce into large pieces. Blanch the tomatoes in boiling water for 1–2 minutes, then drain, skin, and roughly chop the flesh. Shell the eggs and cut into quarters. Cut the tuna into large chunks.

4 Drain the anchovies and the pasta. Put all of the salad ingredients, the beans, and the olives into a large bowl and gently mix together.

5 To make the vinaigrette dressing, beat together all the ingredients and keep in the refrigerator until required. Just before serving, pour the vinaigrette dressing over the salad.

Herring & Pasta Salad

Serves 4

INGREDIENTS

9 ounces dried pasta shells	2 large tart apples	6 dill pickles
5 tbsp olive oil	2 baby frisée lettuces	2 tbsp capers
14 ounces rollmop herrings in water	2 baby beets	3 tbsp tarragon vinegar
6 boiled potatoes	4 hard-cooked eggs	salt and pepper
	6 pickled onions	

1 Bring a large saucepan of lightly salted water to a boil. Add the pasta and 1 tbsp of the olive oil and cook until tender, but still firm to the bite. Drain the pasta thoroughly and rinse in cold water.

2 Cut the herrings, potatoes, apples, frisée lettuces, and beets into small pieces. Put all of these ingredients into a large salad bowl.

3 Drain the pasta thoroughly and add to the salad bowl. Toss lightly

to mix the pasta and herring mixture together.

4 Carefully shell and slice the eggs. Garnish the salad with the slices of egg, pickled onions, dill pickles, and capers, sprinkle with the remaining olive oil and the tarragon vinegar, and serve immediately.

COOK'S TIP

Store this salad, without the dressing, in a container in the refrigerator.

COOK'S TIP

Tarragon vinegar is available from most supermarkets, but you can easily make your own. Add a bunch of fresh tarragon to a bottle of white or red wine vinegar and leave to infuse for 48 hours. It is important to ensure that the tarragon is as fresh as possible and to discard any blemished leaves.

Neapolitan Seafood Salad with Campanelle

Serves 4

INGREDIENTS

1 pound prepared squid, cut into strips

1 pound 10 ounces cooked mussels

1 pound cooked cockles in water

⁵/₈ cup white wine

1¹/₄ cups olive oil

2 cups dried campanelle or other small pasta shapes

juice of 1 lemon

1 bunch chives, snipped

1 bunch fresh parsley, finely chopped

4 large tomatoes, quartered or sliced

mixed salad greens

salt and pepper

sprig of fresh basil, to garnish

1 Put all of the seafood into a large bowl, pour in the wine and half the olive oil, and set aside for 6 hours.

2 Put the seafood mixture into a saucepan and simmer over a low heat for 10 minutes. Set aside to cool.

3 Bring a large saucepan of lightly salted water to a boil. Add the pasta and 1 tbsp of the remaining olive oil and cook until tender, but still firm to the bite. Drain thoroughly and rinse in cold water.

4 Strain off about half of the cooking liquid from the seafood and discard the rest. Mix in the lemon juice, chives, parsley, and the remaining olive oil. Season to taste with salt and pepper. Drain the pasta and add to the seafood.

5 Slice or cut the tomatoes into quarters. Shred the salad greens and arrange them on the base of a salad bowl. Spoon in the seafood salad and garnish with the quartered or sliced tomatoes and a sprig of basil.

Pasta Salad with Red & White Cabbage

Serves 4

INGREDIENTS

2¼ cups dried short-
   cut macaroni
5 tbsp olive oil
1 large red cabbage, shredded

1 large white cabbage, shredded
2 large apples, diced
9 ounces cooked smoked bacon
   or ham, diced

8 tbsp wine vinegar
1 tbsp sugar
salt and pepper

1 Bring a large pan of salted water to a boil. Add the macaroni and 1 tablespoon of the olive oil and cook until tender, but still firm to the bite. Drain the pasta, then rinse in cold water. Drain the pasta again and set aside.

2 Bring a large pan of lightly salted water to a boil. Add the shredded red cabbage and cook for 5 minutes. Drain thoroughly and set aside to cool.

3 Bring a large epan of lightly salted water to a boil. Add the white cabbage and cook for 5 minutes. Drain thoroughly and set aside to cool.

4 Mix together the pasta, red cabbage, and apple. Mix together the white cabbage and bacon or ham.

5 In a small bowl, mix together the remaining oil, the vinegar, and sugar and season to taste with salt and pepper. Pour the dressing over each of the 2 cabbage mixtures and, finally, mix them all together. Serve at once.

VARIATION

Alternative dressings for this salad can be made with 4 tbsp olive oil, 4 tbsp red wine, 4 tbsp red wine vinegar, and 1 tbsp sugar. Or, substitute 3 tbsp olive oil and 1 tbsp walnut or hazelnut oil for the olive oil.

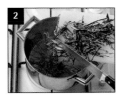

Dolcelatte, Nut, & Pasta Salad

Serves 4

INGREDIENTS

2 cups dried pasta shells
1 tbsp olive oil
1 cup shelled and halved walnuts
mixed salad greens, such as
   radicchio, escarole, arugula,
   corn salad, and frisée

8 ounces dolcelatte cheese,
   crumbled
salt

DRESSING:
2 tbsp walnut oil

4 tbsp extra virgin olive oil
2 tbsp red wine vinegar
salt and pepper

1 Bring a large saucepan of lightly salted water to a boil. Add the pasta shells and olive oil and cook until just tender, but still firm to the bite. Drain the pasta, rinse under cold running water, drain again, and set aside.

2 Spread out the shelled walnut halves on a cookie sheet and toast under a preheated broiler for about 2–3 minutes. Set aside to cool slightly while you make the dressing.

3 To make the dressing, whisk together the walnut oil, olive oil, and vinegar in a small bowl, and season with salt and pepper to taste.

4 Arrange the salad greens in a large serving bowl. Pile the cooled pasta in the middle of the salad greens and sprinkle the dolcelatte cheese on top. Pour the dressing over the pasta salad, scatter with the walnut halves and toss together well to mix. Serve immediately.

COOK'S TIP

Dolcelatte is a semisoft, blue-veined cheese from Italy. Its texture is creamy and smooth and the flavor is delicate, but piquant. You could substitute Roquefort as an alternative. Whichever cheese you choose, it is essential that it is of the best quality and in peak condition.

Vegetables, Salads, & Bakes

Goat Cheese with Penne, Pear, & Walnut Salad

Serves 4

INGREDIENTS

9 ounces dried penne	2 ripe pears, cored and diced	4 tomatoes, quartered
5 tbsp olive oil	1 fresh basil sprig	1 small onion, sliced
1 head radicchio, torn into pieces	1 bunch of watercress, trimmed	1 large carrot, grated
1 Webbs lettuce, torn into pieces	2 tbsp lemon juice	9 ounces goat cheese, diced
7 tbsp chopped walnuts	3 tbsp garlic vinegar	salt and pepper

1 Bring a large saucepan of lightly salted water to a boil. Add the penne and 1 tbsp of the olive oil and cook until tender, but still firm to the bite. Drain the pasta, rinse under cold running water, drain thoroughly again, and set aside to cool.

2 Place the radicchio and Webbs lettuce in a large salad bowl and mix together well. Top with the pasta, walnuts, pears, basil, and watercress.

3 Mix together the lemon juice, the remaining olive oil, and the vinegar in a pitcher. Pour the mixture over the salad ingredients and toss thoroughly to coat the salad greens well.

4 Add the tomato quarters, onion slices, grated carrot, and diced goat cheese and toss together, using 2 forks, until well mixed. Leave the salad to chill in the refrigerator for about 1 hour before serving.

Pasta & Garlic Mayonnaise Salad

Serves 4

INGREDIENTS

2 large lettuce heads
9 ounces dried penne
1 tbsp olive oil

8 red delicious apples
juice of 4 lemons
1 head of celery, sliced
salt

³/₄ cup shelled, halved walnuts
1¹/₈ cups fresh garlic mayonnaise
(see Cook's Tip, below right)

1 Wash, drain, and pat dry the lettuce leaves with paper towels. Transfer them to the refrigerator for 1 hour until crisp.

2 Meanwhile, bring a large saucepan of lightly salted water to a boil. Add the pasta and olive oil and cook until tender, but still firm to the bite. Drain the pasta and rinse under cold running water. Drain thoroughly again and set aside.

3 Core and dice the apples, place them in a small bowl, and sprinkle with the lemon juice. Mix together the pasta, celery, apples, and walnuts and toss the mixture in the garlic mayonnaise (see Cook's Tip, right). Add more mayonnaise, if desired.

4 Line a salad bowl with the lettuce leaves and spoon the pasta salad into the lined bowl. Serve.

COOK'S TIP

Sprinkling the apples with lemon juice will prevent them from turning brown.

COOK'S TIP

To make homemade garlic mayonnaise, beat 2 egg yolks with a pinch of salt and 6 crushed garlic cloves. Start beating in 1½ cups olive oil, 1–2 tsp at a time, using a balloon whisk or electric mixer. When about one-quarter of the oil has been fully incorporated, beat in 1–2 tbsp white wine vinegar. Continue beating in the oil, adding it in a thin, continuous stream. Finally, stir in 1 tsp Dijon mustard and season to taste with salt and pepper.

Fusilli, Avocado, Tomato, & Mozzarella Salad

Serves 4

INGREDIENTS

2 tbsp pine nuts

1½ cups dried fusilli

1 tbsp olive oil

6 tomatoes

8 ounces mozzarella cheese

1 large avocado

2 tbsp lemon juice

3 tbsp chopped fresh basil

salt and pepper

fresh basil sprigs, to garnish

DRESSING:

6 tbsp extra virgin olive oil

2 tbsp white wine vinegar

1 tsp wholegrain mustard

pinch of sugar

1 Spread the pine nuts out on a cookie sheet and toast under a preheated broiler for 1–2 minutes. Remove and set aside to cool.

2 Bring a large saucepan of lightly salted water to a boil. Add the fusilli and olive oil and cook until tender, but still firm to the bite. Drain the pasta and rinse in cold water. Drain the pasta again and then set aside to cool slightly.

3 Thinly slice the tomatoes and the mozzarella cheese.

4 Cut the avocado in half, remove the pit, and skin. Cut into thin slices lengthwise and sprinkle with lemon juice to prevent discoloration.

5 To make the dressing, whisk together the oil, vinegar, mustard, and sugar in a small bowl, and season to taste.

6 Arrange the tomatoes, mozzarella cheese, and avocado alternately in overlapping slices on a large serving platter.

7 Toss the pasta with half of the dressing and the chopped basil, and season to taste. Spoon the pasta into the center of the platter and pour the remaining dressing on top. Sprinkle with the pine nuts, garnish with fresh basil sprigs, and serve.

Pasta-Stuffed Tomatoes

Serves 4

INGREDIENTS

5 tbsp extra virgin olive oil, plus
  extra for greasing
8 beef tomatoes or large round
  tomatoes
1 cup dried ditalini or other very
  small pasta shapes

8 black olives, pitted and finely
  chopped
2 tbsp finely chopped fresh basil
1 tbsp finely chopped fresh
  parsley

²/₃ cup freshly grated
  Parmesan cheese
salt and pepper
fresh basil sprigs, to garnish

1 Brush a cookie sheet with olive oil.

2 Slice the tops off the tomatoes and reserve to make "lids." If the tomatoes will not stand up, cut a thin slice off the bottom of each tomato.

3 Scoop out the tomato pulp into a strainer, but do not pierce the tomato shells. Invert the tomato shells onto paper towels, pat dry, and then set aside to drain thoroughly.

4 Bring a large saucepan of lightly salted water to a boil. Add the ditalini or other pasta and 1 tbsp of the remaining olive oil and cook until tender, but still firm to the bite. Drain the pasta and set aside.

5 Put the olives, basil, parsley, and Parmesan cheese into a mixing bowl and stir in the drained tomato pulp. Add the pasta to the bowl. Stir in remaining olive oil, mix well, and season to taste.

6 Spoon the pasta mixture into the tomato shells and replace the lids. Arrange the tomatoes on the cookie sheet and bake in a preheated oven at 375°F for 15–20 minutes.

7 Remove the tomatoes from the oven and allow to cool until just warm. Arrange on a serving dish, garnish with the basil sprigs, and serve.

Rare Beef Pasta Salad

Serves 4

INGREDIENTS

1 pound rump or sirloin steak in one piece

1 pound dried fusilli

5 tbsp olive oil

2 tbsp lime juice

2 tbsp Thai fish sauce (see Cook's Tip)

2 tsp clear honey

4 scallions, sliced

1 cucumber, peeled and cut into 1-inch chunks

3 tomatoes, cut into wedges

3 tsp finely chopped fresh mint

salt and pepper

1 Season the steak with salt and black pepper. Broil or pan-fry the steak for 4 minutes on each side. Set aside for 5 minutes, then slice thinly across the grain.

2 Bring a large saucepan of lightly salted water to a boil. Add the fusilli and 1 tbsp of the olive oil and cook until tender, but still firm to the bite. Drain the fusilli, rinse in cold water, and drain again thoroughly. Toss the fusilli in the remaining olive oil.

3 Combine the lime juice, fish sauce, and honey in a small saucepan and cook over a medium heat for 2 minutes.

4 Add the scallions, cucumber, tomatoes, and mint to the pan, then add the sliced steak and mix thoroughly. Season to taste with salt.

5 Transfer the fusilli to a large, warm serving dish and top with the steak and salad mixture. Serve warm or allow to cool.

COOK'S TIP

Thai fish sauce, also known as nam pla, *is made from salted anchovies and has quite a strong flavor, so it should be used with discretion. It is available from some supermarkets and from Oriental food stores.*

Beet Cannolicchi

Serves 4

INGREDIENTS

11 ounces dried ditalini rigati

5 tbsp olive oil

2 garlic cloves, chopped

14 ounce can chopped tomatoes

14 ounces cooked beet, diced

2 tbsp chopped fresh basil leaves

1 tsp mustard seeds

salt and pepper

TO SERVE:

mixed salad greens, tossed in
   olive oil

4 Italian plum tomatoes, sliced

1 Bring a large pan of lightly salted water to a boil. Add the pasta and 1 tbsp of the oil and cook for about 10 minutes, until tender, but still firm to the bite. Drain and set aside.

2 Heat the remaining olive oil in a large saucepan. Add the garlic and sauté for 3 minutes. Add the chopped tomatoes and cook for 10 minutes.

3 Remove the pan from the heat and add the beet, basil, mustard seeds, and pasta, and salt and black pepper.

4 Serve on a bed of mixed salad greens tossed in olive oil, and sliced plum tomatoes.

COOK'S TIP

Mustard seeds come from three different plants and may be black, brown, or white. Black and brown mustard seeds have a stronger, more pungent flavor than white mustard.

COOK'S TIP

To cook raw beet, trim off the leaves about 2 inches above the root and ensure that the skin is not broken. Boil in very lightly salted water for 30–40 minutes, until tender. Leave to cool and rub off the skin.

Chili & Bell Pepper Pasta

Serves 4

INGREDIENTS

2 red bell peppers, halved and seeded 1 small fresh red chili 2 garlic cloves	4 tomatoes, halved $\frac{1}{2}$ cup ground almonds 7 tbsp olive oil	$1\frac{1}{2}$ pounds fresh pasta or 12 ounces dried pasta fresh oregano leaves, to garnish

1 Place the bell peppers, skin side up, on a cookie sheet with the chili, garlic, and tomatoes. Cook under a preheated broiler for 15 minutes, or until charred. After 10 minutes turn the tomatoes skin side up.

2 Place the bell peppers and chiles in a plastic bag and set aside to sweat for 10 minutes.

3 Remove the skin from the bell peppers and chiles and slice the flesh into strips, using a sharp knife.

4 Peel the garlic and peel and seed the tomatoes.

5 Spread out the almonds on a cookie sheet and place under the broiler for 2–3 minutes, until golden.

6 Using a food processor, blend the bell pepper, chili, garlic, and tomatoes to make a purée. Keep the motor running and slowly add the olive oil to form a thick sauce. Alternatively, mash the mixture with a fork and beat in the olive oil, drop by drop.

7 Stir the toasted ground almonds into the mixture.

8 Warm the sauce in a saucepan until it is heated through.

9 Cook the pasta in a saucepan of boiling water according to the instructions on the packet, or until it is cooked through, but still has "bite." Drain the pasta and transfer to a serving dish. Pour the sauce on top and toss to mix. Garnish with fresh oregano leaves.

VARIATION

Add 2 tablespoons red wine vinegar to the sauce and use as a dressing for a cold pasta salad, if you wish.

Pizza Margherita

Serves 4

INGREDIENTS

BASIC PIZZA DOUGH:
$1/4$ ounce dried yeast
1 tsp sugar
1 cup lukewarm water
12 ounces strong flour
1 tsp salt

1 tbsp olive oil
TOPPING:
14 ounce can tomatoes, chopped
2 garlic cloves, crushed
2 tsp dried basil
1 tbsp olive oil

2 tbsp tomato paste
$3^1/2$ ounces mozzarella cheese, diced
2 tbsp freshly grated Parmesan
    cheese
salt and pepper

1 Place the yeast and sugar in a bowl and mix with 4 tbsp of the water. Set the yeast mixture aside in a warm place for 15 minutes, or until frothy.

2 Mix the flour with the salt and make a well in the center. Add the oil, the yeast mixture, and the remaining water. Using a wooden spoon, mix to form a dough.

3 Turn the dough out onto a floured surface and knead for 4–5 minutes, or until smooth.

4 Return the dough to the bowl, cover with an oiled sheet of plastic wrap, and leave to rise for 30 minutes, or until doubled in size.

5 Knead the dough for 2 minutes. Stretch the dough with your hands, then place it on a greased cookie sheet, pushing out the edges until even and to the shape required. The dough should be no more than about $1/4$ inch thick because it will rise during cooking.

6 To make the topping, place the tomatoes, garlic, dried basil, olive oil, and salt and pepper to taste in a large skillet and simmer for 20 minutes, or until the sauce has thickened. Stir in the tomato paste and allow to cool slightly.

7 Spread the topping evenly over the pizza base. Top with the mozzarella and Parmesan cheeses and bake in a preheated oven at 400°F for 20–25 minutes. Serve hot.

Gorgonzola Pizza

Serves 4

INGREDIENTS

PIZZA DOUGH:
¹/₄ ounce dried yeast
1 tsp sugar
1 cup lukewarm water
1¹/₂ cups whole-wheat flour
1¹/₂ cups strong white flour

1 tsp salt
1 tbsp olive oil

TOPPING:
3 cups peeled and diced pumpkin
or squash

1 tbsp olive oil
1 pear, cored, peeled, and sliced
1 cup crumbled Gorgonzola cheese
1 sprig fresh rosemary, to garnish

1 Place the yeast and sugar in a bowl and mix with 4 tbsp of the water. Set the yeast mixture aside in a warm place for 15 minutes, or until frothy.

2 Mix both of the flours with the salt and make a well in the center. Add the oil, the yeast mixture, and the remaining water. Using a wooden spoon, mix to form a dough.

3 Turn the dough out onto a floured surface and knead for 4–5 minutes, or until smooth.

4 Return the dough to the bowl, cover with an oiled sheet of plastic wrap, and set aside to rise for 30 minutes, or until doubled in size.

5 Remove the dough from the bowl. Knead the dough for 2 minutes. Using a rolling pin, roll out the dough to form a long oval shape, then place it on a greased cookie sheet, pushing out the edges until even. The dough should be no more than ¼ inch thick because it will rise during cooking.

6 To make the topping, place the pumpkin in a shallow roasting pan. Drizzle with the olive oil and cook under a preheated broiler for 20 minutes, or until soft and lightly golden.

7 Top the dough with the pear and the pumpkin, brushing with the oil from the pan. Sprinkle the Gorgonzola cheese over the top. Bake in a preheated oven, at 400°F for 15 minutes, or until the base is golden. Garnish with a sprig of rosemary.

Onion, Ham, & Cheese Pizza

Serves 4

INGREDIENTS

1 portion of Basic Pizza Dough	9 ounces onions, sliced into rings	3½ ounces mozzarella cheese, sliced
	2 garlic cloves, crushed	2 tbsp rosemary, stalks removed and
TOPPING:	1 red bell pepper, diced	roughly chopped
2 tbsp olive oil	3½ ounces prosciutto, cut into strips	

1 Place the yeast and sugar in a bowl and mix with 4 tbsp of the water. Set the yeast mixture aside in a warm place for 15 minutes, or until frothy.

2 Mix the flour with the salt and make a well in the center. Add the oil, the yeast mixture, and the remaining water. Using a wooden spoon, mix to form a dough.

3 Turn the dough out onto a floured surface and knead for 4–5 minutes, or until smooth. Return the dough to the bowl, cover with an oiled sheet of plastic wrap, and set aside to rise for 30 minutes, or until doubled in size.

4 Remove the dough from the bowl. Knead the dough for 2 minutes. Using a rolling pin, roll out the dough to form a square shape, then place it on a greased cookie sheet, pushing out the edges until even. The dough should be no more than ¼ inch thick because it will rise during cooking.

5 To make the topping, heat the oil in a skillet. Add the sliced onions and garlic and sauté for 3 minutes. Add the diced bell pepper and sauté for a further 2 minutes.

6 Cover the skillet and cook the vegetables over a low heat for 10 minutes, stirring occasionally, until the onions are slightly caramelized. Cool slightly.

7 Spread the topping evenly over the pizza base. Place strips of prosciutto, mozzarella, and rosemary over the top. Bake in a preheated oven at 400°F for 20–25 minutes. Serve hot.

Sun-Dried Tomatoes & Ricotta Pizza

Serves 4

INGREDIENTS

1 portion Basic Pizza Dough	TOPPING: 4 tbsp sun-dried tomato paste ³/₄ cup ricotta cheese	10 sun-dried tomatoes 1 tbsp fresh thyme salt and pepper

1 Place the yeast and sugar in a bowl and mix with 4 tbsp of the water. Set the yeast mixture aside in a warm place for 15 minutes, or until frothy.

2 Mix the flour with the salt and make a well in the center. Add the oil, the yeast mixture, and the remaining water. Using a wooden spoon, mix to form a dough.

3 Turn the dough out onto a floured surface and knead for 4–5 minutes, or until smooth.

4 Return the dough to the bowl, cover with an oiled sheet of plastic wrap, and leave to rise for 30 minutes, or until doubled in size.

5 Remove the dough from the bowl. Knead the dough for 2 minutes.

6 Using a rolling pin, roll out the dough to form a round, then place it on a greased cookie sheet, pushing out the edges until even. The dough should be no more than ¹/4 inch thick because it will rise during cooking.

7 Generously spread the sun-dried tomato paste over the dough, then add spoonfuls of ricotta.

8 Cut the sun-dried tomatoes into strips and arrange them on top of the pizza.

9 Sprinkle the thyme, and salt and pepper to taste over the top of the pizza. Bake in a preheated oven at 400°F for 30 minutes, or until the crust is golden. Serve hot.

Mushroom Pizza

Serves 4

INGREDIENTS

1 portion Basic Pizza Dough	2 garlic cloves, crushed	7 ounces mushrooms
	1 tsp dried basil	1½ cups grated mozzarella cheese,
TOPPING:	1 tbsp olive oil	salt and pepper
14 ounce can chopped tomatoes	2 tbsp tomato paste	basil leaves, to garnish

1 Place the yeast and sugar in a bowl and mix with 4 tbsp of the water. Set the yeast mixture aside in a warm place for 15 minutes, or until frothy.

2 Mix the flour with the salt and make a well in the center. Add the oil, the yeast mixture, and the remaining water. Using a wooden spoon, mix to form a dough.

3 Turn the dough out onto a floured surface and knead for 4–5 minutes, or until smooth. Return the dough to the bowl, cover with an oiled sheet of plastic wrap, and set aside to rise for 30 minutes, or until doubled in size.

4 Remove the dough from the bowl. Knead the dough for 2 minutes. Using a rolling pin, roll out the dough to form an oval or a circular shape, then place it on a greased cookie sheet, pushing out the edges until even. The dough should be no more than ¼ inch thick because it will rise during cooking.

5 Using a sharp knife, cut the mushrooms into slices.

6 To make the topping, place the tomatoes, garlic, dried basil, olive oil, and salt and pepper in a large pan and simmer for 20 minutes, or until the sauce has thickened. Stir in the tomato paste and cool slightly.

7 Spread the sauce over the base of the pizza, top with the sliced mushrooms, and scatter over the mozzarella.

8 Bake in a preheated oven at 400°F for 25 minutes. Just before serving, garnish with fresh basil leaves.

Mini-Pizzas

Makes 8

INGREDIENTS

1 portion Basic Pizza Dough	3¹/₂ ounces tomato sauce	2 tbsp olive oil
	3 cups diced pancetta	
TOPPING:	¹/₂ cup pitted black olives, chopped	
2 zucchini	1 tbsp mixed dried herbs	

1 Place the yeast and sugar in a bowl and mix with 4 tbsp of the water. Set the yeast mixture aside in a warm place for 15 minutes, or until frothy.

2 Mix the flour with the salt and make a well in the center. Add the oil, the yeast mixture, and the remaining water. Using a wooden spoon, mix to form a dough.

3 Turn the dough out onto a floured surface and knead for 4–5 minutes, or until smooth. Return the dough to the bowl,

cover with an oiled sheet of plastic wrap, and set aside to rise for 30 minutes, or until doubled in size.

4 Knead the dough for 2 minutes and divide it into 8 balls. Roll out each portion thinly to form rounds or squares, then place them on a greased cookie sheet, pushing out the edges until even. The dough should be no more than ¹/₄ inch thick because it will rise during cooking.

5 To make the topping, grate the zucchini finely. Cover with

absorbent paper towels and let stand for 10 minutes to absorb some of the juices.

6 Spread 2–3 teaspoons of the tomato sauce over the pizza bases and top each with the grated zucchini, pancetta, and olives. Season with freshly ground black pepper and a sprinkling of mixed dried herbs. Drizzle with olive oil.

7 Bake in a preheated oven at 400°F for 15 minutes, or until crispy. Season and serve hot.

Pizza with Tomato Sauce & Roasted Bell Peppers

Serves 4

INGREDIENTS

2 cups all-purpose flour
1/2 cup butter, diced
1/2 tsp salt
1/2 cup grated Parmesan cheese
1 egg, beaten

2 tbsp cold water
2 tbsp olive oil
1 large onion, finely chopped
1 garlic clove, chopped
14 ounce can chopped tomatoes

4 tbsp concentrated tomato paste
1 red bell pepper, seeded and halved
5 sprigs thyme, stalks removed
6 black olives, pitted and halved

1 Sift the flour and rub in the butter until the mixture resembles bread crumbs. Stir in the salt and 2 tablespoons of the Parmesan. Add the egg and 1 tablespoon of the water and mix with a round-bladed knife. Add more water as necessary to make a soft dough. Cover with plastic wrap and chill for 30 minutes.

2 Meanwhile, heat the oil in a skillet and sauté the onions and garlic for about 5 minutes, or until golden. Add the tomatoes and cook for 8–10 minutes. Stir in the tomato paste.

3 Place the bell peppers, skin side up, on a cookie sheet and cook under a preheated broiler for 15 minutes, until charred. Place in a plastic bag and let sweat for 10 minutes. Peel off the skin and slice the flesh into thin strips.

4 Roll out the dough to fit a 9-inch loose-base fluted flan pan. Line with foil and bake in a preheated oven at 400°F for 10 minutes, or until just set. Remove the foil and bake for a further 5 minutes, until lightly golden. Cool slightly.

5 Spoon the tomato sauce evenly over the pastry base and top with the bell peppers, thyme, olives, and remaining Parmesan cheese. Bake for about 15 minutes, until the pastry is crisp. Serve warm or cold.

Calzone

Makes 4 large or 8 small calzone

INGREDIENTS

1 portion of Basic Pizza Dough	TOPPING:	3¹/₂ ounces mozzarella cheese, cut
freshly grated Parmesan cheese,	2³/₄ ounces mortadella or other	into chunks
to serve	Italian pork sausage, chopped	2 tomatoes, diced
	¹/₂ cup chopped Italian sausage	4 tbsp fresh oregano
	1³/₄ ounces Parmesan cheese, sliced	salt and pepper

1 Place the yeast and sugar in a bowl and mix with 4 tbsp of the water. Set the yeast mixture aside in a warm place for 15 minutes, or until frothy.

2 Mix the flour with the salt and make a well in the center. Add the oil, the yeast mixture, and the remaining water. Using a wooden spoon, mix to form a dough.

3 Turn the dough out onto a floured surface and knead for 4–5 minutes, or until smooth. Return the dough to the bowl, cover with an oiled sheet of plastic wrap and set aside to rise for 30 minutes, or until doubled in size.

4 Knead the dough for 2 minutes and divide it into 4 pieces. Roll out each portion thinly to form rounds. Place them on a greased cookie sheet. The dough should be no more than ¹/₄ inch thick because it will rise during cooking.

5 To make the topping, place both Italian sausages, the Parmesan, and the mozzarella on one side of each round. Top with the tomatoes and oregano. Season to taste with salt and pepper.

6 Brush around the edges of the dough with a little water, then fold over the rounds to form a turnover shape. Squeeze the edges together to seal so that none of the filling leaks out during cooking.

7 Bake in a preheated oven at 400°F for 10–15 minutes, or until golden. If you are making the smaller pizzas, reduce the cooking time to 8–10 minutes. Serve the calzone with freshly grated Parmesan cheese.

Pizza with Creamy Ham & Cheese Sauce

Serves 4

INGREDIENTS

9 ounces flaky pastry dough, well chilled	1/3 cup strong flour	3 1/2 ounces Italian pork sausage, such as Feline salami, cut into strips
3 tbsp butter	1 1/4 cups milk	salt and pepper
1 red onion, chopped	2/3 cup finely grated Parmesan cheese, plus extra for sprinkling	sprigs of fresh thyme, to garnish
1 garlic clove, chopped	2 eggs, hard-boiled, cut into quarters	

1 Fold the sheet of flaky pastry in half and coarsely grate it into 4 individual flan pans, 4 inches across. Using a floured fork, press the pastry flakes down lightly so that they are even, there are no holes, and the pastry comes up the sides of the pan.

2 Line with aluminum foil and bake in a preheated oven at 425°F for 10 minutes. Reduce the heat to 400°F, remove the foil, and cook for a further 15 minutes, or until the pastry shells are a golden color and set.

3 Heat the butter in a pan. Add the onion and garlic and sauté for 5–6 minutes, or until softened.

4 Add the flour, stirring well to coat the onions. Gradually stir in the milk to make a thick sauce. Season well with salt and pepper, and then stir in the Parmesan cheese. Do not reheat once the cheese has been added or the sauce will become stringy.

5 Spread the sauce over the pastry shells. Decorate with the egg and strips of sausage.

6 Sprinkle with a little extra Parmesan cheese, return to the oven and bake for 5 minutes, just to heat through.

7 Serve immediately, garnished with sprigs of fresh thyme.

Olive Oil Bread with Cheese

Makes one loaf

INGREDIENTS

¹/₂ ounce dried yeast	3 cups strong flour	7 ounces pecorino cheese, cubed
1 tsp sugar	1 tsp salt	1¹/₂ tsp fennel seeds, lightly crushed
1¹/₈ cups lukewarm water	3 tbsp olive oil	

1 Mix the yeast with the sugar and 8 tbsp of the water. Set aside to ferment in a warm place for about 15 minutes.

2 Mix the flour with the salt. Add 1 tbsp of the oil, the yeast mixture, and the remaining water to form a smooth dough. Knead the dough for 4 minutes.

3 Divide the dough into 2 equal portions. Roll out each portion to a form a round ¹/₄ inch thick. Place 1 round on a cookie sheet. Scatter the cheese and half the fennel seeds evenly on top.

4 Place the second round on top and squeeze the edges together to seal, so that the filling does not leak during cooking.

5 Using a sharp knife, make a few slashes in the top of the dough and brush with the remaining olive oil.

6 Sprinkle with the remaining fennel seeds and set aside to rise for 20–30 minutes.

7 Bake in a preheated oven at 400°F for 30 minutes, or until golden. Serve immediately or cool before serving.

COOK'S TIP

Pecorino is a hard, quite salty cheese, which is sold in most supermarkets and Italian delicatessens. If you cannot obtain pecorino, use strong cheddar or Parmesan cheese instead.

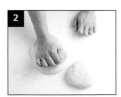

Roman Focaccia

Makes 16 squares

INGREDIENTS

1/4 ounce dried yeast	2 tsp salt	onions, sliced into rings
1 tsp sugar	3 tbsp rosemary, chopped	4 garlic cloves, sliced
1 1/4 cups lukewarm water	2 tbsp olive oil	
4 cups strong white flour	1 pound mixed red and white	

1 Place the yeast and the sugar in a small bowl and mix with 8 tablespoons of the water. Set aside to ferment in a warm place for 15 minutes.

2 Mix the flour with the salt in a large bowl. Add the yeast mixture, half the rosemary, and the remaining water and mix to form a smooth dough. Knead the dough for 4 minutes.

3 Cover the dough with oiled plastic wrap and set aside to rise for 30 minutes, or until doubled in size.

4 Meanwhile, heat the oil in a large pan. Add the onions and garlic and sauté for 5 minutes or until softened. Cover the pan and continue to cook for a further 7–8 minutes, or until the onions are lightly caramelized.

5 Remove the dough from the bowl and knead it again for 1–2 minutes.

6 Roll the dough out to form a square shape. The dough should be no more than 1/4 inch thick because it will rise during cooking. Place the dough onto a cookie sheet, pushing out the edges until even.

7 Spread the onions over the dough, and sprinkle with the remaining rosemary.

8 Bake in a preheated oven at 400°F for 25–30 minutes, or until golden. Cut into 16 squares and serve immediately.

Sun-Dried Tomato Loaf

Makes one loaf

INGREDIENTS

¹/₄ ounce dried yeast	4 cups strong white flour	2 tbsp sun-dried tomato paste
1 tsp sugar	1 tsp salt	12 sun-dried tomatoes, cut
1¹/₄ cups lukewarm water	2 tsp dried basil	into strips

1 Place the yeast and sugar in a small bowl and mix with 8 tablespoons of the water. Set aside to ferment in a warm place for 15 minutes.

2 Place the flour in a bowl and stir in the salt. Make a well in the dry ingredients and add the basil, the yeast mixture, tomato paste, and half the remaining water. Using a wooden spoon, draw the flour into the liquid and mix to form a dough, adding the rest of the water gradually.

3 Turn out the dough onto a floured surface and knead for 5 minutes, or until smooth. Cover with oiled plastic wrap and set aside in a warm place to rise for about 30 minutes, or until doubled in size.

4 Lightly grease a 2-pound loaf pan.

5 Remove the dough from the bowl and knead in the sun-dried tomatoes. Knead again for 2–3 minutes.

6 Place the dough in the pan and set aside to rise for 30–40 minutes. Once it has doubled in size again, bake in a preheated oven at 375°F for 30–35 minutes, or until golden and the base sounds hollow when tapped.

COOK'S TIP

You could make mini sun-dried tomato loaves for children. Divide the dough into 8 equal portions, set aside to rise, and bake in mini-loaf pans for 20 minutes. Alternatively, make 12 small rounds, leave to rise, and bake as rolls for 12–15 minutes.

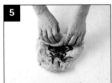

Roasted Bell Pepper Bread

Serves 4

INGREDIENTS

1 red bell pepper, halved and seeded	1 tbsp olive oil	4 cups strong white flour
1 yellow bell pepper, halved and seeded	$1/4$ ounce dried yeast	1 tsp salt
2 sprigs rosemary	1 tsp sugar	
	$1^1/4$ cups lukewarm water	

1 Grease a 9-inch, deep round cake pan with a little butter or margarine.

2 Place the bell peppers and rosemary in a shallow roasting pan. Sprinkle with the oil and roast in a preheated oven at 400°F for 20 minutes, or until slightly charred. Remove the skin from the bell peppers and cut the flesh into slices.

3 Place the yeast and sugar in a small bowl and mix with 8 tablespoons of lukewarm water. Set the yeast mixture aside to ferment in a warm place for about 15 minutes.

4 Mix the flour and salt together in a large bowl. Stir in the yeast mixture and the remaining water and mix to form a smooth dough.

5 Knead the dough for about 5 minutes. Cover with oiled plastic wrap and set aside to rise for about 30 minutes, or until doubled in size.

6 Cut the dough into 3 equal portions. Roll the portions into rounds slightly larger than the cake pan.

7 Place 1 round in the base of the pan so that it reaches up the sides of

the pan by about $3/4$ inch. Top with half the bell pepper mixture.

8 Place the second round of dough on top, followed by the remaining bell pepper mixture. Place the last round of dough on top, pushing the edges of the dough down the sides of the pan.

9 Cover the dough with oiled plastic wrap and set aside to rise for 30–40 minutes. Place in the preheated oven and bake for 45 minutes, until golden and the base sounds hollow when lightly tapped. Serve warm.

5655665

555555555566566665655

556666576

Vegetables, Salads, & Bakes

Green Easter Pie

Serves 4

INGREDIENTS

2 tbsp olive oil
1 onion, chopped
2 garlic cloves, chopped
1 cup risotto rice
3 cups hot chicken or vegetable stock

1/2 cup white wine
2/3 cup grated Parmesan cheese
3/4 cup frozen peas, thawed
3 ounces arugula
2 tomatoes, diced
4 eggs, beaten

3 tbsp fresh marjoram, chopped
1 cup bread crumbs
salt and pepper

1 Lightly grease and then line the base of a 9-inch, deep cake pan.

2 Using a sharp knife, roughly chop the arugula.

3 Heat the oil in a large skillet. Add the onion and garlic and sauté for 4–5 minutes, or until the onion has softened.

4 Add the rice to the mixture in the skillet, mix well to combine, then begin adding the stock a ladleful at a time. Wait until all the stock has been completely absorbed before adding another ladleful of liquid.

5 Continue to cook the mixture, adding the wine, until the rice is tender. This will take at least 15 minutes.

6 Stir in the Parmesan cheese, peas, arugula, tomatoes, eggs, and 2 tablespoons of the marjoram. Season to taste with salt and pepper.

7 Spoon the risotto into the pan and level the surface by pressing down with the back of a wooden spoon.

8 Top with the bread crumbs and the remaining marjoram.

9 Bake in a preheated oven at 350°F for 30 minutes, or until set. Cut into slices and serve immediately or cool and chill.

Spinach & Ricotta Pie

Serves 4

INGREDIENTS

8 ounces spinach	2 large eggs, beaten	9 ounces puff pastry dough, thawed
1/4 cup pine nuts	1/2 cup ground almonds	if frozen
1/2 cup ricotta cheese	2/3 cup grated Parmesan cheese	1 small egg, beaten

1 Rinse the spinach, place in a large saucepan, and cook for 4–5 minutes, until wilted. Drain thoroughly. When the spinach is cool enough to handle, squeeze out the excess liquid.

2 Place the pine nuts on a cookie sheet and lightly toast under a preheated broiler for 2–3 minutes, or until golden.

3 Place the ricotta cheese, spinach and eggs in a bowl and mix together. Add the pine nuts, beat well, then stir in the ground almonds and grated Parmesan cheese.

4 Roll out the puff pastry dough and make 2 x 8-inch squares. Trim the edges, reserving the dough trimmings.

5 Place 1 dough square on a cookie sheet. Spoon the spinach mixture on top, keeping within 1/2 inch of the edge of the dough square. Brush the edges with beaten egg and place the second square over the top.

6 Using a round-bladed knife, press the edges together by tapping along the sealed edge. Use the dough trimmings to make leaves to decorate the pie.

7 Brush the pie with the beaten egg to glaze and bake in a preheated oven at 425°F for 10 minutes. Reduce the oven temperature to 375°F and bake for a further 25–30 minutes. Serve hot.

COOK'S TIP

Spinach is very nutritious as it is full of iron — this is particularly important for women and elderly people who may lack this in their diet.

Desserts

If when you think about cooking with pasta, desserts do not usually spring to the forefront of your mind, you will be amazed by the wonderfully self-indulgent sweet treats made from pasta in this chapter.

The Italians love their desserts, but when there is a special gathering or celebration, then a special effort is made, and the delicacies appear. The Sicilians are said to have the sweetest tooth of all, and many Italian desserts are thought to have originated there. You have to go a very long way to beat a Sicilian ice cream—they truly are the best in the world!

Fresh fruit also features in many Italian desserts— oranges are often peeled and served whole, marinated in a fragrant syrup and liqueur.

Chocolate, too, is popular for a deliciously wicked end to a meal. Whatever your preference, there is sure to be an Italian dessert to tempt and satisfy you—you'll never be disappointed!

Baked Sweet Ravioli

Serves 4

INGREDIENTS

PASTA:
3³/₄ cups all-purpose flour
10 tbsp butter, plus extra for
greasing

³/₄ cup superfine sugar
4 eggs
1 ounce yeast
¹/₂ cup warm milk

FILLING:
²/₃ cup chestnut purée
¹/₂ cup cocoa powder
¹/₄ cup superfine sugar
¹/₂ cup chopped almonds
1 cup crushed amaretti cookies
⁵/₈ cup orange marmalade

1 To make the sweet pasta dough, sift the flour into a mixing bowl, then mix in the butter, sugar, and 3 eggs.

2 Mix together the yeast and warm milk in a small bowl, then, mix into the dough.

3 Knead the dough for 20 minutes, cover with a clean cloth, and set aside in a warm place for 1 hour to rise.

4 Mix together the chestnut purée, cocoa powder, sugar, almonds, crushed amaretti cookies, and orange marmalade in a separate bowl.

5 Lightly grease a cookie sheet with butter.

6 Lightly flour the counter. Roll out the pasta dough into a thin sheet and then cut into 2-inch rounds with a plain pastry cutter.

7 Put a spoonful of filling onto each round and then fold in half, pressing the edges to seal. Arrange on the prepared cookie sheet, spacing the ravioli out well.

8 Beat the remaining egg and brush all over the ravioli to glaze. Bake in a preheated oven at 350°F for 20 minutes. Serve hot.

German Noodle Pudding

Serves 4

INGREDIENTS

4 tbsp butter, plus extra for greasing	½ cup superfine sugar	1 tsp grated lemon rind
6 ounces ribbon egg noodles	2 eggs, lightly beaten	¼ cup slivered almonds
½ cup cream cheese	½ cup sour cream	⅜ cup dry white breadcrumbs
1 cup cottage cheese	1 tsp vanilla extract	confectioner's sugar, for dusting
	a pinch of ground cinnamon	

1 Grease an ovenproof dish with butter.

2 Bring a large pan of water to a boil. Add the noodles and cook until almost tender. Drain and set aside.

3 Beat together the cream cheese, cottage cheese, and sugar in a mixing bowl. Beat in the eggs, a little at a time. Stir in the sour cream, vanilla extract, cinnamon, and lemon rind, and fold in the noodles. Transfer the mixture to the prepared dish and smooth the surface.

4 Melt the butter in a skillet. Add the almonds and fry, stirring constantly, for about 1–1½ minutes, until lightly colored. Remove the skillet from the heat and stir the breadcrumbs into the almonds.

5 Sprinkle the almond and breadcrumb mixture over the pudding and bake in a preheated oven at 350°F for about 35–40 minutes, until just set. Dust with a little confectioner's sugar and serve immediately.

VARIATION

Although not authentic, you could add 3 tbsp raisins with the lemon rind in step 3, if desired.

Honey & Walnut Nests

Serves 4

INGREDIENTS

8 ounces angel hair pasta	½ cup sugar	salt
8 tbsp butter	⅓ cup clear honey	strained plain yogurt, to serve
1½ cups shelled pistachio nuts, chopped	⅝ cup water	
	2 tsp lemon juice	

1 Bring a large pan of lightly salted water to a boil. Add the angel hair pasta and cook until tender, but still firm to the bite. Drain and return to the pan. Add the butter and toss to coat the pasta. Set aside to cool.

2 Arrange 4 small flan or poaching rings on a cookie sheet. Divide the angel hair pasta into 8 equal quantities and spoon 4 of them into the rings. Press down lightly. Top the pasta with half of the nuts, then add the remaining pasta.

3 Bake in a preheated oven at 350°F for 45 minutes, until golden brown.

4 Meanwhile, put the sugar, honey, and water in a saucepan and bring to a boil over a low heat, stirring constantly until the sugar has dissolved completely. Simmer for 10 minutes, add the lemon juice, and simmer for a further 5 minutes.

5 Carefully transfer the angel hair nests to a serving dish. Pour the honey syrup on top, sprinkle with the remaining nuts, and set aside to cool completely before serving. Serve the strained, plain yogurt separately.

COOK'S TIP

Angel hair pasta is also known as capelli d'angelo. *Long and very fine, it is usually sold in small bunches that already resemble nests.*

Raspberry Fusilli

Serves 4

INGREDIENTS

½ cup dried fusilli	1 tbsp lemon juice	3 tbsp raspberry liqueur
4 cups raspberries	4 tbsp slivered almonds	salt
2 tbsp superfine sugar		

1 Bring a large pan of lightly salted water to a boil. Add the fusilli and cook until tender, but still firm to the bite. Drain the fusilli thoroughly, return to the pan, and set aside to cool.

2 Using a spoon, firmly press 1⅓ cups of the raspberries through a strainer set over a large mixing bowl to form a smooth purée.

3 Put the raspberry purée and sugar in a small saucepan and simmer over a low heat, stirring occasionally, for 5 minutes.

Stir in the lemon juice and set the sauce aside until required.

4 Add the remaining raspberries to the fusilli in the pan and mix together well. Transfer the raspberry and fusilli mixture to a serving dish.

5 Spread the almonds out on a cookie sheet and toast under the broiler until golden brown. Remove and set aside to cool slightly.

6 Stir the raspberry liqueur into the reserved raspberry sauce

and mix together until smooth. Pour the raspberry sauce over the fusilli, sprinkle the toasted almonds on top and serve.

VARIATION

You could use almost any sweet, really ripe berry for making this dessert. Strawberries and blackberries are especially suitable, combined with the correspondingly flavored liqueur. Alternatively, you could use a different berry with the fusilli, but still pour raspberry sauce on top.

Italian Bread Pudding

Serves 4

INGREDIENTS

1 tbsp butter

2 small eating apples, peeled, cored, and sliced into rings

$\frac{1}{4}$ cup sugar

2 tbsp white wine

$3\frac{1}{2}$ ounces bread, sliced with crusts removed (slightly stale French baguette is ideal)

$1\frac{1}{4}$ cups light cream

2 eggs, beaten

pared rind of 1 orange, cut into matchsticks

1 Lightly grease a 2-pint, deep ovenproof dish with the butter.

2 Arrange the apple rings in the base of the dish. Sprinkle half the sugar over the apples.

3 Pour the wine over the apple slices. Add the slices of bread, pushing them down with your hands to flatten them slightly.

4 Mix the cream with the eggs, the remaining sugar, and the orange rind, and pour the mixture over the bread. Set aside to soak for 30 minutes.

5 Bake the pudding in a preheated oven at 350°F for 25 minutes, until golden and set. Serve warm.

VARIATION

Try adding dried fruit, such as apricots, cherries, or dates, to the pudding.

COOK'S TIP

Light cream is the type of cream most commonly used for cooking. However, this type of cream should not be boiled as it will curdle. Also, always add hot liquids to the cream rather than the cream to the liquids, in order to avoid curdling. Light cream has an 18 percent fat content.

Tuscan Pudding

Serves 4

INGREDIENTS

1 tbsp butter
½ cup mixed dried fruit
1⅛ cups ricotta cheese

3 egg yolks
¼ cup superfine sugar
1 tsp cinnamon

finely grated rind of 1 orange, plus
extra to decorate
crème fraîche to serve

1 Lightly grease 4 mini ovenproof bowls or ramekin dishes with the butter.

2 Put the dried fruit in a bowl and cover with warm water. Set aside to soak for 10 minutes.

3 Beat the ricotta cheese with the egg yolks in a bowl. Stir in the superfine sugar, cinnamon, and orange rind and mix well to combine.

4 Drain the dried fruit in a strainer set over a bowl. Mix the drained fruit with the ricotta cheese mixture.

5 Spoon the mixture into the bowls or ramekin dishes.

6 Bake in a preheated oven at 350°F for 15 minutes. The tops should be firm to the touch, but not brown.

7 Decorate the puddings with grated orange rind. Serve warm or chilled with a spoon of crème fraîche.

COOK'S TIP

Crème fraîche has a slightly sour, nutty taste and is very thick. It is suitable for cooking, but has the same fat content as heavy cream. It can be made by stirring cultured buttermilk into heavy cream and refrigerating overnight.

VARIATION

Use the dried fruit of your choice for this delicious recipe.

Cream Custards

Serves 4

INGREDIENTS

2 cups light cream
2 tbsp superfine sugar
1 orange

2 tsp grated nutmeg
3 large eggs, beaten

1 tbsp honey
1 tsp cinnamon

1 Place the cream and sugar in a large nonstick saucepan and heat gently, stirring, until the sugar caramelizes.

2 Finely grate half the orange rind and add it to the pan, together with the nutmeg.

3 Add the eggs to the mixture in the pan and cook over a low heat for 10–15 minutes, stirring constantly. The custard will eventually thicken.

4 Strain the custard through a fine strainer into 4 shallow serving dishes. Chill in the refrigerator for 2 hours.

5 Meanwhile, pare the remaining orange rind and cut it into matchsticks.

6 Place the honey and cinnamon in a pan with 2 tablespoons water and heat gently. Add the orange rind to the pan and cook for 2–3 minutes, stirring, until the mixture has caramelized.

7 Pour the mixture into a bowl and separate the orange sticks. Cool until set.

8 Once the custards have set, decorate them with the caramelized orange rind and serve.

COOK'S TIP

The cream custards will keep for 1–2 days in the refrigerator. Decorate with the caramelized orange rind just before serving.

Sicilian Orange & Almond Cake

Serves 8

INGREDIENTS

4 eggs, separated
$^{3}/_{4}$ cup superfine sugar, plus 2 tsp for
   the cream
finely grated rind and juice of
   2 oranges

finely grated rind and juice of
   1 lemon
1 cup ground almonds
$^{1}/_{4}$ cup self-rising flour

$^{3}/_{4}$ cup heavy cream
1 tsp cinnamon
$^{1}/_{4}$ cup slivered almonds, toasted
confectioner's sugar, to dust

1 Lightly grease and line the base of a 7-inch round, deep cake pan.

2 Blend the egg yolks with the sugar until the mixture is thick and creamy. Beat half the orange rind and all the lemon rind into the egg yolks.

3 Mix the juice from both oranges and the lemon with the ground almonds and stir into the egg yolks. The mixture will become quite runny at this point. Fold in the flour.

4 Whisk the egg whites until stiff and fold into the egg yolk mixture.

5 Pour the mixture into the prepared cake pan and bake in a preheated oven at 350°F for 35–40 minutes, until golden and springy to the touch. Cool in the pan for 10 minutes and then turn out. It is likely to sink slightly at this stage.

6 Beat the cream to form soft peaks. Stir in the remaining orange rind, cinnamon, and sugar.

7 Once the cake is cold, cover with the toasted almonds, dust with confectioner's sugar, and serve with the cream.

VARIATION

You could serve this cake with a syrup. Boil the juice and finely grated rind of 2 oranges, 6 tbsp superfine sugar, and 2 tbsp water for 5–6 minutes, until slightly thickened. Stir in 1 tbsp of orange liqueur just before serving.

Orange & Grapefruit Salad

Serves 4

INGREDIENTS

2 grapefruit, pink or plain	4 tbsp clear honey	1 sprig mint, roughly chopped
4 oranges	2 tbsp warm water	1/2 cup chopped walnuts
pared rind and juice of 1 lime		

1 Using a sharp knife, slice the top and bottom from the grapefruit, then slice away the rest of the skin and pith.

2 Cut between each segment of the grapefruit to remove the fleshy part only.

3 Using a sharp knife, slice the top and bottom from the oranges, then slice away the rest of the skin and pith.

4 Cut between each segment of the oranges to remove the fleshy part. Add to the grapefruit.

5 Place the lime rind, 2 tablespoons of lime juice, the honey, and the warm water in a small bowl. Beat with a fork to mix the dressing.

6 Pour the dressing over the segmented fruit, add the chopped mint, and mix well. Chill in the refrigerator for 2 hours for the flavors to mingle.

7 Place the chopped walnuts on a cookie sheet. Lightly toast the walnuts under a preheated broiler for 2–3 minutes, until golden brown.

8 Sprinkle the toasted walnuts over the fruit and serve.

VARIATION

Instead of the walnuts, you could sprinkle toasted almonds, cashews, hazelnuts, or pecans over the fruit, if you prefer.

Zabaglione

Serves 4

INGREDIENTS

5 egg yolks
½ cup superfine sugar

⅔ cup Marsala or sweet sherry

fresh fruit or amaretti cookies, to
serve (optional)

1 Place the egg yolks in a large mixing bowl.

2 Add the superfine sugar to the egg yolks and beat well until the mixture is thick and very pale and has doubled in volume.

3 Place the bowl containing the egg yolk and sugar mixture over a saucepan of gently simmering water.

4 Add the Marsala or sherry to the egg yolk and sugar mixture and continue beating until the foam mixture becomes warm. This process may take as long as 10 minutes.

5 Pour the mixture, which should be frothy and light, into 4 wine glasses.

6 Serve the zabaglione warm with fresh fruit or amaretti cookies if you wish.

VARIATION

Any other type of liqueur may be used instead of the Marsala or sweet sherry, if you prefer. Serve soft fruits, such as strawberries or raspberries, with the zabaglione — it's a delicious combination!

VARIATION

Iced or Semifreddo Zabaglione can be made by following the method here, then continuing to beat the foam while standing the bowl in cold water. Beat ⅔ cup heavy cream until it just holds its shape. Fold into the foam and freeze for about 2 hours, until just frozen.

Sweet Mascarpone Mousse

Serves 4

INGREDIENTS

2 cups mascarpone cheese
1/2 cup superfine sugar
4 egg yolks

14 ounces frozen summer fruits, such
    as raspberries and
    red currants

red currants, to garnish
amaretti cookies, to serve

1 Place the mascarpone cheese in a large mixing bowl. Using a wooden spoon, beat the mascarpone cheese until very smooth.

2 Stir the egg yolks and sugar into the mascarpone cheese, mixing well. Chill in the refrigerator for about 1 hour.

3 Spoon a layer of the mascarpone mixture into the bottom of 4 individual serving dishes. Spoon a layer of the summer fruits on top. Repeat the layers in the same order, reserving some of the mascarpone mixture for the top.

4 Chill the mousses in the refrigerator for about 20 minutes. The fruits should still be slightly frozen.

5 Serve the mascarpone mousses along with amaretti cookies.

VARIATION

Try adding 3 tablespoons of your favorite liqueur to the mascarpone cheese mixture in step 1, if desired.

COOK'S TIP

Mascarpone (sometimes spelled mascherpone) is a soft, creamy cheese from Italy. It is becoming increasingly available, and you should have no difficulty finding it in your local supermarket, or Italian delicatessen.

Lemon Mascarpone Cheesecake

Serves 8

INGREDIENTS

1½ tbsp unsalted butter

2 cups crushed ginger snaps

2 tbsp preserved ginger

2¼ cups mascarpone cheese

finely grated rind and juice of
2 lemons

1 cup superfine sugar

2 large eggs, separated

fruit coulis (see Cook's Tip), to serve

1 Grease and line the base of a 10-inch springform cake pan or loose-bottomed pan.

2 Melt the butter in a pan and stir in the crushed cookies and chopped ginger. Use the mixture to line the pan, pressing the mixture about ½ inch up the sides.

3 Beat together the cheese, lemon rind and juice, sugar, and egg yolks until smooth.

4 Whisk the egg whites until they are stiff and fold into the cheese and lemon mixture, blending well.

5 Pour the mixture into the cookie shell in the pan and bake in a preheated oven at 350°F for 35–45 minutes, until just set. Don't worry if it cracks or sinks–this is quite normal.

6 Leave the cheesecake in the pan to cool. Serve with fruit coulis (see Cook's Tip).

COOK'S TIP

Fruit coulis can be made by cooking 14 ounces fruit, such as blueberries, for 5 minutes with 2 tablespoons of water. Strain the mixture, then stir in 1 tablespoon (or more to taste) of sifted confectioner's sugar. Cool before serving.

VARIATION

Ricotta cheese can be used instead of the mascarpone to make an equally delicious cheesecake. It should be rubbed through a strainer before use to remove any lumps.

Tiramisu

Serves 6

INGREDIENTS

10¹/₂ ounces dark chocolate

1³/₄ cups mascarpone cheese

²/₃ cup heavy cream, whipped until it just holds its shape

1³/₄ cups black coffee with ¹/₄ cup superfine sugar, cooled

6 tbsp dark rum or brandy

36 lady fingers, about 14 oz

unsweetened cocoa, to dust

1 Melt the chocolate in a bowl set over a saucepan of simmering water, stirring occasionally. Leave the chocolate to cool slightly, then stir it into the mascarpone and cream.

2 Mix the coffee and rum together in a bowl. Dip the lady fingers into the mixture briefly so that they absorb the liquid, but do not become soggy and disintegrate.

3 Place 3 lady fingers on 3 serving plates.

4 Spoon a layer of the mascarpone and chocolate mixture over the lady fingers.

5 Place 3 more lady fingers on top of the mascarpone layer. Spread another layer of mascarpone and chocolate mixture and place 3 more lady fingers on top.

6 Chill the tiramisu in the refrigerator for at least 1 hour. Dust with a little unsweetened cocoa just before serving.

COOK'S TIP

Tiramisu can also be served semi-frozen, like ice cream. Freeze the tiramisu for 2 hours and serve immediately, as it defrosts very quickly.

VARIATION

Try adding ¹/₂ cup toasted, chopped hazelnuts to the chocolate cream mixture in step 1, if desired.

Rich Chocolate Loaf

Makes 16 Slices

INGREDIENTS

5½ ounces dark chocolate	2 tsp cinnamon	¼ cup chopped dried no-need-to-
6 tbsp sweet butter	½ cup almonds,	soak apricots
7¼ ounce can condensed milk	1 cup broken amaretti cookies	

1 Line a 1½-pound loaf pan with a sheet of foil.

2 Using a very sharp knife, roughly chop the almonds.

3 Place the chocolate, butter, milk, and cinnamon in a heavy-based saucepan. Heat gently over a low heat for 3–4 minutes, stirring with a wooden spoon, until the chocolate has melted. Beat the mixture well.

4 Add the almonds, cookies, and apricots to the mixture in the saucepan, stirring with a wooden spoon, until well mixed.

5 Pour the mixture into the prepared pan and chill in the refrigerator for about 1 hour, or until set.

6 Cut the rich chocolate loaf into slices to serve.

COOK'S TIP

To melt chocolate, first break it into manageable pieces. The smaller the pieces, the quicker it will melt.

COOK'S TIP

When baking or cooking with fat, butter has the finest flavor. If possible, it is best to use sweet butter as an ingredient in puddings and desserts, unless stated otherwise in the recipe. Reduced fat spreads are not suitable for cooking.

Pear & Ginger Cake

Serves 4–6

INGREDIENTS

⁷⁄₈ cup sweet butter, softened	3 tsp ground ginger	3 eggs, beaten
³⁄₄ cup superfine sugar	1 pound eating pears, peeled, cored,	1 tbsp brown sugar
1¹⁄₂ cups self-rising flour, sifted	and thinly sliced	ice cream or heavy cream to serve

1 Lightly grease and line the base of a deep 8-inch cake pan.

2 Using a whisk, combine ¾ cup of the butter with the superfine sugar, flour, ginger, and eggs and mix to form a smooth consistency.

3 Spoon the cake mixture into the prepared pan, leveling the surface.

4 Arrange the pear slices over the cake mixture. Sprinkle with the brown sugar and dot with the remaining butter.

5 Bake in a preheated oven at 350°F for 35–40 minutes, or until the cake is golden and feels springy to the touch.

6 Serve the pear and ginger cake warm, with ice cream or cream, if desired.

COOK'S TIP

Brown sugar is often known as Barbados sugar. It is a darker form of light-brown sugar.

COOK'S TIP

To test whether the cake is cooked through, insert a knife into the center of the cake. If it comes out clean the cake is cooked through.

Peaches in White Wine

Serves 4

INGREDIENTS

4 large ripe peaches
2 tbsp confectioner's sugar, sifted

pared rind and juice of 1 orange

³/₄ cup medium or sweet white
wine, chilled

1 Using a sharp knife, halve the peaches, remove the pits, and discard them. Peel the peaches, if desired. Slice the peaches into thin wedges.

2 Place the peach wedges in a glass serving bowl and sprinkle the sugar over them.

3 Using a sharp knife, pare the rind from the orange. Cut the orange rind into matchsticks, place them in a bowl of cold water, and set aside.

4 Squeeze the juice from the orange and pour it over the peaches, together with the wine.

5 Marinate the peaches in the refrigerator for at least 1 hour.

6 Remove the orange rind from the cold water and pat dry with paper towels.

7 Garnish the peaches with the strips of orange rind and serve immediately.

COOK'S TIP

There is absolutely no need to use expensive wine in this recipe, so it can be quite economical to make.

COOK'S TIP

The best way to pare the rind thinly from citrus fruits is to use a potato peeler.

Vanilla Ice Cream

Serves 4–6

INGREDIENTS

2¹/₂ cups heavy cream
1 vanilla bean

pared rind of 1 lemon
4 eggs, beaten

2 egg, yolks
⁷/₈ cup superfine sugar

1 Place the cream in a heavy-based saucepan and heat gently, beating. Add the vanilla bean, lemon rind, eggs, and egg yolks and heat until the mixture reaches just below boiling point.

2 Reduce the heat and cook for 8–10 minutes, beating the mixture continuously, until it has thickened.

3 Stir the sugar into the cream mixture and set aside to cool.

4 Strain the cream mixture through a fine strainer.

5 Slit open the vanilla bean, scoop out the tiny black seeds, and stir them into the cream.

6 Pour the mixture into a shallow freezing container with a lid and freeze overnight, until set. Serve when required.

COOK'S TIP

Ice cream is one of the traditional dishes of Italy. Everyone eats it and there are numerous gelato stalls selling a wide variety of flavors, usually in a cone. It is also served in scoops and sliced.

COOK'S TIP

To make tutti frutti ice cream, soak ²/₃ cup mixed dried fruit, such as golden raisins, cherries, apricots, candied peel, and pineapple, in 2 tablespoons Marsala or sweet sherry for 20 minutes. Follow the method for vanilla ice cream, omitting the vanilla bean, and stir in the Marsala or sherry-soaked fruit in step 5, just before freezing.

Granita

Serves 4

INGREDIENTS

LEMON GRANITA:
3 lemons
³/₄ cup lemon juice
¹/₂ cup superfine sugar
2¹/₄ cups cold water

COFFEE GRANITA:
2 tbsp instant coffee
2 tbsp sugar

2 tbsp hot water
2 ¹/₂ cups cold water
2 tbsp rum or brandy

1 To make lemon granita, finely grate the lemon rind. Place the lemon rind, juice, and superfine sugar in a pan. Bring the mixture to a boil and simmer for 5-6 minutes, or until thick and syrupy. Let cool.

2 Once cooled, stir in the cold water and pour into a shallow freezer container with a lid. Freeze the granita for 4–5 hours, stirring occasionally to break up the ice. Serve as a palate cleanser between dinner courses.

3 To make coffee granita, place the coffee and sugar in a bowl and pour in the hot water, stirring until dissolved.

4 Stir in the cold water and rum or brandy.

5 Pour the mixture into a shallow freezer container with a lid. Freeze the granita for at least 6 hours, stirring every 1–2 hours in order to create a grainy texture. Serve with cream after dinner, if desired.

COOK'S TIP

If you would prefer a nonalcoholic version of the coffee granita, simply omit the rum or brandy and add extra instant coffee instead.

Peaches with Creamy Mascarpone Filling

Serves 4

INGREDIENTS

4 peaches	½ cup pecan or walnuts,	1 tsp sunflower oil
1 cup mascarpone cheese	chopped	4 tbsp maple syrup

1 Cut the peaches in half and remove the pits. If you are preparing this recipe in advance, press the peach halves together again and wrap them in plastic wrap until required.

2 Mix the mascarpone and pecan or walnuts together in a small bowl until well combined. Chill in the refrigerator until required.

3 To serve, brush the peaches with a little oil and place on a rack set over medium hot coals. Broil the peach halves for 5–10 minutes, turning once, until they are hot.

4 Transfer the peach halves to a serving dish and top with the mascarpone and nut mixture.

5 Drizzle the maple syrup over the peaches and mascarpone filling, and serve at once.

COOK'S TIP

Mascarpone cheese is high in fat; you can use thick unsweetened yogurt.

VARIATION

You can use nectarines instead of peaches for this recipe, if you prefer. Remember to choose ripe, but fairly firm, fruit which won't go soft and mushy when it is barbecued. Prepare the nectarines in the same way as the peaches and barbecue for 5–10 minutes.

508

Index